Fictional Dialogue

Frontiers of Narrative

SERIES EDITOR
David Herman *Ohio State University*

Fictional Dialogue

Speech and Conversation in the

Modern and Postmodern Novel

BRONWEN THOMAS

University of Nebraska Press | Lincoln and London

© 2012 by the Board of Regents of the University of
Nebraska

Chapter 2, "The 'Idea of Dialogue,'" originally
appeared in *Imaginary Dialogues in English: Explorations of a Literary Form*, ed. Jarmila Mildorf and Till
Kinzel, 203–20 (Heidelberg: Universitätsverlag Winter, 2012).

Chapter 8, "Stuck in a Loop? Dialogue in Hypertext
Fiction," originally appeared in slightly different form
in *Narrative* 15, no. 3 (2007): 357–72. Copyright © 2007
The Ohio State University. Reproduced with permission.

Library of Congress Cataloging-in-Publication Data
Thomas, Bronwen.
Fictional dialogue: speech and conversation in the
modern and postmodern novel / Bronwen Thomas.
p. cm. — (Frontiers of narrative)
Includes bibliographical references and index.
ISBN 978-0-8032-4451-1 (cloth: alk. paper)
1. American fiction—20th century—History and
criticism. 2. English fiction—20th century—History
and criticism. 3. Dialogue in literature.
4. Conversation in literature. 5. Dialogism (Literary
analysis) 6. Modernism (Literature) 7. Postmodernism
(Literature) I. Title.
PS374.D43T46 2012
823'.90926—dc23   2011044492

Set in Minion Pro by Bob Reitz.
Designed by A. Shahan.

Contents

Preface

This study is a direct response to novelist and critic David Lodge's complaint that dialogue novelists "have been somewhat undervalued by academic criticism because their foregrounding of dialogue made them resistant to a method of analysis biased in favour of lyric expressiveness" (1990, 83). Although it has to be allowed that the dialogue novel's chief proponents, including Henry Green, Ivy Compton-Burnett, William Gaddis, and Nicholson Baker, have only attracted a cultish or niche following, the dialogue novel has been and continues to be an important influence on the twentieth- and twenty-first-century novel. Moreover, while studies of some of the individual novelists specializing in dialogue might exist, to date there has been no attempt to contextualize this work as part of a wider movement or shift in the novel form or to analyze the techniques for representing dialogue other than in the most superficial of terms. In this volume I will attempt to provide a new "method of analysis" for fictional dialogue, as well as critiquing existing methods.

I was first attracted to the study of fictional dialogue because I saw in the writing of English comic novelists from the early decades of the twentieth century an infectious enthusiasm for the exhilarating chaos that ensues from giving center stage to the free play of character voices. Scenes of unmediated dialogue seemed to me to provide the reader with precisely that sense of excitement which comes from knowing that "something unforeseen results, something that would not otherwise have appeared" (Morson and Emerson 1989, 4). Of course, this is not to say that scenes of dialogue are not highly stylized and contrived affairs, but the openness and playfulness that characterizes them offers something quite different from novels where a narrative voice or presence guides the reader and provides a sort of lodestar from which events and exchanges may be charted and navigated.

My interest in fictional dialogue also stemmed from a curiosity about what happens to the reading process when we shift from being told a story by a narrating agent of some kind toward seeming to see the action unfold before us in unmediated exchanges between fictional characters. I was fascinated by what distinguishes this experience from that of reading a play text, and by the impact of the "gear shifting" (Page 1988) that we as readers have to negotiate. While many of the dialogues I read were entertaining and fun, I also found that they posed a challenge to the reader, not only in the sense of simply working out who is saying what to whom but also in attempting to figure out what they mean and what their impact is for the interlocutors. Thus Henry Green's stated aim to "create life in the reader" by allowing "the dialogue to mean different things to different readers at one and the same time" (1992, 140) places an onus on the reader to engage in the (re)construction of meaning, even where the inane or mundane utterances of the fictional characters seem to offer scant return for such investment.

Another motivation for my focus on fictional dialogue was the strong sense of frustration I felt with existing studies and approaches. While endless analyses of old stalwarts like Hemingway's "Cat in the Rain" ([1925] 1987) or "Hills Like White Elephants" ([1927] 1987) exist, and while many have been happy to expostulate about such and such a writer's wonderful "ear" for dialogue or to offer blanket prescriptions for what constitutes "good" dialogue, I found that time and again these discussions either focused on isolated utterances or, in many cases, made no attempt to engage in any kind of close analysis of the dialogue at all. They also appeared to overtly or covertly prescribe a certain "idea of dialogue" based on quite narrow grounds, something I will contest in the following pages.

This study should be of interest to anyone who shares my fascination with fictional dialogue, but especially those working in the fields of literary and cultural studies, narratology, stylistics, and linguistics. It is the first of its kind to combine literary and narratological analysis of fictional dialogue with reference to linguistic terms and models, Bakhtinian theory, cultural history, media theory, and cognitive approaches. It is also the first study to focus in depth on the dialogue novel and to bring together examples of dialogue from literature, popular fiction, and nonlinear narratives. For these reasons, I hope to provide the reader with a fresh approach to the study of fictional dialogue, along with some valuable new insights into the innovations and delights provided by a wide range of writers since the early decades of the twentieth century.

Acknowledgments

This book has been a long time in the writing, and I would like to thank my family, friends, and colleagues for waiting patiently for its completion. My friends at the Poetics and Linguistics Association in particular have played a big part in helping me to keep the faith and retain a sense of humor. I am very grateful to Eric Homberger and Patrick Swinden, who guided me through my first forays into fictional dialogue, and to Meir Sternberg, whose meticulous editing of my article on multi-party talk was instrumental in bringing my work to a wider audience. More recently, I would like to thank Jim Phelan for his input on my article on hypertext fiction, and Jarmila Mildorf for inviting me to contribute my piece on the idea of dialogue for *Imaginary Dialogues in English*. I am also deeply indebted to Alan Palmer, who read and commented on several chapters in draft form. At Bournemouth, I am grateful to Karen Fowler-Watt for negotiating the time for me to complete the project. I am also very grateful to my editors at Nebraska for their input. Finally, my biggest thanks go to David Herman, series editor, who first commissioned the volume and has been incredibly generous with his time and his support for the project throughout.

Fictional Dialogue

Introduction

While considerable critical attention has been paid to the representation of speech and thought in narrative, the emphasis of late has swung much more in favor of thought than speech. The thorny issue of how to define and categorize various modes of representation continues to dominate discussions, and the emerging fields of cognitive narratology and cognitive stylistics only seem to further endorse a focus on character consciousness and "fictional minds" (Palmer 2004). Yet Genette (1980, 173) has hailed experimentation with the speech of characters as "one of the main paths of emancipation in the modern novel," while the twentieth and twenty-first centuries have arguably seen the consolidation of dialogue as an ethical ideal or aspiration in many aspects of social and political life.

A major concern of this study is to demonstrate the richness and versatility of dialogue as a narrative technique, by focusing on extended extracts and sequences of utterances rather than plucking lines or snippets of conversation out of context. However, attention will also be paid to the ways in which the versions of dialogue that we are offered may help to normalize or idealize certain patterns and practices, and thereby to exclude alternative possibilities, or to elide "unevenness" and differences.

In his essay on fictional dialogue, Ryan Bishop (1991, 58) expresses frustration with Western culture's tendency to "confuse the map for the territory," and I share his concern that "our judgements regarding 'natural' dialogue are determined by our literacy and literary tradition, not by the event of actual conversation we engage in every day" (58). Bishop is sensitive to the difficulties facing writers in the "making of a thing (a text, in this case) from a process (conversation, or speech)" (59) and suspicious of the consequences of "freezing the flux" and making it manageable (76). But while he accepts the limitations, Bishop also acknowledges the "tremendous rewards" (70) dialogue affords the reader, particularly in offering the sensation of being in the midst of an event, a performance, where boundaries of all kinds are eroded and outcomes uncertain. In the chapters that follow, my analysis focuses on dialogue as process, and on combining skepticism about some of the claims that may be made for the technique, with enthusiasm and joy for the possibilities that it allows.

This study brings together theories and models of fictional dialogue from a wide range of disciplines and intellectual traditions. As we will see, the subject provokes intense debate and often raises profound questions concerning our understanding of narrative and of human communication more broadly. However, to date there has been insufficient cross-fertilization of these issues and debates, or they have taken the form of brief asides on the subject. My study will be informed by existing debates about the nature and functioning of dialogue, but it will also critically reflect on the very terms within which those debates are grounded.

Key Studies of Speech and Dialogue in the Novel

Literary-Historical Accounts

Studies of speech in the novel (e.g., Page 1988; Chapman 1984; Fludernik, 1993, 1996) have contributed greatly to our understanding of the varieties of representation available to novelists and to the historical development of specific forms and techniques. Norman Page's groundbreaking *Speech in the English Novel* provides an invaluable account of how early novelists developed and consolidated their techniques. Moreover, in his discussion of the specific practices of novelists such as Austen and Dickens, Page develops a terminology for the analysis of the wide variety of forms available and offers some interesting insights into the implications of these devices in terms of their perceived relationship with "real speech."

Like Page's, Raymond Chapman's study (1984) mainly focuses on Victorian and early-twentieth-century fiction, though he does interestingly include some discussion of the Tintin and Asterix series of comic books and also makes some reference to advertising. Chapman's approach is similarly grounded in linguistic theory, although Chapman focuses much more on the sounds and prosodic elements related to the representation of speech. As well as providing detailed analysis of the specific methods used to represent speech in the novel, both Page and Chapman pay particular heed to issues of class and how representations of accent and dialect may reflect prevailing attitudes and prejudices.

More recently, Monika Fludernik has provided an almost encyclopedic account of the multifarious ways in which speech has been represented in fiction, while also remaining sensitive to the ways in which the emergence of these techniques is grounded in specific historical and social conditions. Moreover, Fludernik openly confronts the question of why fictional dialogue seems to occupy a privileged status when it comes to representing the "real," opening up a debate that I will return to in the following chapter.

Each of these studies offers those interested in fictional dialogue an invaluable resource when it comes to trying to account for and locate the emergence and use of specific techniques and devices. Nevertheless, the emphasis is predominantly on providing typologies of speech rather than on attempting to understand the dynamic interplay between characters that dialogue may facilitate. Thus, while such studies continue to be invaluable when it comes to understanding the representation of speech, to fully engage with dialogue as interaction we need to turn to other models and approaches.

Stylistic Analyses

Stylistic approaches to fictional dialogue draw on linguistic and ethnographic studies to focus on the mechanisms and forms of organization underlying conversational interaction. Geoffrey Leech and Mick Short's *Style in Fiction* (1981) offers detailed analysis of the range of devices found in the novel for the representation of both speech and thought. But in engaging with pragmatic models, notably speech act theory and Grice's ([1963] 1975) cooperative principle, Leech and Short are able to go beyond the individual utterance to offer insights into the power dynamics and shifts in roles that occur between participants. Similarly, Michael Toolan's (1985, 1987) studies of fictional dialogue have demonstrated how discourse and conversation analysis may provide valuable tools for understanding conversation not as a series of isolated utterances, but as an opportunity for interplay in which all sorts of intricate moves and exchanges are enacted. More recently, attention has turned toward dialogue in the context of a stylistics of drama, drawing on the work of Deirdre Burton in the 1980s, but engaging with developments in corpus linguistics (McIntyre 2010) and cognitive stylistics (Culpeper 2002).

The main contribution of such studies has been to demonstrate that the study of dialogue cannot focus on utterances in isolation but rather must consider talk as socially situated and grounded in specific social contexts. The unit of analysis is no longer the individual utterance but sequences of utterances in which the characters' social relations are dynamically enacted by their interactions, rather than merely being illustrated by them. In the chapters that follow, my own analyses of scenes of dialogue will draw on terms and models derived from the fields of pragmatics and from conversation and discourse analysis, demonstrating how my approach is heavily indebted to the ongoing work of literary stylisticians. At the same time, I recognize the limitations of such approaches, and particularly the fact that they often appear to neglect the historical and cultural contexts of the extracts and examples chosen. While it will be impossible always to do justice to issues of context in a study of this nature, I hope to be able to focus some attention on the wider shifts and forces that have helped to shape the development of fictional dialogue over the period covered.

Thus while this study is informed by both literary-historical and stylistic approaches to the analysis of speech in fiction, the emphasis is less on exploring how fictional representations may or may not be like naturally occurring or "real" speech and more on analyzing the specific ways in which novelists have responded to changing attitudes to and modes of speech, and on questioning and problematizing any attempt to schematize or provide universals.

The Influence of Bakhtin

Interest in dialogue not just as a technique but as a stance, a philosophical and ethical "idea" (or "ideal"), stems largely from the theories of Mikhail Bakhtin and his circle. It was Bakhtin who first gave expression to the fact that an important part of the appeal of the novel is its heteroglossia, its ability to foreground the speech and interactions of characters and to encompass a wide variety of speech genres (1986, 1981). But theorists have perhaps been too ready to acquiesce with Bakhtin's apparent lack of regard for directly represented speech as a narrative technique (1984, 187–88). Bakhtin seems to characterize unmediated scenes of dialogue as little more than a masquerade or puppet show, yet it is precisely the interrelation between showing and telling in scenes of dialogue that make them so fascinating and so complex. Where the narrator seems to step back or stand in the wings while the characters take center stage, it is the arrangement and organization of their utterances and the timing and sequencing of their exchanges that contributes so much to the effectiveness of such scenes. There is no reason, therefore, why such a technique should be any less interesting or relevant than Voloshinov's concept of "quasi-direct discourse" which was so influential on Bakhtin, given that here we may just as readily find that "between the reported speech and the reporting context, dynamic relations of high complexity and tension are in force" (Voloshinov [1930] 1973, 119). Moreover, scenes of dialogue ensure that there is always an "answering word" (1981, 280) and element of "addressivity" (1986) which demands active involvement from the reader.

As I will argue more fully in chapter 2, while Bakhtin's theories remain influential, the idealistic tone of some of his pronouncements has come in for criticism. It can be tempting to fall for a rather utopian vision of dialogue as a democratizing force or as a staging of the "drama of escaping our individualism" (Young 2001, 4), yet characters in novels no more have free and unrestrained access to scenes of talk than do any of us. Novelists such as Ivy Compton-Burnett and William Gaddis have amply demonstrated how conversations can be tortuous and painful affairs for those involved, where the stakes may be incredibly high in terms of what the participants have to gain or lose. Moreover, the idea that a narrator can ever just be one voice among many in a text, as Bakhtin seems to suggest, is questionable, even where that organizing presence appears to cede control or authority to other voices in the text.

Challenges to Existing Approaches

In the chapters that follow I will be drawing on the work of narratologists such as Fludernik (1993, 1996) and Sternberg (1982b), who have consistently challenged and exposed the "direct discourse fallacy," which seems to afford direct speech a kind of authenticity and immutability denied to other forms of representation. I will also be engaging with studies that foreground the ideological implications of the notion of dialogue (Davis 1987; Middleton 2000) and with recent reappraisals of Bakhtin's work that critique the "ethico-political baggage" (Hirschkop 1992, 105) implicit in his theories.

In the field of narratology, postclassical approaches that engage with issues of contextualization and ideology and that embrace interdisciplinarity have made it possible to move beyond purely formalist or typological concerns. In particular, this has led to a shift away from constantly refining and redefining the categories by which we understand the workings of narrative and toward asking searching questions about the kinds of assumptions and preconceptions carried by these categories and how their influence may extend way beyond the story worlds themselves.

Many of these key shifts are discernible in the work of David Herman and his attempt to provide a more holistic approach to narrative, drawing on linguistic terminology and models and also embracing recent developments and theory from within the field of cognitive science. Herman's holistic approach demonstrates the need to focus on scenes of talk where utterances can only be understood "as part of a larger environment for sense-making" (2006, 81) rather than being artificially isolated from that "larger environment" in which speech and thought intersect and occupy a "fuzzy rather than a clear cut boundary."

Herman's interest in how participants approach these "interactions-in-progress" (82) helps to convey why the very "slipperiness of talk" is what entrances, fascinates, and involves readers of these texts in such a powerful way. Herman's approach highlights how our characterization of what constitutes talk, and the relationship between talk and surrounding activities and behaviors, requires a "Copernican revolution" (84). Indeed, the "dominant norms for talk" (85) that emerge from literary representations require intense scrutiny and a process of denaturalization and defamiliarization. I will take up this challenge more specifically in chapter 2, where I will explore how the "idea of dialogue" may bring on board its own baggage and ethical as well as social and behavioral norms. But the notion that we need to contest and question *why* the speech and interactions of characters in novels are presented as they are informs the analysis throughout this study and underpins the ways in which that analysis aims to be critical and reflexive rather than purely descriptive.

Contesting the separation of inner and outer worlds in fiction is also central to Alan Palmer's theory of fictional minds (2004) in which Palmer challenges the speech category approach of classical narratology. His analysis demonstrates how crude previous studies of speech and thought have tended to be in delineating separate spheres for the two activities and in providing such narrow categories for what might constitute speech or thought. Instead, he demonstrates how the narrator's descriptions and the characters' utterances convey the sense of their having continuing consciousnesses and of their engaging in mental events even in the absence of any direct or specific reference. He also demonstrates how novels are full of references to joint or group thinking, suggesting the possibility of a "Bakhtinian emphasis on the shared, social and dialogic nature of mental functioning" (328).

Like Palmer's, my analyses will often focus on scenes where it appears that the characters may have little opportunity or even inclination to engage in introspection and where they may similarly have little concern or regard for the thoughts and feelings of their interlocutors. While I share Palmer's conviction that such scenes often prompt and provoke the reader to engage in the kind of mental mapping he describes, I will also be contesting the idea that somehow there must always be something of import or significance behind the characters' words, something interesting or noteworthy going on in the characters' minds. Moreover, the notion that thoughts and emotions can be communicated either to others or to oneself unproblematically and coherently is often put to the test in novels that trade for the purposes of humor or suspense on the verbal inadequacies of characters or which powerfully hint at the characters' alienation from the social settings in which they find themselves.

The Cultural Context

An interest in dialogue as a concept or ideal as much as a narrative technique is not confined to the novel; it embraces all kinds of popular cultural texts and practices. Bakhtin's influence has extended beyond the fields of linguistics and literary criticism to help shape and define theories of representation and discourse in media and film texts as well as the analysis of popular cultural forms and practices. Equally, film theory (Kozloff 2000) and the analysis of media genres such as the talk show (Shattuc 1997) have increasingly turned to discourse and conversation analysis in an effort to expose the power relations affecting the dynamic interrelations of those involved. Such approaches have also signaled a shift away from conceptualizing meaning as something that is imposed on participants or audiences, toward exploring the ways in which meaning may be jointly produced and emergent. Although the specific features of such speech genres and modes may be very different from those represented in the novel, I will nevertheless be drawing on work in these areas, particularly as it may help to illuminate wider social and cultural practices and discoursal norms in a way that the preoccupation with form and close analysis has tended to sideline in literary criticism and narratological approaches.

An increased interest in verbal interaction has also been associated with the rise of a "therapy culture" (Furedi 2004), where the promise of a "talking cure" drives interpersonal exchanges in which the goal is some kind of truth or enlightenment, primarily about the self. Irene Kacandes's *Talk Fiction* (2001) has provided interesting insights into the "talk explosion" in modern culture and has usefully demonstrated how important it is to connect the work of writers with extraliterary cultural developments. However, the notion that talk is of itself cathartic and "good" for those involved has also come in for some critique, particularly where it becomes a kind of marketing tool or means of applying pressure on people to communicate in certain socially sanctioned ways, as I will explore further in chapter 2.

The Scope of This Study

This study seeks to place the emphasis squarely on dialogue as a key narrative device in the novel of the twentieth and twenty-first centuries. Building on studies of dialogue from previous literary periods and exploring the specific ways in which certain conventions and practices have become inscribed and normalized, the analyses that follow will seek to contextualize the practice of individual writers within larger historical, cultural, and aesthetic movements. For example, evidence suggests that the early decades of the twentieth century marked a shift away from focusing on dialogue as an "art" toward engaging with the idioms and jargons of the day. In her study of the reading public during this period, Q. D. Leavis ([1932] 1965) bemoaned this shift and took issue with writers such as P. G. Wodehouse on the basis that the language found in his novels made her "wince." I have argued elsewhere (Thomas 1995) that this period was also important in establishing a sense of common ground among writers experimenting with dialogue, particularly insofar as they were prepared to foreground the banal and the routine and to engage with the mishaps and miscommunications that characterize so much of our day-to-day interactions with one another. Part of the appeal of dialogue during this period rested on the fact that it was perceived as a means of capturing the idiom of the day, "speeding up the contemporary scene so that there is none of that slight yellowing of the edges that marks the period piece" (Stopp 1958, 74).

No study of twentieth-century fiction can ignore the twin movements of Modernism and Postmodernism and the ways in which they radically disrupted prevailing notions of meaning and truth and how these might be represented. Experimentation with dialogue, I will argue, can be identified not only as a key constituent of these movements but also, at times, as a reaction against them, particularly as they are perceived to distance themselves from the popular or the everyday. The novel's response to major technological changes affecting the twentieth century will also be discussed in depth (chapter 7), as these affect our understanding of human communication and offer up new possibilities for narrative and storytelling.

The attempt to capture the cadences and idioms of one's time perhaps necessarily connects the dialogue novelist with a specific period or locale and suggests that he or she may be able to offer the reader insights into the defining communicative and popular cultural practices of a particular age. Of course, treating literary texts as windows into past worlds or cultures and their communicative habits and practices would be a highly dubious enterprise, but it is nevertheless possible to explore the ways in which dialogue in the novel has a metacommunicative function (Herman 1994), reflecting not just on how groups of characters choose to behave toward and interact with one another but also to suggest how those forms of talk are socially situated and become socially sanctioned.

Structure and Organization

Each chapter will relate theoretical discussions about the forms and functions of dialogue to in-depth analyses of extracts from novels that consciously foreground dialogue and often push its boundaries as a narrative device. Chapter 1 considers how existing studies of dialogue have tended to focus on locating the representation of character speech within some kind of continuum usually predicated on the basis of the realism of the representation, and the implications of this for our understanding of the device and its functioning within specific narratives. The discussion then extends in chapter 2 to a fundamental reexamination of the "idea of dialogue," drawing on work from cultural and literary theory, postclassical narratology, and recent reappraisals of Bakhtin's theories. These more theoretical chapters are complemented by a consideration of how an analysis of fictional dialogue may prompt us to revisit fundamental cornerstones of narrative theory, particularly our understanding of character, plot, and the role of the narrator.

In chapter 3, I examine the role dialogue plays in helping to construct and maintain a sense of consistency and recognizability for literary characters. However, I also demonstrate that the notion that a character's mind and actions are always consistent, coherent, private, and knowable to oneself is fundamentally challenged by examining extended interactions and looking at what happens between not just within utterances. This chapter explores theoretical challenges to the concept of character and draws on cognitive approaches to fundamentally reexamine how we conceive of inner and outer worlds and attempt to keep them distinct.

Chapter 4 analyzes the role dialogue plays in establishing the action of a novel, particularly where conversations between characters may be center stage and provide more or less all the action that there is. Drawing on speech act theory and cognitive approaches once more, I explore the relationship between speech and action but also contest the notion that the events of a novel must be either noteworthy or readily definable within certain static boundaries.

While much of this study concerns itself with novels where dialogue is foregrounded to such an extent that it may seem irrelevant to talk of a narrator shaping and directing the action, chapter 5 analyzes the variety of means by which the speech of characters may be framed for us. This chapter explores theoretical accounts of framing from a wide range of sources and argues that we need to revisit many of these theories and concepts if we are to begin to account for the complex and dynamic interrelations that exist between narrative discourse and dialogue in many fictional texts.

The final three chapters focus on questions of genre and medium, exploring how dialogue is not only shaped by but also helps to shape various forms and norms of representation. Considered as a distinct genre, the dialogue novel of the early twentieth century, as developed and refined by the likes of Ronald Firbank, Evelyn Waugh, and Henry Green, aligned itself with the traditions of comedy and satire and often flaunted its vulgarity and common touch. A close association between the dialogue novel and comic writing persists to the present day in the writing of Philip Roth or Nicholson Baker, for example. Chapter 6 will explore why it is that dialogue as a technique seems to be such an intrinsic feature of certain genres, focusing specifically on the hard-boiled crime thriller.

Chapters 7 and 8 consider how new communication technologies have affected how we conceptualize and manage our verbal dealings with one another and how artists and writers try to react to and map these changing mechanisms and contexts of interaction. In chapter 7, I challenge traditional definitions and boundaries placed upon dialogue by exploring online and para-social communication. I also contest the possibility of separating inner and outer worlds, arguing that these new technologies often offer us an "alibi of interaction." Chapter 8 focuses on the use of dialogue in hypertext fiction and on the difficulty of holding onto a notion of context in nonlinear narratives where conversations are experienced as recurring within some kind of endless "loop."

This study aims to provoke new debates about fictional dialogue and to readdress the neglect of dialogue as a narrative technique especially in the fields of literary and narrative theory. In so doing, it draws attention to some neglected literary classics, paying particular attention to the dialogue novel as a subgenre that has been largely overlooked by both literary critics and narratologists. Such has been the neglect of this topic that its scope is at times overwhelming, so there are inevitably notable omissions here that I will address in my conclusion in the hope that they will form the subject of many future studies. I have also included an appendix as a means of demonstrating how the main issues and theories explored in the study can inform and complement a detailed analysis of the language and structure of a scene of fictional dialogue. This should provide a helpful and practical guide for those wishing to embark on the analysis of fictional dialogue themselves.

PART I | *Theory*

1   Debates about Realism

This chapter will explore one of the more contentious issues raised by fictional dialogue: the extent to which the efficacy of novelistic representations can or should be measured against naturally occurring speech. As I argued in the introduction, critics and theorists have always been fascinated by the range of devices employed by novelists for capturing the speech varieties and stylistic quirks of fictional characters, and they tend to judge their success in terms of how finely tuned the writer's "ear" for dialogue is. As we will see in later chapters, dialogue plays a crucial role in helping to create and populate credible fictional worlds and in contributing drama and vitality to the actions and situations located within those worlds. Thus it seems that the representation of speech and conversation in the novel brings with it certain inevitable expectations and implications in terms of the reality of what is being portrayed and the extent to which this corresponds to recognizable lived experiences. But it is also important to recognize that fictional dialogue is often highly stylized and that what passes for an accurate reflection of "real speech" may be simply the product of a "linguistic hallucination" (Fludernik 1993, 453) in which the reader readily participates.

Defining Our Terms

Recent theory has wrestled with the muddle surrounding terminology in this area, and particularly the distinction between mimesis and realism. Many critics openly acknowledge the difficulty of arriving at adequate definitions. For example, Meir Sternberg (1981, 237) playfully contends that "the trouble is that, unlike the proverbial old dog, mimesis has been taught so many new tricks and has such an aptitude for learning new ones, that its performance can hardly be reduced to a single univocal bark." Sternberg wants to "retain mimesis as the most comprehensive term for the relationship between reality and its modeled representation" (237), but with a sensitivity to its capacity for "flexibility, mobility and protean changes." In his analysis of polylingualism and issues of translation, Sternberg distinguishes between the literalness of reproduction and the stylization and selectivity of mimesis, and both he and Fludernik have attacked the "direct discourse fallacy," which perpetuates the notion that what is being represented is some kind of exact copy of a preexisting utterance or conversation (Sternberg 1982b; Fludernik 1993).

In narratology, dialogue has tended to be associated with mimesis (in the sense of "showing") rather than diegesis ("telling"), because the presence of the narrator is minimized, and it appears as though the characters' speech is almost unmediated. Genette's (1980) concept of "scene," for example, has dialogue facilitating an almost exact equivalence between story time and discourse time, perpetuating the association between dialogue and "showing" rather than "telling" and implying that the reader may be given direct and unmediated access to events without the intervention of a "teller."

Recently, however, narratologists have become suspicious of the idea that somehow fictional dialogue is more "direct" than other forms of representation because it purports to "show" what is being said and because the narrator seems to withdraw to the sidelines. For example, McHale (1978, 257) has criticized what he calls "derivational" accounts of speech and thought representation, while Fludernik (1993, 281) attacks the "ingrained" belief that "direct discourse is in every sense of the word primary or originary to other types of quotation." In his account of the direct discourse fallacy, Sternberg (1982b, 140) exposes the "idealization" inherent in taking at face value a form so seemingly dependent on "superhuman powers" of recall. Instead, Sternberg argues, any analysis of fictional dialogue must be alert to the fact that "the most potent effects of direct speech . . . turn on various strategies of interference and montage" (1982a, 69). Alongside his attacks on the direct discourse fallacy, Sternberg develops his quotation theory to distinguish between frame and inset and to expose how the relations between quoter and quotee may range from the empathetic to the wholly dissonant. The emphasis shifts, therefore, from the fallacious notion that what we have is a direct, authentic copy of the "original" to examining how the report we are offered is filtered down to us by the reporter.

The direct discourse fallacy raises some crucial issues having to do with the status and ideology of the "direct" in narrative fiction and with guarding against relying too much on reading fictional representations against some kind of template based on naturally occurring conversation. Nevertheless, the language in which the debate is conducted can itself betray how "ingrained" are our responses to the "direct," and the danger is that it can distract us from attempting to explore why and how the fallacy continues to have such a hold over us.

When it comes to the notion of realism, it appears we are no closer to reaching "a conclusive state or a clear definition," despite the fact that the debates have "preoccupied philosophers, literary theorists, and art theorists for generations" (Ronen 1995). Ronen claims that disciplinary differences contribute to the lack of consensus and that in the field of literary studies, things are complicated by the fact that realism can be equated with the object of representation, a mode, or a style. Of course it is also associated with a distinctive literary movement, particularly in relation to the novel, as I will discuss more fully later.

What we have to allow, according to Ronen (1995), is that any discussion of realism involves adopting a philosophical position toward what we accept as our reality. The notion of realism as a mode of representational practice that carries with it certain ideological assumptions has perhaps made it more important than ever to keep mimesis and realism distinct. Jan Bruck (1982) sees the confusion as one between imitation and representation and argues that realism is both much more recent and much more circumscribed as a concept than mimesis. Bruck holds that realism is the product of a bourgeois ideology that only fully emerges in the nineteenth century and which responds to the demand for representing "real life" as part of a growing sense of social consciousness.

It is also important to recognize that what passes for realism varies considerably according to the prevailing aesthetic and cultural norms of the day. For example, Fludernik (1993) points out that whereas the early novel had to tread carefully in representing the rude language of the common people, by the time James Joyce was writing this had become not so much an ideal as a requirement. Similarly, according to Bishop (1991), the amount of background information to his characters' speech supplied by Henry James seems somewhat superfluous compared to contemporary authors such as Munro, Carver, or Olsen, for whom "curtness equals reality" (69).

The Need for a New Approach

A particular problem with notions of realism with regard to fictional dialogue is that all too often the focus is on isolated utterances and not on the flux and process of conversational interaction. Thus, as I said in the introduction, while others (Page 1988; Fludernik 1996) have provided thoroughgoing typologies for the range of devices for representing speech available to novelists, for me the fascination of fictional dialogue has never been about measuring its accuracy or authenticity but rather about trying to understand why the experience it offers me as a reader is so unique and so exhilarating. Thus while I fully accept the need to interrogate the stance toward the real which these representations offer us, my emphasis is not on tabulating current practice or evaluating it according to how far it approximates to the real, but on arguing for a wholesale shift of attention away from what can often be a sterile debate about the putative authenticity of this or that isolated instance of speech, toward establishing a new approach that allows for the active involvement of the reader in participating in bringing scenes of dialogue to life.

Increasingly, theorists have come to realize that the problem with some of the rhetoric in these debates is that "the whole concept of realism . . . is often based on an inadequate or inaccurate notion of what spontaneous speech is really like" (Page 1988, 3–4). As we saw in the introduction, many studies of dialogue in the novel have turned to linguistic models in order better to understand spontaneous speech, particularly how we need to focus not just on the surface features of talk but on the way in which what we say affects the world around us and those with whom we come into contact. For example, in her discussion of speech act theory, Rossen-Knill (1999, 42) argues that "during the act of reading, fictional speech . . . becomes 'real speech,' and as such, it works in and on the fictional world. At the same time, fictional speech works on the real world, continually shaping a new entity for the reader." Furthermore, the work of discourse and conversation analysts has focused attention on the need to analyze the underlying organization and management of talk and to approach conversation as a microcosmic social system with far-reaching implications for its participants.

It has to be recognized that this approach has itself come in for criticism, mainly from narratologists, both for naively trying to map fictional representations onto "real life" parallels and for perpetuating the illusion that there is some originary source on which the representations are based. But stylisticians are often precisely concerned with highlighting the fact that "we neglect the artifice in fictional dialogue, the ways in which it is non-naturalistic, is not a full transcription, at our peril" (Toolan 1988, 58). Moreover, alongside analyzing the relations between participants in a fictional exchange, stylisticians such as Toolan or Leech and Short (1981) are just as concerned with exploring the metacommunicative relationship existing between narrator and reader, which frames and shapes how we respond to what the characters are saying and doing to one another.

For the remainder of this chapter I will begin with a brief account of the emergence and development of key techniques and devices for the representation of speech. Then I will outline how and why a new focus on conversational interaction may be both possible and desirable. Finally, I will explore how writers associated with the key literary movements of the twentieth and twenty-first centuries, Modernism and Postmodernism, have redefined the territory of the "real" in their representational practices and experimentation with form.

Forms and Conventions: A Brief History

Studies of speech in the novel often set out to provide exhaustive, but usually descriptive, surveys of the varieties depicted and the methods used for their representation. Such studies can, however, provide useful reminders that devices we may take for granted are the product of a particular set of conventions and accepted practices for the representation of speech. For example, Norman Page (1988) has demonstrated how early novelists took their cue from the theater, setting out the speech of their characters much as in a dramatic script. Traces of the practice persist into the twentieth century, for instance in the Nighttown section of Joyce's *Ulysses* ([1922] 1985) and in Irvine Welsh's *Trainspotting* ([1993] 1996, 181–84), where a conversation between Renton and his psychiatrist is laid out in script form. Nicholson Baker's *Checkpoint* (2004) appears to be almost entirely set out in script form, as if to challenge the reader in terms of how to place and how to respond to what he or she is reading.

Page notes that whereas quotation marks have become fairly ubiquitous, they are far from universal, and what he calls the "continental" practice of using dashes has been employed by writers such as Joyce and

Welsh as less obtrusive and more flexible in terms of blurring the bound-aries between speech and thought and between character speech and the discourse of a narrator (see chapter 5). Jonathan Rée (1990) links the use of quotation marks to commercial considerations such as printing costs and points out that they remained relatively casual until becoming much more "fussy" (1044) in the Victorian period. Rée goes on to rather play-fully suggest that this signified "a fall from a sunlit realm of joyous verbal freedom, into a squalid, loveless world where the poison of possessive individualism has spread even to people's relations to their own words." He notes that in postmodern fiction the quotation mark has "lost its hyp-ocritical veneer of respect for other people's words; it functions primar-ily as a scare quote" (1053), reinforcing the idea that even this seemingly innocuous functional device for the delimiting of speech carries with it a whole load of ideological and aesthetic baggage.

In his study of Dickens, Mark Lambert (1981) argues that quotation marks perform the function of preserving the integrity of speech and that characters whose words are seemingly reproduced for us directly appear in a kind of spotlight that is favorable, compared with those characters who remain in the background, their words only given in paraphrase. According to Lambert, character speech in Victorian fiction is privileged; he even claims that Dickens displays aggression and antagonism toward his fictional constructs for taking some of the attention and limelight away from his narrator.

Lambert also notes that the layout rules for fictional dialogue changed in the nineteenth century. Whereas previously the speech of more than one character could be incorporated in the one paragraph, the prefer-ence became for a new paragraph to denote each change of speaker. For Lambert this shift only serves to further underline the privileged status of character speech, but he also claims that this new layout suggests to readers that they will have to invest less work and less imaginative ener-gy in these sections of the novel than in those composed of narrative description or commentary. Another by-product of this shift, according to Lambert, is that the novelist can use paragraphing to denote a change of speakers without having to label each speaker for the reader by means of speech tags.

Speech tags mark off dialogue from the surrounding discourse and contribute to the framing of the dialogue (discussed more fully in chapter

5). The device also owes a debt to the theatrical, performing the function of "stage directions" (Page 1988) in providing paralinguistic information to the reader about how the utterance is spoken (e.g., "softly"), where it takes place ("in the orangery"), and what action or gesture accompanies it ("pacing up and down"). Even the most seemingly bland speech tags can serve to establish control over the dialogue and distance the reader: the French writer Nathalie Sarraute called them "symbols of the old regime" (1963). But novelists have always found ways of having fun with speech tags: Fludernik (1993) notes how in *Ulysses*, Joyce opts for the deliberately obsolete alongside the downright provocative ("ejaculated surprised"), while P. G. Wodehouse is a master of the overelaborate ("in one of those gruff assumed voices that sound like a bull-frog with catarrh" (*Heavy Weather*, [1933] 1988, 572). This suggests that speech tags are not necessarily either "cumbersome" (Sarraute 1963) or a purely functional accompaniment to what the characters "actually" say. Instead, as Lambert's (1981) study of the "suspended quotation" suggests, they may themselves be stylistic tours de force, reclaiming some of the attention back from the characters, as suggested earlier, and often signaling to the reader that what the author puts in quotation marks should in no way be regarded as some kind of sacred trust. The specific feature of the "suspended quotation" is that it leaves a gap between parts of the same utterance, sometimes for the purposes of suspense, but also, Lambert claims, so that the narrator can maintain some semblance of control over the discourse.

In P. G. Wodehouse's *Summer Lightning* ([1929] 1988, 273), the reader is brought up to date on the ongoing feud between the Hon. Galahad (or "Gally," as he is affectionately known) and Sir Gregory Parsloe over the matter of Gally's yet-to-be-published *Reminiscences*, in which Sir Gregory fears exposure over a story involving some prawns. When Gally turns up at his home to accuse him of stealing his brother's prize pig, the Empress of Blandings, Sir Gregory mistakenly assumes that when Gally says "your sins have found you out!" he is referring to his youthful indiscretions. Between Sir Gregory's initial reaction ("Eh?") and the slightly more composed "What the devil do you mean?" the narrator intervenes both to provide a running commentary on how the interactants perceive the ongoing exchanges ("the Squire of Matchingham's bewilderment gave way to wrath") and to colorfully convey their paralinguistic jousting ("regarding him through his monocle rather as a cook eyes a black-beetle on discovering it in the kitchen-sink"). Here the device of the suspended quotation acts to draw out the humor of the scenario and particularly the reactions of the participants involved. Elsewhere the device might be employed to heighten dramatic tension or emotion in a scene by focusing on the gestures and reactions of those involved or by delaying a revelation or reaction for maximum impact.

Lambert's study demonstrated how what surrounds speech in the novel merits close analysis, both in terms of the variations used and in terms of helping to shape the reader's interpretation of what is being represented. Thus Lambert shows that speech tags are often highly colored and subjective in how they portray the speaker: only the speech of respected and dignified characters is left untagged, as though this requires no explanation or justification. Moreover, Lambert suggests that certain speech tags ("return," "continue") can help to create a sense of interaction between characters and help shift the emphasis from the production of speech to its perception. They also create a "model of human speech" (15), suggesting that particular ways of speaking and of interacting with others constitute the norm within a given fictional world. But speech tags also reflect already existing customs and practices: Lambert claims that readers of Dickens would have been discomfited by constant interruptions to speech, further confirming the risks the novelist took in persevering with the technique.

The extent to which any representation aims for mimesis reflects on both aesthetic and cultural values. Thus the choice of whether to represent a particular dialect or language directly rather than indirectly may imply certain value judgments not just about the character involved but also about the prestige and status attaching to that speech variety. In addressing the specific issues involved in translation, Sternberg (1981) provides a useful scale by which to measure the degree of mimesis aimed for, including a homogenizing convention, whereby all the characters seem to speak the same, and selective reproduction, where only the odd word or idiom is reproduced. In addition to considering the incorporation of wholly different languages into a text, Sternberg also raises the question of what happens when a writer creates his or her own fictive language, such as the language of the Houyhnhnms in *Gulliver's Travels*, and the extent to which these are made to appear plausible and convincing to the reader.

Written prose comes closest to replicating spoken language where something approximating a phonetic transcription is attempted. Changes to the spelling of words and the use of punctuation and other graphic devices can go some way toward evoking the sounds and rhythms of naturally occurring speech. Sumner Ives (1971) has coined the term "eye dialect" to refer to the various ways in which a writer visually signals to the reader that the dialect or language represented is not his or her own, for example, by changing "the" to "de" or "ze." Such devices may provide the reader with "vocal scores" (Rée 1990, 1046) that permit them to rehearse and perform these lifeless marks, to provide the vocalization required to bring a writer's "word-music" to life (Chapman 1984, 196). However, controversy haunts the practice, especially where it is felt that this may contribute toward a "linguacentric, prescriptive attitude" (Preston 1982, 306) when the dialects of those perceived to be uneducated receive this kind of treatment disproportionately.

It is clear that fictional dialogue looks nothing like a full phonetic transcription, and in fact focusing only on selective and partial features of a speaker's vocal repertoire may be necessary to avoid detracting from the reality effect (Fludernik 1993). According to Abercrombie (1966, 4), "nobody speaks at all like the characters in any novel, play or film. Life would be intolerable if they did; and novels, plays or films would be intolerable if the characters spoke as people do in life."

Fictional representations of speech do not record every hesitation, pause, and false start in speech; instead, they offer us a "tidied up" version where participants appear remarkably fluent and transitions between speakers are remarkably smooth. Indeed, Page (1988, 12) insists that "most readers are so conditioned by long experience of reading and listening to fictional and dramatic dialogue of many kinds that they would probably not recognize 'the real thing' if they saw or heard it, and would not much care for it in any case."

Comparisons with linguistic transcriptions of speech highlight how much is "tidied up" in fictional dialogue. But the extent to which linguistic transcriptions are themselves accurate or neutral has been brought into question, for example, when transcription conventions across different languages are compared (Kress 2003). Most notably, Elinor Ochs's (1979) analysis of the limitations of transcription conventions for recording children's speech showed that transcription is a selective process full of blind spots and biases. Demonstrating how transcription conventions separate the verbal and the nonverbal and how layout enforces an expectation of relevance between utterances, Ochs's study reminds us that every aspect of the process of purporting to record speech is deserving of much closer scrutiny.

While changes to spelling, typography, and punctuation can help to convey some of the sounds of speech, there are limitations. Chapman (1984) argues that written representations fall short in terms of conveying pitch, elision between word boundaries, and sounds that are outside language, such as the sigh or the grunt. Much work also remains to be done on understanding how far written representations are able to capture the rhythms and pace of speech. Walter Nash (1985) has suggested that the tempo of comic dialogue in the late nineteenth and early twentieth centuries was heavily influenced by the jaunty rhythms familiar to contemporary readers from the Victorian and Edwardian music halls and parlor recitals. However, as I will argue in chapter 7, no such work has been attempted to date with film, television, or radio talk. Meanwhile, Ron Scollon's (1981) analysis of everyday conversation has shown that entrances and exits are intricately timed affairs depending on a regular meter of regular beats, and conversational analysts have also focused on "precision timing" (Jefferson 1973) in managing turns at talk. As we will see in the analyses to follow, fictional dialogue often relies on timing to build up its effects, and a distinctive rhythm may be established between co-conversationalists, especially where they are familiar or intimate with one another. Related to this is the issue of how the rhythms and tempo of a scene of dialogue relate to the surrounding discourse and affect the reader's engagement and immersion in a narrative, though as Franz Karl Stanzel (1984, 68) acknowledges, "We know much too little at this point about what goes on in the reader's imagination when he is led in his reading from a fairly long narrative passage to a fairly long dialogue passage and then back again."

In addition to recognizing the limitations of fictional dialogue, most critics agree that when trying to capture a particular speech variety, writers draw on previous literary representations rather than on "the real thing": according to Page (1988), Dickens set the standard for representing the Cockney dialect for generations to come. For Page this is only to be expected where a writer is trying to convey in one medium the effect of language used in another, and he debunks the idea that precision and accuracy are necessary by pointing out that only very minimal changes in spelling are required to signal to the reader that we have a dialect or non-standard variety of speech. Page also claims that it can be very difficult to distinguish one dialect from another without any other overt cues or prompts.

The fact that contemporary novelists still rely on techniques developed by the earliest proponents of the form has led some critics to claim that the novel only affords the writer "a very poor range of mimetic possibilities" (Davis 1987, 180), especially when it comes to group or multi-party talk (see chapter 4), where we might expect more problematic transitions between speakers and perhaps a higher incidence of interruptions and overlaps. In *Carpenter's Gothic* ([1985] 2003) William Gaddis employs marks of omission and dashes to convey the interruptions signaling Liz and Paul's constant war of wills. Meanwhile, A. S. Byatt has experimented with parentheses as a way of marking overlaps in *Possession* (1990). In *Blindness* (1997), the Portuguese novelist José Saramago chooses not to use line breaks to denote speaker transitions, so dialogue is simply absorbed into the narrative discourse rather than being set off from it. However, such experiments are rare, and even where novelists make heroic efforts to capture new spoken varieties or to foreground taboo forms of speech, it seems that orderliness and politeness are somehow taken for granted when it comes to the organization and management of talk in fiction.

It has been claimed that the "ear" of the reader may be just as important as that of the "writer" (Chapman 1984) and that how readers respond to a particular speech variety may depend on their preexisting familiarity with that variety (Page 1988). It has also been claimed—for example, by Roger Fowler (1989)—that the vast majority of readers will assume that any variety of speech deviating from the standard represents the speech of a social class beneath their own. The whole question of the social stratification of speech varieties in fiction needs to be explored more fully, but for Chapman (1984), at least, this does not necessarily signify a failure on the writer's part so much as demonstrate that the reader is aware of the limitations and conventionality of fictional dialogue and is prepared to interpret the representation accordingly rather than just perform the dialogue as though from a script. Moreover, Chapman maintains that writers may draw attention to the difficulties they face in their attempts at representation so that they "may succeed by the very audacity of presenting the problem and showing how it may be overcome" (195).

Representing Conversational Interaction

The attempt to provide a typology and description of methods and varieties of speech presentation in the novel came largely from within the field of linguistics. However, these studies rarely draw on specific models for the analysis of conversational interaction and have been accused of treating fictional dialogue as just another aspect of the writer's prose style (Burton 1980). Stylisticians have relied more overtly on work from within the fields of conversation analysis, discourse analysis, and pragmatics in their analyses of fictional dialogue, often applying terms and principles directly to extracts from novels "in the expectation that such principles may contribute to an account of how and why, as readers, we have the intuitions we do, make the judgments we do, concerning fictional dialogues" (Toolan 1985, 199).

Toolan draws on Deirdre Burton's (1980) pioneering work in applying the concept of conversational "moves" derived from discourse analysis to the analysis of dramatic texts. Such an approach, which focuses on identifying supporting or challenging moves in a conversation, can help illuminate the characters' pursuit of conversational goals and thereby the power relations existing between the characters. However, Toolan is critical of this model's implicit notion that the intentions of speakers are non-conflicting and transparent, and he looks to Grice's cooperative principle ([1963] 197) and to conversation analysis as a means of demonstrating how conversations are the result of a mutually negotiated process jointly achieved by participants.

Toolan argues that the notion of conversations as locally managed systems, central to the conversation analysts' model, facilitates an analysis that is sensitive to the ways in which participants react and interact with another. Conversation analysis also shifts the emphasis from the purely personal knowledge participants may have to the social norms governing conversation (Gumperz 1982); further, conversation analysis attempts to understand conversation based not on abstract hypotheses but on the conduct of participants, which is observable and available for inspection (Atkinson and Heritage 1984). Conversation analysis insists on analyzing utterances in sequences rather than in isolation or paired strings, and so the allocation and organization of turns at talk becomes crucial to understanding how conversations are managed and how power and control over the conversation are distributed among its participants.

In Toolan's (1987) analysis of a dinner-party conversation from Joyce's *A Portrait of the Artist as a Young Man* (1916) or Leech and Short's (1981) analysis of the authoritarian regime overseen by Nurse Duckett in Kesey's *One Flew Over the Cuckoo's Nest* (1962), recourse to discourse analysis, to speech act theory, or to Grice's cooperative principle facilitates an exploration of the ways in which what emerges from the contributions of interactants is far greater than simply the sum of their parts. For critics of such approaches, the problem is that they tend to treat fictional conversations just like any other data. To pursue that criticism, however, would be to ignore that the sole purpose of this kind of analysis is to better understand how representations foreground and exploit *all* of the resources of conversational interaction for drama and for the illumination of character and character interrelations.

In the following chapters I will draw on theoretical terms and concepts from the fields of linguistics and stylistics while also acknowledging the limitations of these approaches, particularly with regard to their claims to universality and attempts to define what counts as a speech event (chapter 4). In addition, I will be contesting Toolan's claim that literary texts only deal with non-routine talk. On the contrary, openings and closings, phatic communion and the routines of institutions and social groups can be foregrounded, for example for the purposes of humor. In P. G. Wodehouse's novels, characters often seem to get "stuck" carrying out what should be fairly simple and straightforward exchanges such as greetings and partings. Sometimes this is exacerbated by some external or mechanical factor, as in *Summer Lightning* ([1929] 1988), where the chapter "Over the Telephone" graphically portrays the perils and anxieties of initiating and terminating a conversation by means of this unfamiliar "instrument":

"Hugo?"
"Millicent?"
"Is that you?"
"Yes. Is that you?"
"Yes."

Granted, the effectiveness of this exchange relies on the contribution of the narrator, who sardonically interjects, "Anything in the nature of misunderstanding was cleared away. It was both of them" (362). However, because the novelist is prepared to give up so much time and space to these seemingly banal utterances and to shape this unprepossessing material into something that is exquisitely timed and balanced, such exchanges remain memorable.

But the routine and the banal can also be employed to expose petty displays of power and covert displays of control, or simply to dramatize the tedium and frustrations of the characters' lives. For example in *Howards End* ([1910] 1986, 63–64), E. M. Forster uses a conversation between Leonard Bast and Jacky to painfully express the gulf between his aspirations and the reality of his domestic arrangements.

> "What ho!" said Leonard, greeting the apparition with much spirit, and helping it off with its boa.
>
> Jacky, in husky tones, replied, "What ho!"
>
> "Been out?" he asked. The question sounds superfluous, but it cannot have been really, for the lady answered, "No," adding, "Oh, I am so tired."
>
> "You tired?"
>
> "Eh?"
>
> "I'm tired," said he, hanging the boa up.
>
> "Oh, Len, I am so tired."

Here the mirroring of utterances lacks the exuberance of the extract from Wodehouse and seems only to underline Leonard's entrapment. The narrator's sarcastic interventions and later reference to Jacky's lack of skill in the "art of conversation" suggest that our sympathies should lie with Leonard, who at least tries to initiate a topic ("I've been to that classical concert I told you about") and attempts to put on a brave face with his "spirited" opening. But Forster's skill here lies not just in conveying the exhaustion and futility of Leonard's attempt to retain some semblance of communication. Jacky's inability or refusal to cooperate is also hinted at, and the scene's power comes from the almost unbearable tension that exists between the couple.

It is precisely with regard to such exchanges that the linguistic models come into their own, allowing us to focus on the underlying mechanisms that drive these exchanges as much as on what the characters might be saying. In this instance we might draw on John Laver's (1975, 1981) analyses of phatic communion in order to try to understand who has the real power in this scene. Thus, although Leonard appears solicitous of Jacky's welfare, inquiring about her day and "hanging the boa up," such other-oriented tokens are usually only used in "downward" interactions where a socially superior character addresses an inferior. Moreover, employing terms taken from speech act theory, we can see that there is a gap between the literal meaning and the illocutionary force of Leonard's question ("Been out?"), which could just as easily be an accusation as a request for information. The narrator's comment that it "sounds superfluous, but it cannot have been really" also suggests that there is a subtext to the conversation that belies its seemingly banal surface.

This scene offers plenty of evidence that Forster's sympathies lie with the "boy," Leonard Bast, and that Jacky represents the "abyss" (58) into which he might at any time descend. In addition, as has already been suggested, the narrator's comments seem to become more wordy and pompous as the characters' problems in communicating with one another are made evident. Nevertheless, the reader is left discomfited by the scene precisely because the dialogue allows us to appreciate that the relationship is far more complex than the narrator's cutting remarks would seem to suggest.

Thus, just as the study of speech in the novel can highlight the extent to which the fictional world reflects and foregrounds forms of social stratification, so an analysis of the local management systems of conversation may provide valuable insights into the work carried out by those who participate in this system to keep it going. However, as the scene from Forster's novel also exemplifies, we cannot rely on simply reading off fictional dialogue against some kind of "real template," as the history of previous exchanges between participants, and a sensitivity to their nonverbal behavior may be just as important.

Speech Categories and Fictional Minds

This study largely concerns itself with direct speech and free direct speech, terms derived from a typology of forms of speech and thought representation originally devised by Leech and Short (1981). *Direct speech* purports to present a character's actual words, enclosed within quotation marks and framed by speech tags or narrative commentary. *Free direct speech* refers to stretches of dialogue without accompanying speech tags or, less commonly, without quotation marks. *Ulysses* provides many examples of the latter, with dashes replacing quotation marks and with stretches of dialogue only intermittently being marked by speech tags. Leech and Short's model has equivalent terms for the representation of thought (direct thought, free direct thought), so that directness is seen as central to how both the utterances and mind-sets of the fictional characters are conveyed to the reader.

However, the attempt to categorize the representation of speech and thought in this way is highly problematic and contentious. Fludernik (1993) has claimed that such models are not sufficiently flexible to deal with the wide variations in practice we find in the novel; she also attacks them for perpetuating the notion that indirect forms must be derived from direct ones. It seems, then, that the attempt to impose categories carries with it all sorts of assumptions and even biases for and against certain forms of representation. According to Sternberg (1986, 296), "the study of represented discourse has from the beginning privileged the representation of thought over speech, monologue over dialogue," and has been guilty of a bias toward the producer, neglecting the contribution of the "angle of hearing" to the discourse.

In his study of fictional minds in the novel, Alan Palmer (2004) also critiques the speech category approach for privileging direct forms of representing thought as being more mimetic and for implying that consciousness and speech, thought and action are somehow separated by an impermeable barrier. Instead, Palmer calls for a holistic view of the social mind in action, which would allow for speech and thought to be conceived as interpenetrable rather than distinct realms. For example, he demonstrates how even where the focus is on the outward actions and utterances of characters, there may be ample suggestion of how the character experiences, reacts to, and is motivated by what is being said and by what is happening to him or her. Likewise, Palmer argues that the conception of minds as private and passive denies the extent to which thought is social and thinking is a form of social interaction.

Palmer's challenge to the speech category approach and his holistic approach to the representation of speech and thought offer another important means by which we can begin to move beyond the level of the individual utterance in analyzing fictional dialogue and toward focusing on the interplay and interpenetration that takes place in scenes of conversational interaction. In the next section I will argue that this is crucial where we attempt to engage with literary movements and artistic practices where the possibility of distinguishing between internal and external, mediated and unmediated, becomes ever more problematic.

Realism, Modernism, and Postmodernism

In the Victorian period, the heyday of the classic realist novel, the development of techniques for the representation of speech went hand in hand with the attempt to offer readers an accurate portrayal of contemporary society. Critics such as Page (1988) and Chapman (1984) have demonstrated how the representation of non-standard speech varieties in the novels of this period is usually reserved for comic or minor characters and that what passes for realism may be only fairly minor tinkering with spelling or syntax. Steven Marcus (1965) goes further in arguing that in Dickens's novels being well spoken is invariably associated with virtue, while other peculiarities of Dickens's representations include the fact that characters brought up in lowly circumstances somehow manage to rise above their peers linguistically as well as in moral virtue.

N. F. Blake (1981) identifies the Great War as a turning point in the representation of non-standard speech varieties within the novel, writing that this is because the war brought into contact people from different regions and social classes to a greater extent than had been the case previously. This did not necessarily mean that novelists aimed for more verisimilitude in their representations or that prejudice and snobbery somehow disappeared without trace. Yet it is easy to point to examples of experimentation with characters' speech patterns and with fictional dialogue in the first half of the twentieth century. As I will argue in chapter 6, the novels of P. G. Wodehouse and Evelyn Waugh relied heavily on dialogue for their humor, while alongside them, writers such as Ivy Compton-Burnett and Henry Green were working on developing full-blown dialogue novels in which there is virtually nothing other than the characters' utterances and their verbal interplay to amuse or intrigue the reader. Again, the dialogue we find in these novels is often highly stylized, with words acting as a "smokescreen" (Page 1988, 140) rather than a window onto the characters' inner worlds, and with repetition and "linguistic poverty" (141) as the norm rather than eloquence and verbal virtuosity. Rather than reproducing existing forms of talk, Compton-Burnett and Green create for their characters social dialects that are echoes of the past as much as they are reflective of the present.

In the same period, writers more closely aligned with the Modernist movement experimented with representing speech and thought to explore new forms of meaning-making and new ways of understanding human communication. In his study of Dorothy Richardson, John Mepham (1998) maintains that Modernist writers are interested less in what is said than in the process of saying it, with all of the difficulty and self-consciousness that may entail. In doing so, they cannot rely solely on conventional dialogue but must work toward developing "some device . . . that renders this proximity of the spoken and the unspoken on the printed page" (118). Thus although Modernism is most prominently associated with the development of techniques for the representation of consciousness, the idea that interiority is somehow privileged as a result may easily be contested with reference to the "scenes of talk" presented by such writers as Virginia Woolf (Herman 2006) and by understanding that speech and consciousness do not have to be conceived of as bounded activities. Melba Cuddy-Keane (1996) has shown that Woolf was able to draw on a rhetorical tradition in which conversation is associated with conscientious political action so as to attempt to create an alternative to the authorial dominance of patriarchal discourse. Meanwhile, Aaron Fogel (1985) sees in Conrad's poetics of dialogue a refusal to ignore the extent to which force and danger play a part in our conversational interactions and a challenge to what he calls the "conversational idealism" (174) of the "great tradition." Such practices may leave us more discomfited than reassured about the pleasures and possibilities of conversational interaction, but they are important in reminding us that not to recognize these truths and realities would be to subscribe to a partial and narrow conceptualization of what such interactions may entail.

But it is perhaps Joyce's writing that effected the most obvious challenge to prevailing conventions and conceptualizations of speech and dialogue in the novel. As Chapman (1984) has demonstrated, Joyce goes beyond modifying spellings of words to make subtle adjustments to syntax, lexis, and idiom. More significant, perhaps, was his attempt to blur the boundaries between narrative discourse and character speech and to blend speech and consciousness. Conversations taken from Joyce's novels have provided fertile ground for analysis (e.g., Toolan 1987) because they are so effective in "forcing us to reflect on our canons for conversational coherence" (Herman 1994, 219). Nevertheless, even here it may be that when it comes to how talk is organized and managed by fictional interlocutors, those canons remain virtually intact. Moreover, Davis (1987) claims that if Modernist literature is prepared to present us with the incoherent and the incompetent, this only serves to further underline the power of art, and of the artist, to rise above this and to comprehend and effectively communicate that vision through his or her command of language.

In contrast, it has been claimed that the novel of the mid- to late twentieth century increasingly focuses our attention on "micro-social transactions" (Mepham 1997, 419) in which the means by which a conversation is conducted and organized itself becomes a major focus. Mepham argues that the contemporary novel displays a change of attitude toward speaking as an activity. The novel continues to be fascinated by what makes a character's speech distinctive, what Mepham calls his or her "verbal style" (415), and since the 1950s and 1960s, Mepham claims, there has been significant expansion in the rendering of these styles, signaling a shift away from the "condescension or neglect" (416) of previous representations. However, Mepham sees during this period a more significant shift in the form of increased sensitivity to what he calls "conversational style," which relates to what is being done or achieved in a conversation, and which considers speech from an interactional perspective.

The importance of conveying the fabric of our verbal interactions vividly and authentically has therefore not diminished, especially for members of marginalized groups who may feel that their voices and interactional styles have not been given an adequate hearing (M. Bradbury 1992). Writers continue to try to develop ways to celebrate oral cultures and immerse readers in the verbal worlds of their characters, even if this can sometimes pose difficulties of comprehension. These issues are perhaps most apparent in the postcolonial novel, where writers may incorporate varieties of English unfamiliar to the reader, as in the use of pidgin, Creole, or Black Vernacular English. However, the fact that writers may be aiming for realism in their representations does not mean that they subscribe to the kinds of aesthetic and ideological assumptions inherent in the modes and practices of classic realism. Postcolonial critics also question whether it may be inherently patronizing and even racist to assume that writers from emerging nations must all adopt the same "naive" techniques.

Indeed, postcolonial writing is often influenced by traditions and genres of storytelling that carry their own inflections and takes on realism, as in the case of magical realism. Furthermore, contemporary realism may be informed and influenced by Modernism and Postmodernism and may be characterized by anxiety, irony, and speculation rather than confident assumptions or assertions about how the world is (M. Bradbury 1992).

In postmodern fiction, the grounds establishing what constitutes the "real" are even more unstable, as novels present us with a plurality of fictional worlds, blurring genres and the boundaries between the fictional and the real. Louise Barnett has even claimed that "postmodern characters either have nothing to say or are resigned to the impossibility of saying it" (1993, 220); in contrast to Modernist fiction, she argues, postmodern fiction offers the reader no relief from the linguistic failures on display. Nevertheless, Postmodernism's playfulness and engagement with popular cultural forms opens up new opportunities for the novel in terms of the speech varieties that may be represented. Moreover, postmodern fiction often disrupts linearity and facilitates experimentation with narrative structure, challenging and disrupting the ways in which scenes of dialogue relate to one another and to some sense of an ongoing, stable context for the characters' talk, as I will explore more fully in chapter 8.

Conclusion

When we begin to scrutinize the conventions and devices for representing speech that have become naturalized over time, it becomes clear that these are subject to stylistic, historical, and cultural variation. The emphasis shifts from simply trying to pinpoint a formalist preoccupation with *how* the effect of the real may be created to trying to understand *why* readers are prepared to accept lifeless marks on the page as somehow sufficient to evoke the complex sounds, nuances, and dynamics of face-to-face communication. Moreover, approaches that draw on linguistic models of conversational interaction have demonstrated that "it is not how the characters 'really' speak that matters, but rather how their speech shows them to stand in relationship to others" (Chapman 1989, 168).

In the chapters that follow I will be focusing on analyzing fictional dialogue as a mode of social interaction, instead of attempting to add to the already substantial body of work on varieties of speech in the novel. I will be drawing on some of the theories and approaches discussed in this chapter, including stylistic analyses of fictional dialogue and developments in cognitive narratology, in order to aim for a more "holistic" account of existing novelistic practices. But as will become more evident in chapter 2, I will throughout be using these approaches and my own analyses to scrutinize and challenge the extent to which they help support a partial, but nevertheless incredibly powerful and dominant, "idea of dialogue."

2 The "Idea of Dialogue"

The previous chapter argued that the study of fictional dialogue has been overly preoccupied with charting the varieties of speech presentation available to novelists and with debating the "realism" of particular representations. As I will argue more fully in chapter 4, the tendency has also been to focus on the "duologue of personal encounter" (Kennedy 1983) and on isolatable "scenes" where the characters' talk has clear boundaries and identifiable outcomes. For some critics and theorists, however, it is necessary to reflect on whether fictional representations themselves help to instantiate an "idea of dialogue" that has an impact not only on how we conduct our everyday verbal interactions but also on our wider social and political relations. Central to such rethinking is work drawing on Bakhtin's (1981) dialogical principle and the influence of linguistic theories and models that have demonstrated the importance of approaching conversational interaction as a microcosmic social system in which the distribution of power may be uneven. Cultural and literary historians have also explored the ways in which conceptions of the "art of conversation" may be subject to historical and cultural change and may be both reflected in and shaped by novelistic representations. Finally, the idea of dialogue may be revisited in terms of the versions of the self and of the mind that it helps perpetuate, for example, in recent work drawing on cognitive theories or in debates surrounding the concept of intersubjectivity. This chapter will outline and engage with debates in each of these areas, beginning with some of the important historical antecedents and contexts, before exploring the idea of dialogue with specific reference to *Deception* ([1990] 1992) by Philip Roth.

In the Beginning . . .

Most studies of dialogue begin with analysis of the etymology of the term and with some discussion of the classical tradition from which it stems.

The appeal to tradition seems designed to provide a kind of validation of dialogue and to elevate it beyond the everyday. For example, in her study of dialogue in the genre of romantic comedy, Kay Young (2001, 19) takes us back to the Socratic dialogue as "something like the 'first' or model conversation of Western thought." Although Young acknowledges that this model "both reveals and obscures the nature of conversation" (19), she maintains that its legacy persists in the assumption that conversational exchanges will somehow bring us to knowledge and truth. The implications of such an idea of dialogue are left unchallenged, and instead, as is so often the case, Young goes on to trace a line of development from the classical tradition through to models of conversation from philosophy and contemporary linguistics, suggesting continuity and stability, universality and consensus. Perhaps because of her subject matter, Young's analysis retains a rather idealized view of conversation as facilitating "betweenness" (4) and as exhibiting the "energy of give and take." While these qualities of dialogue are not in dispute, what is more contentious is the absence of any critique of the forms of talk discussed and the ways in which they may disseminate and perpetuate certain values and social norms.

Conversation and Conduct

Another important source for those interested in the history of conversation and dialogue are the conduct books and manuals produced across Europe from the seventeenth century onward. In his study of "the art of conversation," Peter Burke (1993) argues that these attempts to formulate how conversation should be conducted were part of a wider cultural shift toward exercising self-control and that these print models influenced not only attempts to write down speech but also how people comported themselves in everyday conversation. Moreover, Burke claims that the novels and plays of this period "affected the speech habits of at least some of their readers . . . offering them not only ready-made phrases but paradigms of good and bad talk, which may appear no more than 'common sense' but are actually culturally determined norms" (120). The association between moral virtue and good practice in conversation has a long lineage, therefore, and is at the heart of other, more explicit attacks on the idea of dialogue, as we will see. Although Burke charts how the precepts attempting to fix and define good practice may diverge across different time periods and cultures, he demonstrates how an idea of dialogue emerges that is still recognizable in current formulations of conversation, from conversation or discourse analysis to the work of philosophers like Paul Grice.

The modern novel continues to pay lip service to the notion of conversation as an "art," especially in examples of "table talk," where characters come together in usually fairly formal circumstances, such as a dinner party or social gathering, to engage in competitive but usually well-regulated discussions of weighty matters. In the novels of D. H. Lawrence and Aldous Huxley, for example, set-piece scenes are given over to intellectual and philosophical debates of various kinds and are seen as both ennobling and enriching for participants. Even where the situation may be less formal, we may find characters delighting in crafting their contributions and critically reflecting on the conduct and quality of their exchanges, as is often the case for the couple in Roth's *Deception*.

In many respects the very conventions developed by novelists for representing fictional dialogue could be said to carry ideological meaning, and in the nineteenth century in particular, various devices helped consolidate what Mark Lambert has called the "integrity of speech" (1981, 23), whereby directly recording characters' utterances came to be accepted as a mark of authenticity but also of value. Lambert even claims that layout and the visual appearance of dialogue on the page help contribute to dialogue's prestigious status, as it flaunts its luxuriousness in leaving so much white space unused. Similarly, David Herman (2006) has shown how typography and layout help shape how we approach fictional dialogue as identifiable and discrete sequences of "turns," without, it seems, any unseemly jostling for the floor or any unevenness in terms of the rights of those who may wish to participate and contribute to the talk. By these means, therefore, it is clear that the expectation of good conduct and decorum in conversation is not confined to the past but is continually being reinforced as the preferred framework within which both individual contributions and exchanges between characters may be understood.

Resisting the Idea of Dialogue

One of the most polemical attacks on the idea of dialogue is offered by the critic Lennard J. Davis as part of a more generalized critique of the practice of novelists engaged in "creating humans in the image of an idealized, middle-class image of themselves" (1987, 120). Like Burke, Davis looks to the seventeenth and eighteenth centuries to explain "how these sets of signs and arrangements on the page, which actually look and sound almost nothing like real conversations, got to be accepted as the rule for conversation rather than the exception" (163). Davis, too, holds that as a consequence of this process "readers then tend to think of their own natural speech as a replica of that printed form" (163) and come to conceive of conversation as crucial to the pursuit of truth and knowledge.

Davis seeks to distinguish between conversation, as the product of the immediate context, and dialogue, which he characterizes as monolithic, non-negotiable, and non-egalitarian and subject to the absolute control of the novelist. Thus for Davis the free-flowing, rational exchanges we find represented in novels serve "to display for us that there is really no problem in social organization" (177), but this is only because they are "denuded of most of the heteroglossia and popular strength of actual conversation" (178). In particular, Davis holds that the novel displays a "prejudice against the group" (180), relegating any collective voice to the "less than admirable" form of rumor, gossip, or paraphrase. Davis rails against the duplicity of the novel in helping to perpetuate "the illusion of a group practice and a multiplicity of voices without the attendant obligations and responsibilities of membership in a group" (181).

Davis offers a passionate and persuasive critique of the idea of dialogue, but his concept of fictional dialogue is almost wholly based on pre-twentieth-century fiction, and the realist novel in particular. Although Davis stresses that he is calling for resistance toward rather than outright rejection of novels, he offers few examples of writers who may have experimented with or challenged the idea of dialogue, and indeed he does very little to engage with or analyze specific scenes or representations. Thus while Davis's argument is important and thought-provoking, it is not difficult to find examples to challenge and contest some of his claims.

Conversation and Coercion

The notion that models of dialogue and conversational interaction may conceal or deny the operation of power is also explored by Aaron Fogel (1985) in his analysis of what he calls the "coercion to speak" in the novels of Joseph Conrad. Fogel offers a critique of theories of dialogue that associate it only with the "fun" and "free," arguing that they neglect the extent to which conversation can be coercive and authoritarian. In Conrad's novels, Fogel contends, dialogues are *made* to happen and are often brutal encounters that display a "recognition that communication itself is by nature more coercive and disproportionate than we think when we sentimentalize terms like *dialogue* and *communication*." Fogel goes on to explicitly reject the notion that dialogue is somehow inherently "mutual," "sympathetic," or "good." Although he claims that Conrad is unique in the particular ways in which he exposes this coercive aspect of dialogue, we will see that Roth's novel similarly reveals how seemingly innocuous exchanges can be difficult and even cruel affairs.

But Fogel is not merely concerned with suggesting that existing forms of talk in the novel may not present the full picture. He also argues that dialogue scenes return "home" to a "unified idea of dialogue" (14) that constitutes "a picture of the social covenant" (193). According to Fogel, "dialogues display a kind of miniaturized, static social constitution" (13) that is "used and imposed" (233–34) on those who do not have power by those who do. Like Davis, therefore, Fogel connects the idea of dialogue with the exercise of social and political power and with false notions of freedom: "Conversation itself, though we like to think of it as a freedom, may be a complex form . . . learnable only by an elite, an implicit set of rules of freedom, devices for appearing free" (13). In contrast to what we see in most novels, Fogel maintains that "most real speech between classes is probably not conversational" (174–75), and he finds in Conrad's fiction—in scenes of coercion within the domestic sphere as much as in displays of institutionalized or official power—a novelist who is prepared to challenge and expose the "conversational idealism" (174) for which these other forms of communication appear not to exist.

The Politics of Dialogue

Implicit in studies such as Fogel's is the belief that how dialogue is represented in fiction is important because of what it tells us about our social relations and because these representations in turn help fix and naturalize those social relations in ways that are inevitably partial and uneven. Such an approach often develops as a riposte to philosophical theories such as those of Habermas or Bakhtin, in which dialogue is made to stand for a certain kind of democracy (Hartley 2000). In particular, recent work on Bakhtin has focused on highlighting the blind spots in his theories, especially what many see as its tendency toward idealism.

Foremost among these critiques is Ken Hirschkop's (1992) attempt to set out the limits of dialogue in response to what he sees as some of the "fantasies" (113) prompted by Bakhtin's theories. Hirschkop challenges the ways in which those following Bakhtin attempt to "smuggle in" (106) liberal values and a kind of "ethico-political baggage" (105), resulting in the worst kind of naive populism. Recognizing that the term *dialogue* has a political charge that distinguishes it from conversation or chat, Hirschkop also acknowledges its allure: "Dialogue is so powerful a value in a liberal democratic political culture, so evident a political value, that the invitation to find it in literary works may prove impossible to refuse" (102). Hirschkop's aim is to rescue Bakhtin's work from this kind of hijacking and to challenge the tendency of critics to conflate dialogism and dialogue. He demonstrates that the exchange of ideas and positions we routinely associate with dialogue is not a necessary or inevitable good and is in fact "unrealisable in all but a few situations" (111).

Peter Middleton (2000) shares Hirschkop's impatience with the misappropriation of the idea of dialogue, but he locates his critique of Bakhtin's theory as part of a robust attack on what he calls dialogue's "hegemonic" (31) hold over the contemporary novel. In setting out to explore the "politics of dialogue in fiction" (34), Middleton questions whether "dialogue is the linguistic modality most representative of the human condition" (31), despite the fact that so many "current beliefs about language, speech, and conversation contribute to its inevitability" (31). Like Fogel, Middleton claims that other "socially significant forms of interaction" (33) are sidelined because of the dominant belief in "the polity of communication" (38) that dialogue exemplifies. And, like both Davis and Hirschkop, Middleton believes that "the means of representing sociality has ethical consequences" (39), ensuring that it is much more than a matter of stylistic preference.

As well as critiquing Bakhtin's theories, Middleton turns his attention to what he calls the "prosthesis" of the Habermasian ideal speech situation, on the grounds that it too perpetuates an "ethical ideal of unimpeded communication" (41). For Middleton, then, analysis of the role of dialogue in the novel entails examination "into the limits and possibilities of dialogue in politics, public spheres and public spaces" (44), and he, like Davis, argues that our understanding of intersubjectivity and social relations is, at least in part, "trained" by novels, films, and television. According to this view, analyzing dialogue is no longer just a matter of deciding how true to life or effective a particular representation may be. Instead, the stakes are incredibly high, as "understanding the history of dialogue in the twentieth century novel can help us learn more about the political efficacy of idealized self-images of interaction and intersubjectivity which underwrite our politics" (56).

Increasingly, therefore, it seems that the analysis of fictional dialogue entails engaging with a concept of dialogue that has long-established but still contentious philosophical roots. In particular, theorists set out to question the seeming freedoms that dialogue offers and the extent to which our notions of dialogue rely on a conceptualization of language that is very much open to debate. For her part, Lucy Hartley (2000, 71–72) explores the possibility that "dialogue is something like a neutralizing linguistic space within which opposing voices are reconciled and the activity of conversation takes on the regulating form of a linguistic ideal." She associates dialogue with "an idealized understanding of language" (71) in which "communication seems to depend upon a straightforward exchange of meaning" and a belief that participants always say what they mean. Moreover, she contests the implicit assumptions that dialogue is a model of "right" communication and "the exemplary means of linguistic harmony and social cohesion" (72).

Critiquing the idea of dialogue in this fashion thus necessitates a radical rethinking of how we conceive of language and communication more broadly as well as how we understand language in relation to wider social and political formations. All too often this kind of argument is conducted at a very abstract theoretical level, without reference to the actual practices of novelists or writers. But in her study of Shakespeare's "social dialogue," Lynne Magnusson (1999) combines detailed linguistic analysis of specific dramatic scenes with reference to discourse theorists such as Bourdieu and Bakhtin in order "to relate linguistic texture to social, cultural and ideological practices" (6). Magnusson focuses on what she calls "relational scripts"—for example, those for personal friendship or service—as these are subject to cultural variation and value, and she demonstrates how these scripts, which often center on two speakers, cannot be understood without reference to the larger social forces that help shape them as discourses. Magnusson's work demonstrates that revisiting and contesting the idea of dialogue need not mean that we dismiss literary representations or merely point out their limitations. Instead, understanding how specific forms and norms of representation both reflect and help shape existing social practices and structures only serves to underline how scenes of dialogue are perhaps far richer and more complex than previously thought, and therefore that there is still much to be gleaned from their closer analysis.

The Lessons from Linguistics

Magnusson's study draws on recent work in linguistics and demonstrates how this has gone beyond formalism and description to provoke just the kind of questioning of the idea of dialogue that we have been considering. In calling for a radical rethinking of how we approach fictional dialogue, Middleton (2000) likewise draws on linguistic theories that offer a way of exploring alternative conceptualizations, especially of intersubjectivity. He notes how conversation analysts conceive of intersubjectivity as being locally managed, and he supports Deborah Schiffrin's (1990) attempts to shift discussion of intersubjectivity away from a simplistic reliance on mutual understanding. Certainly, the work of conversation and discourse analysts has been hugely influential in allowing us to analyze and demonstrate how conversations enact rather than simply display power, and how the social relations between participants are constituted by, rather than merely being reflected in, their conversations.

Increasingly, those working with theories and models concerned with the operation and management of conversational interaction have become skeptical of claims of universality. For example, despite recognizing the value of Grice's cooperative principle ([1963] 1975) for the analysis of fictional dialogue, Michael Toolan (1985, 199) has argued that "it may be that (in Western culture at least) cooperativeness is a more widely applied norm of conversational behavior than any other, but this does not mean that other principles—e.g. of submission, coercion, resistance, tact—do not exist, nor that they are not quite central to understanding particular types of interaction." Meanwhile, Carole Edelsky's study of turn taking in conversation ([1981] 1993, 201) has demonstrated that "one-at-a-time is . . . not a conversational universal, nor is it essential for the communication of messages," suggesting that we may need to revisit how we approach multi-party talk and account for its relative neglect in novelistic representations (Thomas 2002).

Work on cross-cultural and cross-gender interactions also challenges claims of universality by highlighting the fact that "when a certain kind of interaction is the norm, those who feel comfortable with that type of interaction are drawn to participate, and those who do not feel comfortable with it recoil and go elsewhere" (Tannen 1998, 22). For example, Tannen's study of overlapping speech in the talk of New York Jews (1999) offers an alternative to the "turn-taking mechanism" (Sacks, Schegloff, and Jefferson 1978) of conversation analysis, where the norm is that only one person speaks at a time. Tannen demonstrates that in the context of New York Jewish table talk, overlapping is an important expression of enthusiasm and interest, a token of involvement and engagement with the ongoing interaction. What Tannen and others seek to demonstrate is that conversation and the context in which it takes place is never static but is dynamic, and even those who participate in the talk might not always be in agreement as to how it may be characterized. In Roth's *Deception*, the Jewish "Philip" and his English lover often comment on their cultural differences and the misunderstandings these may cause, while gender and age differences equally provide grounds for some of their conversational mismatches.

In a similar vein to Tannen, linguist Sara Mills (2004) has challenged the universality of politeness principles, especially the idea that politeness means the same for all regardless of their social class. On the contrary, Mills claims, behavior deemed polite in certain class contexts would be considered impolite and rude in others. She argues forcefully that linguists need to start to address the implications of this as it extends to judgments that go beyond those about the linguistic competence and appropriateness of speakers and hearers in conversation. Such work has important implications for the idea of dialogue and the kind of value judgments we make about characters' contributions and behavior. There is also much work to be done in examining the extent to which novelistic representations even allow for the display of impoliteness, especially when it comes to the management of conversations and the virtual invisibility of interruption and overlapping in scenes of direct speech.

The Talking Cure

Once conversation is approached as "a little social system" (Goffman 1967, 113), rather than as a universal given based on fixed principles and modes of conduct, we can begin to probe not just what conversation *is* but also what it is *for*, as well as how we value it within a particular cultural framework. For example, many theorists have suggested that the late twentieth and early twenty-first centuries display a faith in a "talking cure" (Shattuc 1997), wherein self-expression and trying to make oneself understood are seen as necessary goods (Zeldin 1998), and where successful communication can be taught by self-appointed experts and gurus. John Mepham (1998) discusses the emergence of some of these ideas in relation to Modernist fiction and the influence of psychoanalytic theories on the representation of speech and thought. He reminds us that "the therapeutic speech situation is an invention, historically novel and with specific cultural origins, which has now become so commonplace and with so many variants (of therapy and counselling) that we have lost sight of how strange and new and unlikely it must have seemed" (105). Mepham argues that many novelists in the Modernist period were resistant to this "new and unlikely" speech situation and the demands it placed upon speakers and those who chose not to speak. It could equally be claimed that this resistance and skepticism has persisted beyond the Modernist novel into late-twentieth-century and postmodern fiction, as I will explore further in my analysis of *Deception*.

Deborah Cameron (2000) focuses her attack on norms and beliefs about speech and conversation emerging from corporate communication and observes that the privileging of disclosure and shared intimacy in contemporary culture means that other qualities, such as reticence, have become socially dispreferred. While Cameron acknowledges that there has always been a connection between being a good talker and being a good person, she goes on to point out that "whether some person, or group of people, has good, bad or indifferent communication skills is entirely dependent on what 'communication' is taken to be, and what is thought to constitute 'skill' in it" (145). Again, Cameron insists on a link between communicative practices and prevailing social relations, maintaining that "co-operation and consensus are strategies that work best in a context of basically egalitarian social relations; where relations are unequal, however, the norm of co-operation may in practice serve the interests of the more powerful party—in other words, reproduce the status quo" (173). Such work is important not only for providing us with an understanding of the contexts and conditions in which certain notions of communication and consensus come to prevail, and in which writers and artists create their representations, but also in reminding us that these notions need to be contested and challenged at every turn.

The Role of the Addressee

Implicit in many of our models of interaction is the assumption that conversational behavior is always a reflection of the true intentions of participants, and that what one person says (and means) is readily available and comprehensible to the other. Yet Gadamer ([1975] 2004, 385) reminds us that "we say that we 'conduct' a conversation, but the more genuine a conversation is, the less its conduct lies within the will of either partner." Accepting such a view does not entail subscribing to an idea of dialogue as some idealized realm of mutuality and reciprocity, as the display of "will" may be spirited and even antagonistic to the other. However, it does point to the need to focus on the role of the addressee in conversation, which has become a central concern of both linguistic and narratological approaches.

Speech act theory demonstrated that what we do in our day-to-day interactions has important consequences for ourselves and others, but much of its emphasis was on what kind of action is being performed by the speaker. Michael Toolan (1985) argues persuasively for an analysis that takes into account the perlocutionary effects of speech acts, allowing us to move beyond a preoccupation with speaker intention toward an understanding of how utterances are used and taken up by participants in specific situations. Meanwhile, an emphasis on sequentiality in conversation analysis means that participant roles are recognized as being interchangeable and in flux. Utterances display "recipient design" (Sacks, Schegloff, and Jefferson 1978), and the "turn-taking mechanism" relies on participants being sensitive to next as well as prior contributions. As Heritage and Watson (1979, 139) explain, "For every about-to-be-produced next utterance, members must locate a methodic basis for the previous utterance's production and assess the prospective consequentiality of that basis for the production of a next utterance. Similarly, for many just-produced utterances, a methodic basis for their selection may be found in some relationship to an immediately preceding utterance." Although the "methodic" nature of this process has been disputed, such a model clearly demonstrates that participants' contributions to conversation are not confined to their verbalized expressions but consist just as much in the work they conduct in constantly anticipating and revising their responses and reactions to the ongoing talk.

In the field of narratology, Meir Sternberg (1986) has forcefully contested what he sees as the bias toward the producer in accounts of direct speech, arguing that instead we need to pay heed to the "angle of hearing" (302). In particular, Sternberg challenges the "assumption that only those who make an overt contribution to the discourse can impose on it their voices and perspectives" (96). To contest such an assumption necessitates revisiting how we approach and analyze dialogue, as it forces us to reexamine how we define what counts as a contribution and, by implication, who counts as a participant in the talk. Meanwhile, the principle that any analysis must focus on the reception of as well as the exchange of utterances is crucial to unseating an idea of dialogue in which certain forms of participation and involvement are privileged over others.

Cognitive Approaches

Perhaps most radically of all, postclassical narratology argues for a shift away from isolating stretches of dialogue as text and treating participants as disembodied voices (Herman 2006), toward recognizing how talk and what surrounds it is situated and rooted in specific social conditions. In particular, as was discussed in the previous chapter, cognitive approaches (e.g., Herman 2003, 2006; Palmer 2004) not only contest the notion that speech and thought exist as distinct and impermeable categories but also demonstrate that what is verbalized by characters in conversational interactions is only ever part of the story. Drawing on recent developments in cognitive psychology but also embracing literary theory, linguistics, and philosophy, cognitive narratology demonstrates that intentionality is multi-layered (Zunshine 2003) and that characters' outward behavior and verbalized utterances form a continuum with their inner consciousnesses and both verbalized and unverbalized thoughts. For the analysis of dialogue, such an approach means that conversations are not necessarily easily detachable from the ongoing action, and that what characters do as well as what they say and what they take others to be saying, can tell us a great deal about what they are thinking and feeling, or at least invite us to speculate as to what they may be thinking or feeling. In a novel like Roth's *Deception* this is key to understanding how such a seemingly sparse narrative can convey a richness and complexity to the interplay between the characters that is both involving and intriguing to the reader.

Cognitive approaches also draw on the concepts of scripts and schemata from psychology to suggest that narrative texts depend upon the reader having access to a store of situational and contextual knowledge (Jahn 2005a) that acts as a kind of shorthand facilitating communication in this instance between novelist and reader. The idea of dialogue might in some senses be described in these terms. Typography and layout usually function as visual cues that we are entering into scenes of dialogue, from which the figure of the narrator appears to take a leave of absence. The pattern of give-and-take that we expect from scenes of dialogue also helps to convey that we are entering into a familiar script (almost literally at times) from which we might expect certain behaviors (only one person speaks at a time) and familiar outcomes (someone wins an argument, declares his love, reveals her secret).

Yet while cognitive approaches often concern themselves with describing what may seem like commonsense notions and patterns of behavior, they also demonstrate how the skills and resources we have evolved are there to facilitate and enhance our ability to interpret and be sensitive to what those around us may be doing or thinking. Cognitive narratologists are thus concerned to go "beyond the skin" (Palmer 2004) to try to account for the work that we as readers do in negotiating interactions between characters, work that is much richer and more nuanced than has hitherto been recognized. Thus in interpreting a scene of talk between a group of characters, a cognitive approach concerns itself not with an internalist view of the mind as some kind of discrete container but rather with social minds in action and with the kind of intermental thought that occurs where groups of people are brought together (Palmer 2004). Such an approach suggests that our idea of dialogue needs to be expanded to consider the situatedness of talk not just in terms of the physical environment but also in terms of the ongoing interconnectedness of the characters, whether or not this is something that is within their choosing, and the ways in which what they say or do may be taken up and interpreted by others.

The Idea of Dialogue in the Modern Novel

In many senses it may seem counterintuitive to talk of a prevailing idea of dialogue when we survey the sheer variety and experimentation with the representation of speech that is such a defining feature of the twentieth- and twenty-first-century novel. Along with Conrad's "coercive" poetics (Fogel 1985) we could point easily to the Modernists' blurring of the boundaries between speech and thought, or the absurdists' experiments with sense and structure both on the stage and in prose fiction, as ample evidence against any suggestion of conformity or conservatism. Meanwhile, novels in the comic tradition (Thomas 1995) happily foreground exchanges that are banal, awkward, uneven, and sometimes just plain confused, thereby disrupting as much as they may reinforce prevailing notions of what might make conversations successful, meaningful, or fulfilling for participants. Nevertheless, while engaging in dialogue may be portrayed as tortuous or embarrassing, the assumption is often that such a process is necessary and worthwhile, that talking things through, sometimes just talking, is cathartic, enlightening, or at the very least a means of marking time.

Deception

Philip Roth's late-twentieth-century experiment in writing a novel entirely in dialogue seems to support Peter Middleton's (2000) argument that the dialogue technique has become almost ubiquitous in contemporary fiction. Indeed, Roth seems to relish the challenge of making dialogue do all the work, such that the novel has virtually no plot or characterization in the conventional sense. Even speech tags are kept to an absolute minimum, leading to occasional ambiguity as to exactly who is saying what. Gradually we piece together that the two characters are lovers conducting an extramarital affair and that one of the characters, Philip, is a writer who may or may not be embellishing or inventing the whole scenario for his own amusement. Although we do discover aspects of the characters' individual and shared histories and see the relationship evolve and gradually disintegrate, the novel offers us few certainties in terms of how we might begin to evaluate the characters' behavior or apportion blame.

Roth's experiment was not terribly well received by the critics. Fay Weldon (1990), reviewing the book in the *New York Times*, described it as "a brilliant radio play for a minority audience," while Mark Schechner (2003, 122) reacted against what he saw as the book's contrivances ("cryptic fragments served up a little too reverentially"), finally dismissing it as "too much yadda yadda" (121). Negative reactions to Roth's technique have been accompanied by a mixture of frustration and bemusement with the game of hide-and-seek set up by the novel's central conceit, namely, that the intense and erotic interactions taking place between the two central characters may be nothing more than a ruse concocted by the writer, "Philip," who reveals that "where the real exchange ends and the invented one begins I can't even remember anymore" (181). But I want to suggest that Roth's textual and metafictional maneuvering also has the effect of inviting us to engage with complex ethical issues raised both by the content of the characters' conversations *and* by the very idea of dialogue against which their contributions may be judged.

In many respects, *Deception* appears to reinforce rather than overtly challenge the idea of dialogue as discussed in this chapter. Structurally, the novel takes the form of a series of vignettes based on the characters' duologues, some of which are no more than the "cryptic fragments" that Schechner objects to, while others are more fully developed scenes built around recognizable themes or issues, such as the treatment of Jews in England or the woman's marital difficulties. As there is no action or description as such, the characters' exchanges stand metonymically for a kind of intimacy as they complete each other's sentences and echo and match their words. In this regard, the characters' interactions closely resemble the repartee and banter of lovers familiar from both romantic and comic traditions in the novel and drama, where talking is seen as intrinsically erotic and sensual and is key to the lovers' gaining mutual knowledge and understanding. The total reliance on dialogue seems to set up a kind of "social covenant" (Fogel 1985, 193) with the reader which promises that the experience of deciphering these fragments will be ultimately rewarding and fulfilling, particularly insofar as they may illuminate or make transparent the characters' feelings and interrelations.

The novel opens with the two protagonists indulging in a conversational game that relies on their collaboration as well as their mutual fondness for playacting and for dancing around their true feelings for one another and the realities of their lives outside of this game. The familiar model of lovers' banter is established by means of a punch/counterpunch structure ("You're not middle-aged"; "I certainly am" 10) that soon escalates into an increasingly excited, almost frenzied, exchange of questions. The tone appears playful, and the characters seem to enjoy the freedom to ask each other questions of a personal nature ("Are you entirely heterosexual?" 10) that contribute to the sense of intimacy between them. But at times the questions seem designed to be confrontational or to strike a raw nerve, both in their sheer provocativeness ("What are your real feelings about Jews?" 11) and in hinting at tensions that the bravado and the game-playing only paper over. For example, the subject of the truthfulness of their conversations is broached early on ("Do you tell lies? Have you lied to me already?" 11), as is the suspicion that each is being deliberately evasive ("What things don't you tell me?" 11). Thus although the idea of dialogue as a game persists throughout the novel, as we discover more about the characters and grow more familiar with the pattern of the game and how they play it we recognize that it has become a kind of trap for them, so that the joy and erotic charge they might once have felt is something they can only increasingly despairingly try to re-create.

Roth's novel also plays with the idea of dialogue as a "talking cure," as the relationship between "Philip" and his lover increasingly mirrors that of the therapist and the patient, where he takes on the role of expressing concern and offering reassurance ("How are you doing?" 151) and she offloads her anxieties ("I'm much fatter," 129). Here talking is characterized as a release, carefully prepared for and managed in a safe environment dependent on mutual trust and a shared belief in the efficacy of the process. Philip's control of the conversations and his fondness for questions also cast him in a Socratic and paternalistic role, which is reinforced by his use of diminutive terms of address for "my sweet girl" or "toots." While both participants play up to their roles ("You've come for your lesson" 144) in a highly self-conscious fashion, it becomes clear that Philip's control extends far beyond their sex games and erotic fantasies. He also takes it upon himself to make judgments about his lover's other relationships ("It's beneath you to stay in a marriage because you think you can't get another job" 153) and to refer to abstract concepts such as her "dignity" (153) so as to keep her under his moral control.

Roth therefore reveals a much darker side to these exchanges, so that the reader becomes aware that the relations between the characters are far less harmonious, and less even, than may at first appear. In particular, we see how Philip extracts confessions and disclosures without offering anything in return, and how his utterances are dominated by questions and commands ("Talk about it" 20). His manipulation of the conversations toward frank but often humiliating confessions of a sexual nature, combined with references to being "tied up" (39) and to fetishes (44), serve to frame the exchanges within the context of a kind of sadomasochism where submissive and dominant roles seem to be clearly demarcated.

Here, then, the "coercion to speak" is not simply something that is imposed by one party on the other but is the complex product of those "larger governing shapes" of which Fogel (1985, 195) speaks. The novel might be seen to lend itself to an analysis based on the uncovering of imbalances in gender relations or in cultural variations between the conversational style (Tannen 2005) of a New York Jew and an Englishwoman. But beyond this, the novel provocatively locates the will to talk, or more precisely to make others talk, as part of the pressure to externalize and make public, to perform one's self for others in the expectation of some kind of reciprocation. The "deception" in Roth's novel rests on the abrogation of such responsibility, as "Philip" seems to have very little conscience about exploiting the material he has gathered, to the point of leaving those he supposedly cares for vulnerable and cruelly exposed. Indeed, if we consider the novel nothing more than a metafictional game, Philip emerges as a kind of twisted puppeteer, toying with our responses and emotions as the characters play out their carefully choreographed verbal dance for our amusement.

Nevertheless, as readers we are drawn into the characters' world as we work hard to piece together the "cryptic fragments" we are offered and to construct from these our responses to the characters, their situation and interrelations. As a consequence, we move beyond an internalist view of character and beyond simplistic judgments about blame and guilt, innocence and responsibility. In particular, Roth invites us to imagine the impact that the characters' utterances have on one another, both overtly, where a character verbalizes the other's reactions ("You are getting more and more resentful with every word I say," 112), and covertly, by means of the blank physical spaces that exist between their interactions on the page.

But the "deception" of the title also of course includes that of the reader, drawn into this fictional world only to discover that as far as "Philip" is concerned, the characters are just words, intimacy just a "subject" (187). The game we have been involved in does not provide us with enlightenment, insight, or knowledge but rather with doubt, uncertainty, and even a certain despair. Thus Roth's novel exploits the idea of dialogue only to expose it as a deception, a dangerous game we play to convince ourselves that we can come to know others and ourselves, or to find some kind of "cure" for our anxieties and insecurities, through question and answer, give and take. The negative reactions of critics to the revelation of this deception only serves to underline how much is bound up with the idea of dialogue and how resistant we are to confronting and contemplating its full implications.

Conclusion

As we have seen, the idea of dialogue carries with it assumptions of an aesthetic, ethical, and political nature. Debates about what we mean by "dialogue" inevitably spill over into discussions about language, communication, and meaning and about the rights and freedoms of participants, as well as the responsibilities that participation and representation bring. In the chapters that follow my analysis of fictional dialogue will continue to engage with concepts and debates from politics and the philosophy of language and to aim for greater reflexivity when it comes to trying to theorize and discuss the terms in which these debates are conducted.

This chapter is not intended to be an attack on dialogue or on the ability of artists and writers to challenge and break free from the "hegemonic" (Middleton 2000) or "regulating" (Hartley 2000) forms and practices that prevail at any given time. As we will see, the twentieth- and twenty-first-century novel provides plentiful examples of scenes of interaction that are far from ideal, where cruelties and injustices are powerfully enacted, and where characters struggle to communicate with one another in a meaningful way. Experimentation with the formal conventions and constraints of fictional dialogue has also continued to push the boundaries in terms of what is and is not acceptable or possible in terms of the representation of speech and interaction. However, I believe that a heightened sensitivity to the notion of a prevailing idea of dialogue may have important implications in terms of how we approach the analysis of scenes of talk in the novel. At the micro level it would involve examining how far the characters monitor their own utterances or those of others, while at the macro level we might focus on the narrator's framing of the characters' utterances and the extent to which these "repeatedly fall together" into "whole, strict forms of dialogue" (Fogel 1985, 13), as I will explore further in chapter 5.

PART II   *Narrative Cornerstones*

3 : Speech, Character, and Intention

The speech of fictional characters is often perceived as offering the reader direct, unmediated access to that individual's emotions, desires, habits, and predilections. If a novel does not offer us direct access to a character's thoughts, then speech is the next best thing, providing a "linguistic fingerprint" in the form of an idiolect (Page 1988) that is distinctive and unique to that individual. From this, it is claimed, "our practised eyes will make up the larger patterns of which such indications can be read as parts," so that "it takes very little to make a character" (Kermode 1976, 18).

Such a view presupposes not only that what characters say can be taken to reveal what they are feeling or thinking but also that characters must always mean what they say if we are to be able to trust and place our faith in their speech as somehow an indicator of who they "really" are. In Jerzy Kosinsky's satire *Being There* ([1970] 1997), the gullibility of the political elite is demonstrated when they assume that Chauncey Gardiner is some kind of visionary, when in fact all he is doing is mimicking phrases and expressions he has heard on television. In the case of Chauncey there is no intent to deceive, but elsewhere fictional dialogue often reminds us that "human speech conceals far more than it reveals; it blurs much more than it defines; it distances more than it connects" (Steiner 1975, 229). In particular, Modernist and Postmodernist fictions have disrupted faith in the transparency of character speech, and as new techniques for representing characters' consciousnesses have developed, the boundaries between speech and thought have become ever more blurred. Indeed, Modernist and Postmodernist writing have provoked many debates about the usefulness of the notion of a fictional "character" understood as some kind of stable textual coordinate. Instead, many critics and theorists prefer to talk of "subjectivities" that are fluid, contradictory, and much more clearly *subject to* social and historical forces.

Bakhtin's dialogic theory has raised important questions pertaining to the speaker's ownership of an utterance, showing instead how each utterance carries within it traces of other utterances and always anticipates the response of an "answering word" (1981, 280). It is important, too, to consider how far the context of speech determines whether the characters are free and able to express themselves, as well as the extent to which verbalizing their innermost thoughts is culturally sanctioned or preferred, given that "a word in the mouth of a particular individual person is a product of the living interaction of social forces" (Voloshinov [1930] 1973, 58). As I will discuss more fully in chapter 7, Adam and Nina's fondness for the telephone in Waugh's *Vile Bodies* ([1930] 1987) allows them to avoid discussing anything too "intense." However, in Nicholson Baker's *Vox* ([1992] 1994), the same instrument becomes the ideal conduit for the most intense and frank of sexual revelations. Context is even more significant in Puig's *Kiss of the Spider Woman* ([1976] 1991), where the prison setting means that the characters do not know how much they can trust one another or how much of their conversations is monitored by their guards. Even if a speaker does have freedom of expression, therefore, it does not follow that the speaker can choose or control how his or her utterances and disclosures are received and rearticulated by others.

In this chapter I will be arguing that focusing on dialogue as interaction raises important new questions concerning the representation of character and consciousness in fiction. Drawing on models of verbal interaction and on approaches influenced by cognitive and discursive psychology, I will be critiquing both literary-historical "pictorial" accounts of the speech of fictional characters, and recent attempts to focus on intersubjectivity as a way of avoiding the static and intentionalist connotations of the whole concept of the literary "character." An analysis of a novel by Ivy Compton-Burnett will be used to illustrate the potential of the dialogue technique for opening up new possibilities in the way we conceive of fictional characters and their interrelations.

Speech and Character: Literary-Historical Accounts

To date, most studies of dialogue focus on the ways in which the speech of fictional characters helps to individualize them and provides them with their own distinctive linguistic "fingerprint" (Page 1988, 97). Typically, the analysis is descriptive, with the critic outlining the various techniques employed by novelists for creating distinctive speech patterns and verbal tics for their characters. Such an approach can be very beguiling, as critics often focus on comic traits and idiosyncrasies and revel in the wealth of speech varieties on offer. Page devotes two chapters to characterization, mainly focusing on the nineteenth century and the origins of certain key devices. He argues that many of these derive from the stage, as in the theater speech is vital for helping an audience to recognize and locate characters in relation to one another. Thus characters may reveal details of their past lives in their conversations, but how they address one another may also tell us a great deal about their mutual relations, such as whether they are on a first-name basis. They may also employ certain catchphrases and verbal mannerisms that help to fix them in the reader's mind and help make their speech easily transportable across texts and even across different media. In addition to providing the reader with a means of recognizing and identifying characters, such repetition provides readers with "more of" (Pugh 2005) what they find pleasurable and appealing in a particular character and his or her verbal style.

Page and others (e.g., Chapman 1994; Blake 1981) also consider the sociolinguistic context of character speech, particularly with regard to representations of social and regional dialects. Characters' accents and dialects provide important information about their social status and geographical origins and may prompt some consideration of the extent to which varieties of speech are socially stratified in a given society, as we saw in chapter 1. Although analysis tends to dwell on the realism of the representations, this approach does at least have the virtue of making us examine how wider social and historical factors may influence the representation. In the late-twentieth-century novel, for example, the associations between certain dialects and educatedness or virtue are increasingly problematized, especially in novels such as Alice Walker's *The Color Purple* (1983) or Irvine Welsh's *Trainspotting* (1996 [1993]), where non-standard varieties are foregrounded at the expense of standard forms.

Existing studies of dialect in the novel focus almost exclusively on the nineteenth century. Raymond Chapman (1994) analyzes the ways in which nuances of dialect can be used to convey important changes in a character's social standing, paying particular attention to how the changing status of Henchard in Hardy's *The Mayor of Casterbridge* (1886) is revealed in his speech. Such analyses are important in reminding us that the speech of fictional characters does not exist in a vacuum but is located within social and economic networks in which all sorts of prejudices and imbalances may exist. Nevertheless, the preoccupation with realism means that all too often the analyses treat speech as something that is static and fixed, rather than dynamic and interactive, with the tendency being to refer to the social networks and hierarchies in which this speech exists as being equally fixed and unchallengeable.

Character through Interaction

More recently, critics have demonstrated how focusing on speech in interaction may call for a radical rethinking of traditional conceptions of character and intentionality. Film critic Sarah Kozloff (2000) defends the idea that dialogue reveals character but does at least consider the possibility that seeing character speech as a transparent window to the character's personality and psyche may make dialogue the "handmaid of a bourgeois humanistic ideology" (29). Her analysis moves far beyond the pictorial, taking into account the ways in which predominant speech patterns can emerge in certain films and genres and the vital role that the management of the turn-taking system plays in conveying to the reader key power relations and dynamics. Although Kozloff allows that the verbalization of emotional states in film can be somewhat artificial, she demonstrates how certain set-piece dialogue scenarios—for example, the interrogation of a killer—are vital if the audience is to begin to understand the complex motivations underlying extreme forms of behavior.

In her analysis of Shakespeare's dramatic dialogue, Lynne Magnusson (1999, 4) is much more openly critical of studies that "regard the speech as issuing from within the character rather than from interactions among characters." Magnusson contends that we need to understand character speech not so much as the expression of an individual but as "the locus of social and power relations" (181). She also argues powerfully for a transactional concept of selfhood, in which the self is constituted in what is mirrored back to us in the responses of others. Character is thus not something that can be found "in" isolated utterances or even exchanges but rather something that emerges out of the "history" of utterances the text sets up. Similarly, identity is conceived as something that is always undergoing maintenance and repair.

The shift away from the pictorial approach in recent studies of dialogue demonstrates the influence of those theories and models of conversational interaction outlined in chapter 2. In particular, conversation analysis offers a view of "selves or statuses which are temporarily and specifically claimed and attributed as part of a currently sustained communication arrangement" (Schegloff 1967, 30) and suggests that all the evidence we need for understanding others is to be found in terms of their conversational behavior. The notion of the self as a "reflexive project" (Giddens 1992) that involves the individual actively constructing his or her own biography and social bonds has become very influential in the fields of sociology and media studies, and I will return to it in chapter 7. But a danger of this approach is that it assumes that this kind of project is always productive or empowering. With specific reference to conversational interaction, the assumption is often that communication between individuals is somehow the ideal mechanism for the discovery and emergence of a self that has always been latent, waiting to be discovered or to emerge. As we will see in the analysis that follows, conversational interaction may in fact hinder self-expression, and it may also be the case that the version of the self that emerges is one that is constructed and imposed by others rather than being freely chosen.

As we have seen, John Mepham's (1997) study of fictional dialogue sets out a clear distinction between the character's verbal style—what makes his or her speech distinctive in terms of accent, idiom, and so forth—and the character's conversational style, which is concerned with what his or her words do or achieve within an interactional context. To illustrate this distinction, Mepham offers an analysis of *Carpenter's Gothic* ([1985] 2003) by William Gaddis, a novel written mainly in dialogue that provides the reader with an uncomfortably close insight into the relationship between the central characters, Liz and Paul. Mepham argues that "the pattern and rhythm of speaking can be as indicative of the nature of the transaction which is taking place between the characters as is the explicit content of their speech" (422), and notes in particular the ways in which pauses, interruptions and repetition are used to convey the central relationship and its complex balance of power. Mepham argues that Gaddis's novel displays "an interest in what happens to make conversations go wrong" (424), and indeed very little seems to go right in the exchanges between Liz and Paul, even at the most basic level of being heard and understood. Although Mepham's claim that this kind of emphasis on conversational style is new to the twentieth-century novel seems somewhat overstated, it could perhaps be said that novelists such as Gaddis are prepared to go further than before in foregrounding the ways in which his characters manipulate every conversational resource at their disposal to inflict pain and humiliation on each other.

Studies such as Mepham's still tend to focus on speech acts and the intentions of speakers, meaning that the conceptualization of the interactional context may be rather limited. Goffman's (1981, 9) work on ratified and non-ratified participants and Sternberg's (1986) critique of the ways in which the role of the addressee is neglected in narrative discourse have contributed greatly to challenging the notion that it is only the producers of speech, or those who overtly contribute, that count in verbal interactions. Schiffrin (1990, 133) has also challenged the ways in which analyses of conversational interactions tend to divide up the roles of speaker and hearer, relying on the "tacit assumption that communication is typically verbal and dyadic, and that communicative roles can be neatly segregated as to relatively active vs. passive roles." Schiffrin argues instead for a notion of conversation as a "negotiated accomplishment" (143) in which "even those aspects of self which participants might regard as relatively stable features (e.g. role, status) are interactively negotiated, as are aspects of social relationships (e.g. power, solidarity)" (144).

Rethinking Intersubjectivity

What Schiffrin (1990) calls "the principle of intersubjectivity" has proved vital in enabling theorists to look beyond fixed and static conceptualizations of the roles of participants in conversational interactions, toward an understanding of how subjectivities are constructed and negotiated in the course of those interactions. Here dialogue is conceived as not just being helpful in revealing the self to others but as necessary to the very discovery of that self and to its expression. As Coste (1989, 205) puts it, "dialogue creates a space that gives more meaning to the unsaid." The principle of intersubjectivity can therefore also be used to try to provide some kind of bridge between speech and thought, for example, in Goffman's (1981, 71) claim that "talk brings people together in some sort of intersubjective, mental world."

But if intersubjectivity remains a key principle, it has also increasingly come to be seen as a "problematic" (Schegloff 1992, 1296), defensible only as something that is "*locally managed, locally adapted* and *recipient designed*" (1338). Schiffrin herself calls for a rethinking of intersubjectivity as "not a static assumption of communication, but a negotiated accomplishment of conversation" (143). She also suggests that intersubjectivity should not be tied to the intentions of speakers but must focus more on listener's interpretations and allow for the fact that interactional roles and alignments often change and overlap.

Like Schiffrin, Mepham (1998, 112) draws on the notion of intersubjectivity as a way of moving beyond a wholly private conception of consciousness, but he too recognizes that in the novel "it is accomplished within particular speech regimes which regulate expectations, norms of reticence, what can and cannot be said without discomfort or discourtesy," illustrating that in certain fictional worlds at least, there may be obstacles and resistance to the free expression and sharing of ideas and meanings. In *Carpenter's Gothic*, Mepham points out, Paul dominates most of the conversations between the couple, barely letting Liz speak and apparently not even listening to her when she does so that she has to resort to testing him ("I wanted to see if you heard me" [72]). Whether or not one is being listened to is clearly an important aspect of the dynamics of any conversation, but it is rarely if ever explicitly addressed in theoretical accounts. Gaddis's novel skillfully demonstrates how over time Paul's behavior has worn Liz down to the point where every time she does speak she anticipates being ignored, misheard, or put down in some fashion. Indeed, all of the characters in Gaddis's novel seem hypersensitive, frequently commenting reflexively on the acts of saying, telling, and hearing, highlighting their anxieties about their ability to communicate and be heard. As well as dominating the conversational floor, Paul also ventriloquizes on Liz's behalf, repeating her words back to her and attempting to impose his own meaning on them, forcing Liz to occasionally protest ("I didn't say nobody was home Paul" [75]). Here, intersubjectivity is far from the utopian vision of many accounts and is suggestive more of power and domination than of a free and mutually enriching connection.

Studies of interactions within the family have demonstrated how speakers make full use of every resource within their environment to attempt to gain or maintain control over the discourse and manage conflicts. Tannen (2004) has shown how family pets may be framed as interactional resources, while Alla Tovares (2006) focuses on conversations based around television shows, in which voices from the public sphere are incorporated within conversations about private issues, often directly affecting the participants' own relationships. Such work once again highlights the problematics of attributing intentionality and subjectivity where conversational interactants may routinely be ventriloquizing and giving voice to other perspectives.

Another problem with intersubjectivity is that just because one or more parties *thinks* they have formed some kind of connection, it does not follow that the other party sees things in quite the same way. Studies of conversational interaction have increasingly demonstrated the need to focus on the roles of addressees in negotiating and even shaping the meaning of the ongoing talk; for example, Goodwin and Goodwin (1982, 1) claim that "next utterances transform prior talk." Yet as discussed previously (chapter 2), such studies rarely dwell on the ways in which participants' words may be deliberately twisted and distorted, their intended meanings usurped. Nevertheless, as we will see in my analysis of a novel by Ivy Compton-Burnett, fictional dialogue often focuses on how meaning may be wrested from speakers in a conversation by their interlocutors to the point that it is almost impossible to tell what the speaker may or may not have intended.

It is important, therefore, to be wary of always characterizing intersubjectivity as something consensual or equitable, and we must be sensitive to the ways in which "participation rights may be socially and culturally allocated" (Schiffrin 1990, 133). We should never forget the possibility that seemingly shared understandings may carry at least some degree of "coercion" (Fogel 1985), and as we will see, representations of multi-party talk in particular remind us that participant "rights" in a conversation may be locally managed and subject to huge unevenness.

Peter Middleton (2000, 43) declares himself irritated by the "extreme abstraction" and hidden politics of the "burden" of intersubjectivity and proposes instead that we should see it as "an open-ended set of possible means people have of relating to one another, which is open to many kinds of manipulation." In many fictional dialogues we see that the selves claimed and constructed in verbal interactions may be imposed or shaped by more powerful or dominating personalities or by sets of social relations that make resistance difficult or impossible.

The Problem with Intention

It may also be the case that speakers deliberately distort or conceal their "true" intent. This may be revealed to the reader by the intervention of a narrator in the form of direct commentary or speech tags that expose the deception or dissembling. However, in the dialogue novel, where we are reliant purely on the characters' verbal exchanges, it can be much more difficult to know when the characters are playing games, for example, uttering a particular form of words to provoke a reaction or create some kind of show. In the novels of Ronald Firbank, the reader cannot even rely on the sequencing of utterances to help identify how one utterance relates to or responds to any other, especially in his trademark "babel of voices" scenes (*Vainglory* [1915] 1988, chapter 22), where random exclamations ("Rabbits!") are given no context or where utterances are often left unfinished. In this fictional world, utterances may not have any specific premeditated or deep intent other than to provide the speaker with a momentary diversion or opportunity for display. Moreover, the speaker might not want to reach out to, or even engage with, potential addressees. Firbank's technique in these scenes helps create the impression that speakers have no need or even desire to be listened to or to listen to others, and they often appear quite happy for others to interpret their utterances however they choose, relying heavily on innuendo and suggestion.

Although we tend to think of conversations in works of fiction as being tied to specific scenes or events, their impact may extend well beyond the specific time frame in which they unfold. So often in fiction, what characters intend to say or do in uttering their words on a specific occasion only offers us a partial insight into who they are and how they relate to others in their social sphere. Instead, speakers and hearers may willfully misinterpret, manipulate, and distort their words, possibly long after they have been uttered and in contexts far removed, ensuring that our hold on "character" is both fragile and temporary.

The Relationship between Speech and Thought

Recognizing how the self emerges in interaction with others cannot be isolated from how we understand the relationship between speech and thought or from our very concepts of self and identity. As discussed earlier, Modernist and Postmodernist fictions have problematized any absolute separation of speech and thought and have radically disrupted the notion of character as something stable and consistent. Although the dialogue novel seems to eschew offering the reader any insights into the minds of fictional characters beyond what they consciously and intentionally verbalize, the reader is inevitably drawn into imagining and inferring what lies "behind" the characters' words, their motivations and desires.

Many studies of conversational interaction deal with the relationship between speech and thought and offer conceptualizations of the "self" as something that is constructed within and between verbal exchanges, rather than as something that is already fully formed. Indeed, some approaches (e.g., Antaki and Widdicombe 1998) characterize identities in talk as something that conversationalists *use* to achieve certain ends, rather than something that they "are." Goffman's (1959) work on the presentation of the self in verbal interaction highlights the extent to which the self is something that is performed rather than some kind of essence to be made visible and accessible through verbalization. Similarly, many contemporary studies of discourse directly challenge what Toolan (1985, 195) calls the "idealizing myth of transparent human behavior," focusing instead on how subjectivity is constructed in the course of verbal interactions rather than being revealed through them. For example, Schiffrin (1990) contends that "what is often seen as relatively stable features of self and social life are often found to be interactive achievements that are realized through conversation" (147).

Fictional Minds

Ernest Hemingway's oft-quoted "iceberg" theory[1] (1932, 192) suggests that readers will always try to look for the meanings behind characters' words and deeds and will build their own mental maps for what the characters may be thinking and feeling. But this does not necessarily mean that the minds and consciousnesses of fictional characters are stable, fixed, and available for inspection. Narratologists have seized upon theories of mind from cognitive psychology in an attempt to understand how notions such as those of "the mind beyond the skin" (Palmer 2004) may be evidenced in prose fiction. Moving away from the self conceived as a kind of "Central Headquarters" (Dennett 1996), such approaches facilitate new ways of thinking about the relationship between narrative and identity that have important implications for the concept of character.

Palmer argues that one of the defining pleasures of novel reading is that it draws on our ability to imagine what other people are thinking and to imagine that characters also engage in this kind of mind reading in their interactions with one another. But Palmer takes issue with the overestimation of the verbal component in critical accounts of representations of thought and inner speech in fictional texts, arguing that vast areas of the mind not suitable for the speech category approach tend to be left to a very loose and baggy conceptualization of "character."

Instead of conceptualizing thought as always private and passive, Palmer proposes that it should be conceived of as "purposeful, engaged, social interaction" (2004, 32) and that we understand consciousness as continuous and continuously evolving rather than fixed and static. Such an approach also suggests that we need to reassess how the "gear shifting" (Page 1988) that takes place between speech and thought in prose fiction perpetuates a conceptualization of the two as being entirely separate and distinct. Palmer interestingly chooses to try out his theories on the "behaviorist" novel *Vile Bodies*, not so much to suggest that Waugh's characters have any kind of hidden depths as to show how readers "feel compelled to pour meaning" (317) into the "space or vacuum" they occupy. Even where there appears to be little or no direct reference to the workings of the characters' minds, therefore, Palmer demonstrates that the characters' speech and the framing narrative may provide the reader with ample material for building up a picture of their mental states. Palmer (2007) later draws on attribution theory (Edwards and Potter 1992) to further help to account for how readers attribute mental states and emotions to characters based on what they do and say. Importantly, he allows that this is also something characters themselves do in their dealings with one another, especially in their verbal exchanges, as we will see in the analysis of Ivy Compton-Burnett's *Brothers and Sisters*.

Characterization in the Dialogue Novel

In the dialogue novel, readers often have to work especially hard to unearth even the most basic information about characters. Indeed, at the end of a novel such as Roth's *Deception* we still don't know the full names of the characters or have much of an idea about what they look like, despite having listened in on their intimate conversations. Instead, we have to focus carefully not just on what is said but on how it is said so that we can at least recognize speakers from their verbal mannerisms and feel that we may be getting to "know" them to some degree. We can also infer a great deal about the characters in terms of how they manage their conversations and, according to who initiates exchanges, who asks most questions, as well as other dynamics (Thomas 2007).

Many contemporary dialogue novels, such as Roth's *Deception* and Puig's *Kiss of the Spider Woman*, are composed primarily of duologues between two central characters. Creating the effect of intimacy, as though we are overhearing private conversations, the implication is that we are being given privileged access to the characters and have all that we could possibly require for understanding their emotions and motivations. Such novels also implicitly suggest that the more the characters talk to one another, the more intimate they are likely to be, and the more engaged the reader will be in turn with their stories. Nevertheless, the issue of what we can "know" about other people from their verbal input is often foregrounded and problematized in such novels, as the title of Roth's fiction suggests. Indeed, it could be argued with both of these novels that it is only in the gaps within and between the characters' conversations that they approach true intimacy.

Paradoxically, therefore, the volume and apparent frankness of the characters' talk may be no more than a mask, a device whereby, under the guise of conversing and communicating with one another, they continually dance around the surface of their relationships. It is vital, therefore, not only to focus just on what the characters say, or even how their words are framed, but to examine how their utterances are received and subject to reinterpretation as subsequent conversations and events unfold. Equally, we must be alert to the ways in which other characters may manipulate or distort the intention behind someone's words and consider how humor and irony may affect our evaluation of the extent to which a speaker is committed to what he or she is saying.

Brothers and Sisters ([1929] 1984)

In the dialogue novels of Ivy Compton-Burnett, as Coste (1989) has demonstrated, a distrust of words affects nearly all of the characters, especially when it comes to what they say about themselves or about those nearest to them. Instead, as Coste goes on to argue, the characters attempt to occupy the speech of others with their own meanings, both as a means of controlling others and as a means of ventriloquizing their own desires and frustrations. Although Compton-Burnett's fictions are unique in many ways, they also raise important questions concerning the relationship between speech and intention, speech and thought, and the use of conversation for manipulation, cruelty, and abuses of power.

According to Alan Wilde (1980), Compton-Burnett's novels engage with many of the epistemological concerns of late Modernism, and even prefigure those of Postmodernism. Wilde aligns Compton-Burnett with those "proponents of surface" who reject earlier conceptions of character that cling to "faith in some central core of being," preferring "not to see more deeply but differently" (211). Wilde argues that although Compton-Burnett's narrator seems to offer the reader insights into her characters' minds, this is at an ironic distance. Moreover, he claims that Compton-Burnett's self-conscious and artificial dialogue acts as a "fictional circuit breaker" (213), ensuring that her novels are "reflexive rather than referential" and that her characters remain "unmistakably verbal constructs" (213). Wilde concludes that Compton-Burnett's technique encourages "a view of character as discontinuous and, if not incoherent, still as no more than an assemblage of surface contiguities" (215). Thus Compton-Burnett is a key figure not just in trying to map changing conceptions of "character" in the twentieth century but also in understanding how well the dialogue technique lends itself to "proponents of surface."

As many critics have pointed out, one of the defining features of Compton-Burnett's novels is that the characters commonly vocalize what is conventionally left unsaid. More interestingly, perhaps, the addressees probe and look for hidden meanings, ensuring that the process of uncovering is ongoing (Iser 1978). Thus, although her work is often dismissed as "Victorian," the characters' conversations touch on such subjects as incest, infidelity, homosexuality, and even murder. Although the characters rarely consciously disclose much about themselves, they are more than happy to expose the secrets of others, especially if this involves some kind of public humiliation. They also cannot help but reveal the worst sides of themselves when given an opportunity to inflict pain or humiliation on others, so that often their actions contradict their avowed intentions (Iser 1974). Many of the characters are unashamed of listening behind closed doors, and they know each other so well that they can tell exactly how and when to inflict the most harm. Thus, while it is difficult to engage with or even to like Compton-Burnett's characters, her novels offer a fascinating insight into the ways in which conversations and silences may be manipulated to expose secrets and frailties and to deflect attention away from one's own shortcomings.

In *Brothers and Sisters*, the incestuous relationship between Christian and Sophia is gradually exposed and has repercussions for all of the other brothers and sisters in the novel. As in all of her fiction, Compton-Burnett relies almost entirely on dialogue, but she uses speech tags to maintain ironic distance and hint at the duplicity of the characters; for example, she describes Latimer, one of the more elusive characters, as "covering with these light words the depths of him beneath" (42). Nathalie Sarraute (1963, 119) writes that Compton-Burnett's novels play out "somewhere on the fluctuating frontier that separates conversation from sub-conversation" and uses this distinction as the basis for much of her own theoretical thinking about dialogue. Sarraute's theory seems to imply that the characters themselves are unsure where this frontier lies, as they verbalize and give open expression to sentiments and emotions that might be better hidden. But in a sense Compton-Burnett's fictions are also about exposing the futility of trying to "keep hidden" those "depths beneath," especially in the context of the dangerous conversational games the characters play where they constantly probe at and toy with each other's sensitivities and inadequacies.

Most of Compton-Burnett's novels deal with revelations and traumas of various kinds affecting small groups of people bound together in some way, usually through family connections. Many critics (e.g., Iser 1974, 1978) claim that her characters are barely distinguishable from one another in terms of their speech, and certainly the emphasis is on the interplay between them as an ensemble rather than on their stylistic quirks and idiosyncrasies. Indeed, characters rarely appear alone, and instead the reader is thrust into the midst of scenes, having to negotiate who is saying what as well as what is happening.

The novels often make overt reference to Greek tragedy and to the theatrical; for example, Dinah in *Brothers and Sisters* (102) comments that "We are all of us acting," reinforcing the impression that the characters play versions of themselves and see even the most trivial of actions and utterances as capable of having momentous repercussions. What makes Compton-Burnett's dialogue so distinctive is the openness and sheer lack of tact that the characters display in their interactions with one another; as Robin tells Sophia, "You and I are adepts at saying just the thing at the moment, that a decent person would not say" (153). This is most striking where these exchanges take place between members of the same family, where it seems they can dispense with the mask of politeness and irony employed in more public arenas. Another interesting aspect of Compton-Burnett's style here is the way Robin skillfully attacks Sophia under the guise of attributing motivation to "you and I" jointly. As mentioned earlier, theories of attribution are especially useful in reading Compton-Burnett's fictions, because the characters constantly try to second-guess each other's mental states and motivations, usually as a means of exerting some kind of control. Such behavior challenges the idea that the self is something private or inviolable, as the characters use their interactions to threaten and (re)construct each other's sense of selfhood, usually in such a direct fashion that there seems little room for any contradiction.

In his analysis of Compton-Burnett's style, Iser (1978) maintains that although the characters are continually asking each other questions, this rarely, if ever, results in their achieving any kind of mutual understanding. This is because, according to Iser, the speaker of an utterance may have little or no control over its implications. Indeed, Iser claims that the addressees of utterances in these fictions play a crucial role, because "the process of self-discovery is no longer left to a person entangled in his own interior monologue, but is brought about by someone else. There are times when this revelation is quite brutal" (1974, 152–53). Although the idea of the characters attaining "self-discovery" is highly questionable, Iser's recognition that this might be brought about—even forced—by others and that "the characters themselves seem to be virtually indifferent" to this process demonstrates once again how the dialogue technique forces us to reassess our concept of the characters' inner selves and the impossibility of abstracting this from the complex dynamics and power plays of their often difficult interrelations.

One of the key sources of tension for Compton-Burnett's characters is the frustration that comes from realizing that family ties not only bind them to others whom they can barely tolerate but also bind them to dispositions and behaviors that they cannot choose or alter. The claustrophobia of the settings is also evident in the way characters speak for one another, rephrase what others have said, and generally show complete disregard for each other's privacy and individuality.

Within the Stace family, relations between Sophia and her children are especially problematic, and this is primarily conveyed through their speech. In their own company the children refer to their mother as Sophia; they seem much closer to their nurse, whom they affectionately refer call "Patty." Although Miss Patmore insists on referring to her employer as "Mother," her actions—listening behind doors and acting as a go-between—give her a great deal of influence within the family. Sophia has all the appearance of power: she is constantly issuing orders to those around her and attempting to manage their conversations. She also employs the tactic of referring to herself in the third person and playing the victim ("we poor women" [29]), not realizing how intensely irritating this is even to her own family. But even this supreme manipulator is unable to control how others perceive her, and her increasingly desperate attempts to do so underlie our sense of the pain and frustration this must be causing her.

Although the characters appear pathologically unable to steer clear of taboo subjects, they are highly self-conscious about what can and cannot be said and about how their exchanges with one another are conducted. According to Wilde (1980, 224), they are "creatures of language, caught reflexively in a web of words." When the incestuous relationship between Sophia and Christian is exposed, the pompous Edward comments, "This is a thing to be absolutely silent about . . . to be so silent about, that it does not come to our lips when we are alone, does not enter into our thoughts" (186), but the news soon spreads and provides the subtext for many of the discussions and realignments between the characters that follow. Yet Compton-Burnett in no way presents talk as a "cure" or therapy for the characters. Although Sarah at one point claims that "Everything is less depressing when it is talked of" (97), the experiences of most of the characters seems to contradict this, and their exchanges seem to bring them little joy or relief.

Although they seem to play with and manipulate the surface of words, the conversational stakes are extremely high for Compton-Burnett's characters because the worlds in which they move are so confined that they cannot escape the judgments of others. Although her technique only offers a glimpse of the "depths beneath" her characters, it lays bare all the ways in which one's sense of self is constantly being undermined and challenged, especially by those who are closest to us. If it is the case that "Each individual relies on others to complete one's picture of one's self" (Collins 1988, 49), and that self is constantly being performed, then Compton-Burnett's novels show how the success of that performance can only ever be measured by its reception, and for most of the characters this seems much more likely to be hostile than affirming. Compton-Burnett's fictions do not show us selves emerging from conversations morally improved or enriched by the experience; more often they are damaged and bruised but somehow unable to remove themselves from the arena.

Conclusion

A novelist's reputation may be built almost entirely on his or her ability to capture the speech patterns of individual speakers. For readers and critics, too, endless pleasure can be derived from revisiting favorite characters and their verbal mannerisms. However, all too often the effectiveness of these representations is evaluated on highly subjective grounds, with little effort being made to look beyond the surface of the dialogue other than to catalog the means by which "real" speech is emulated. We have seen in this chapter that dialogue plays a much more complex role in characterization than this would suggest. When we examine the utterances of characters in context, the responses to those utterances, and how they may be manipulated by others, the idea that characters' speech offers us an uncomplicated insight into their personalities and consciousnesses becomes much more problematic. This is not to say that this in any way detracts from our engagement with those characters and their interrelations. Indeed, novels that foreground verbal interactions and show their reverberations may draw us much more closely into the characters' worlds, helping us appreciate more fully the complex forces and circumstances that help drive their behavior and motivations.

4 : Dialogue in Action

As we saw in the previous chapter, dialogue can play a crucial role in immersing us in the social worlds of the characters in a novel. Dialogue also plays a vital role in advancing the plot, both in terms of informing us about the actions of characters and providing what "action" there may be in the guise of important revelations, disputes, and discussions. As with character, in the Modernist and Postmodern novel there is often a shift away from both the depiction of large-scale events and from the attempt to force events to fit into some kind of logical order or design. This can mean that conversations between characters come instead to take center stage, possibly as meaningful "events" in themselves, but equally as diversions from anything too momentous or even purposeful. As we will see, the dialogue novel can be especially provocative in this regard, as is the case in Henry Green's *Nothing* ([1950] 1979b), where the title itself sets up the challenge for the reader to search for something of substance in the characters' seemingly vapid and repetitive interactions.

This chapter will explore the complex relationship between speech and action in narrative fiction, drawing on narrative theory, linguistic models of speech acts and their contexts, and approaches influenced by cognitive science. Specific attention will be paid to the ways in which "action" is conceived in the dialogue novel, and the chapter will also critique static conceptions of context, which focus exclusively on the performance of actions and their immediate effects. The chapter will conclude with an analysis of *Checkpoint* by Nicholson Baker (2004) which specifically addresses issues of intentionality and the implications of talk.

Speech, Action, and Plot

Although it might be thought that foregrounding talk, especially informal conversation, must inevitably result in the action of a novel being halted or pushed to the background, this very much depends on how we define what constitutes "action" in this context. With narrative fiction, action is most often associated with the concept of plot, carrying with it the notion that everything that happens is directed toward some goal or climactic point and that events are interrelated in a meaningful and logical fashion, arousing a sense of expectation and anticipation on the part of the reader. As we will see, dialogue may play a vital role in ensuring the forward momentum and cohesion of plot, but it may also divert and disrupt—for example, by foregrounding the inconsequential or offering different versions and accounts of the same "event" that may not be reconcilable. In this respect it is perhaps no surprise that experimentation with dialogue is a key feature of the postmodern novel's rejection of grand narratives and linear plots and that the dialogue novel has once more come into its own thanks to the work of Philip Roth, Don DeLillo, Manuel Puig, and Nicholson Baker, among others. If indeed contemporary fiction focuses more and more on the dynamics of micro-social transactions (Mepham 1997), then approaches derived from linguistics become even more important for analyzing and dissecting the ways in which these transactions are managed and organized.

Contemporary dialogue fiction draws on a long tradition of verbal repartee in the novel, wherein narrative action is constituted almost entirely by character speech. Here the dialogue is center stage, and the narrative may focus exclusively on the characters' verbal actions and interactions. In the novels of D. H. Lawrence and Aldous Huxley, the "verbal duels" (McDowell 1985) between the central characters are often highly stage managed, closely resembling Socratic dialogues in the way opposing arguments or philosophies are balanced against one another, with the characters devoting all of their energies and drawing on all of their verbal skills to try to gain the upper hand. As was said earlier, such representations draw heavily on conceptualizations of the "art" of conversation, particularly the genre of "table talk" that dates back to the earliest origins of the novel. Alan Palmer (2005, 426) has argued that this tradition closely corresponds to Northrop Frye's (1957) concept of the anatomy, "characterized by exuberant displays of learning" where the characters act as mouthpieces for certain philosophical positions. Palmer traces the influence of the anatomy through to the modern novel, specifically to the work of James Joyce and Iris Murdoch. In such instances the characters may be placed in a context that deliberately restricts their movements and heightens the intensity of their exchanges. This may involve physical restrictions, such as the characters being enclosed together in some isolated or remote spot, as well as social or cultural restrictions that circumscribe what may or may not be said and done.

When dialogue dominates a narrative in this way, there are implications for both structure and pace. The relationship between dialogue and action may therefore be discussed in relation to the distinction made in narrative theory between story and discourse and between the events that constitute the story and how and when these are related to the reader. As discussed in chapter 1, in Gérard Genette's (1980) concept of "scene," stretches of "pure" dialogue represent the closest approximation of discourse time to story time, so that the time of reading is roughly equivalent to the time the action would take to unfold in reality. Although this notion has come in for much criticism (e.g., Brooke-Rose 1978), it remains one of the few theories to engage with the narrative possibilities of dialogue, not just in terms of time, pace, and so forth, but also in terms of what such scenes contribute to the reader's knowledge of and engagement with the narratives in which they are contained. The term "scene" also takes us back to the close links between fictional dialogue and the theatrical. A key concern in this chapter will be to examine and question the extent to which novelists have explicitly organized their fictional conversations into specific "events" or "scenes" and the implications of this for our idea of dialogue. The chapter will also address how far theoretical approaches to fictional dialogue contribute to and perpetuate the idea that exchanges between characters are always bounded, discrete, and purposeful.

Wolfgang Iser (1974) has argued that action in the dialogue novel is all in the present, as we are offered no perspective from which to view events with hindsight. Certainly, as will be discussed in the next chapter, dialogue novels often thrust us into the midst of the ongoing action in a bewildering fashion, sometimes making it difficult at first to orient ourselves in relation to what is happening. Nevertheless, as we will see, even if there is no clear narrative presence to guide us through the events of the novel, the characters' accounts of events from their pasts, cross-references between conversations, and the sequencing and ordering of exchanges ensure that we can gain some perspective on events and evaluate the characters' actions and reactions accordingly.

In her (2000) analysis of film dialogue, Kozloff pays considerable attention to narrative structure, and while the relationship between dialogue and action may be very different in a film as opposed to a novel, much of what she has to say has important implications for the analysis of prose fiction. Among her nine functions of film dialogue, Kozloff includes "communication of narrative causality" and "enactment of narrative events" (33). She argues that dialogue is crucial for providing the audience with a backstory, but her analysis also demonstrates that dialogue plays a key part in terms of both the cohesion of the plot and the audience's ability to piece together the narrative threads. This is most evident where characters discuss or analyze events in the fictional world, offering their own commentary and evaluation of what has taken place and suggesting connections between what might otherwise appear to be disconnected events. Kozloff further suggests that key narrative events in film are often almost entirely verbal, for example, the confession of a secret or a declaration of love. The extent to which the narrative relies on verbal events may vary from genre to genre, but in every genre the relationship between speech and action helps determine the pace of the narrative. Thus, where the action is intense or frenzied, dialogue may be at a minimum, whereas endless discussion of unfolding events may lead to a slowing down of the pace, closely corresponding to Genette's (1980) concept of "scene."

Although Kozloff allows that dialogue in film may function as a kind of "verbal wallpaper," she demonstrates how seemingly endless and empty repetition may represent "a play of reiteration and controlled difference" (188) that contributes hugely to the atmosphere or effects created by the film. Thus, although in scenes of dialogue it may at first appear that nothing much is happening, actions reported by the characters in the course of their utterances, along with the "action" constituted by their engagement with one another, may be an economical and unobtrusive way to create the effect of motion and pace in the viewer's imagination.

Speech Acts

Our language is full of phrases which suggest that talk is somehow less valuable or productive than action (for example, "talk is cheap"; "talking the talk but not walking the walk"). Yet in literary fiction, Lennard J. Davis (1987, 189) suggests that "giving language a priority over action . . . distracts from involvement in actual social conditions, defends against alienation, and reinforces the individual against the group." Pragmatic approaches to language have always tried to bridge this divide, and ever since speech act theory set out "how to do things with words" (Austin 1962) we have become accustomed to thinking about the consequences and implications our everyday conversations might have and of the actions that we perform in participating in them. Peter Middleton (2000, 33) recognizes that "most of what people do to one another is done through speech" and provocatively claims, "Get rid of the dialogue and you have pornography or violence." But it is also important to avoid focusing exclusively on the "doing"; as Toolan (1985) reminds us, we can often only tell "what is going on" in a conversation by focusing on the perlocutionary effects of what is being said. In this respect, as was argued in the previous chapter, we need to extend the analysis of the relationship between speech and action beyond what the speaker intends and focus on the microdynamics of how what takes place between participants in an exchange affects their mutual relations. Analyzing dialogue in relation to action in this way helps to highlight and expose the power relations underlying conversational exchanges while remaining sensitive to how those relations are dynamic and constantly shifting.

The influence of speech act theory on studies of fictional dialogue, especially stylistic approaches (Toolan 1985; Leech and Short 1981), has already been recognized. However, this can result in a rather crude and schematic approach to speech in action, whereby what counts as contributing to the interaction and what counts as a speech event is narrowly circumscribed. Sternberg (1986), among others, has taken issue with the preoccupation with what speakers may be "doing" in uttering their words, arguing that we also have to take into account how the interlocutors receive, respond to, use, and recycle those locutions. Approaches to narrative influenced by cognitive science (Herman 2006) have also argued for a shift away from the atomistic tendencies of speech act theory to a more holistic view in which speech acts are understood within a much wider discourse context as participating in some kind of social drama. Herman (84) stresses the importance of understanding "talk as inextricably embedded in activities rather than viewing activities as a more or less extraneous backdrop for speech."

Such refocusing involves a rejection of static conceptualizations of "context" (e.g., Schiffrin 1994; Emmott 1997), instead recognizing the active role participants play in helping to construct context. Studies of talk in workplace contexts (e.g., Grosjean 2004) have demonstrated how in many situations speech is subordinated to action and that participants may be engaged in a whole range of physical and other activities while a conversation is going ahead. This has important implications for the analysis of fictional dialogue, because in order to understand how speech is socially situated we have to look beyond individual utterances, or even pairs of utterances, focusing instead on whole exchanges and taking into account every aspect of the discourse context. By concentrating on scenes of *inter*-action, therefore, we have to recognize how characters react to one another and take their cues from one another. Other key theoretical influences here include the emphasis on talk as social action in the work of Voloshinov ([1930] 1973) or Bakhtin's concept of dialogism (1981). Discursive psychology (Edwards and Potter 1992) has also usefully highlighted how "what really happened" is an outcome of how people formulate events in their talk, such that the meaningfulness and coherence of those events is not given but constructed.

Speech, Thought, and Action

As outlined in chapter 1, Alan Palmer's (2004) critique of the "speech category approach" highlights the importance of recognizing how speech reflects the mind in action, in opposition to critics' prevailing tendency to conceptualize thought as private and passive rather than as socially situated in a specific context. "Action," according to Palmer, thus needs to be understood even more broadly to accommodate the mental functioning and motives of characters as well as the literal "acts" they perform. His analysis demonstrates how difficult it is to find descriptions of actions in novels that do not carry with them some suggestion of the speaker's state of mind, pointing to the impossibility of sealing conversations off as bounded "events."

Narrative Devices for Contextualizing Speech

Palmer focuses in particular on speech tags that help contextualize speech in terms of some kind of action ("he murmured, moving away from her") but which may also hint at the emotions or attitudes of participants toward what is going on around them ("he conceded, getting up wearily") or their motives for acting ("she insinuated, slyly"). As was said earlier, Norman Page (1988) calls these "stage directions," once again taking us back to the theatrical paradigm and making explicit the extent to which dialogue unfolds within an environment and social context where there may be a good deal going on, affecting both what is said and how interlocutors respond to it.

Where we have the more extended "suspended quotation" (Lambert 1981), the narrator may make even more explicit both the context and the actions surrounding the ongoing talk, creating an effect not unlike that of the camera zooming out from a conversation or an exchange to take in what is going on around it. The suspended quotation also facilitates the representation of discontinuous talk, in contrast to scenes composed wholly of direct speech that most commonly give the impression of participants being fully focused on a homogeneous, directed, and cohesive set of exchanges. Suspended quotations frequently serve the function of delaying the denouement or punch line to a story, to great comic effect. For example, in Ronald Firbank's *Valmouth* ([1919] 1988, 407) we are momentarily sidetracked from Lady Parvula's account of when she "peeped under a bishop's apron" by the narrator's description of her "resolutely refusing a stirring salmis of cockscomb *saignant* with *Béchamel* sauce" but "helping herself to a few *pointes d'asperges à la Laura Leslie*." After such a sensual and mouthwatering interlude, it somehow seems appropriate, and much more comic, that the story ends with the vague but suggestive "I saw . . . the dear Bishop!"

Of course, the extent to which narrative description accompanies scenes of dialogue may vary considerably, some novelists providing the reader with only very minimal cues in terms of what the characters are doing, how they look, and so forth. But even if there are no explicit "contextualization cues" (Gumperz 1982), typography and punctuation may convey a great deal about the situation in which the characters find themselves. For example, capitalization can convey that characters are in a situation where they need to raise their voices, and brackets may be used to convey that more than one conversation is going on at the same time. Puig's *Kiss of the Spider Woman* ([1976] 1991) uses punctuation in a highly stylized way, often to draw attention to the limitations of the dialogue. Puig uses marks of omission repeatedly in conversations between Molina and Valentin, especially in their most intimate scenes, as though to afford them some privacy and leave the reader to imagine what is taking place between them. Although the characters are not speaking to one another at this point, the device somehow manages to suggest that they are in communication, even sometimes what their emotions may be, though we "see" or "hear" nothing of what is going on.

Another link between speech and context occurs where the utterances of one character carry within them references to the actions and reactions of others. We saw how in *Deception* ([1990] 1992) the characters are acutely aware of each other's responses and often provide the verbal equivalent of the visual "reaction shot," as when one character says to the other, "You're trembling" (27). Performing the deictic function of pointing to acts going on in the immediate environment, such a technique powerfully draws the reader in so that these micro movements and gestures take on an intensity that is far greater than if the same action were reported to us by a narrator.

Action and Reaction

In the dialogue novel, key events may take place offstage, with the focus resting firmly on the responses of characters or their attempts to divert attention away from what is happening elsewhere. In the previous chapter we saw how the novels of Ivy Compton-Burnett rely on melodramatic revelations of incest, illegitimacy, adultery, and even murder. Although these revelations are shocking enough in themselves, it is most often the way in which the revelations are managed that is most shocking, with the violence and cruelty of the characters' words only ramping up the pain and the misery. As Nathalie Sarraute (1963, 109) puts it, here words are "the daily, insidious and very effective weapon responsible for countless minor crimes." With the resurgence of interest in the dialogue technique in more recent fiction, there is yet more evidence of these "crimes" and their ability to sustain a narrative, as in the bruising exchanges taking place between husband and wife in Gaddis's *Carpenter's Gothic* ([1985] 2003) or in the corporate sparring at the heart of Don DeLillo's *Cosmopolis* (2004). Indeed, the title of Roth's novel, *Deception*, signals to the reader that suspicion and jealousy between two people can be more than enough to sustain a narrative.

In Evelyn Waugh's tragicomic *A Handful of Dust* ([1934] 1987), it falls to Jock Grant-Menzies to relay to Brenda Last the news of her young son's death. In an excruciatingly painful scene, Brenda has to drag the information from a reluctant Jock, whose efforts to try to break the news gently only contribute to the subsequent confusion. However, the emphasis is on how Brenda receives the news and initially misinterprets what Jock is telling her, and Waugh refuses to let us be diverted from this by any mawkish sentimentality about the boy or his untimely end. Waugh skillfully draws out the full horror of Brenda's faux pas as she gradually realizes that it is not her lover but her son who has been killed, and utters an unfortunate, perhaps involuntary, exclamation of relief ("thank God" [118]). Jeffrey Heath (1982) even argues that the scene is emblematic of what is at the heart of this novel: the human need to apportion blame for events we cannot understand and to try to cope with the most painful of experiences. Here, then, the suggestion is that where events are so painful and tragic, we may never understand the "full story" of why they happened but have to content ourselves, as the characters try to do, with the mantra "it was nobody's fault" (105).

Oral Narratives

Where acts and events such as these take place "offstage," they may be recounted by one or more characters as a piece of oral storytelling in which how events are related and received may be just as interesting and significant as those actions themselves in terms of the unfolding narrative. As suggested by Kozloff (2000), dialogue here is crucial in creating a sense of cohesion, suggesting subtle connections and echoes between events and characters across time and space, for example, where characters recount past events that may have affected them or that may in turn have some impact on their audience(s).

Oral accounts of events may be constructed and told collaboratively, both as a means of creating or reinforcing bonds between the co-narrators, or as a means of creating or consolidating divisions within a social group. In *Kiss of the Spider Woman* ([1976] 1991), much of the narrative is made up of Molina recounting to his cellmate, Valentin, the plots of various B-list movies. Initially, this is largely a way for the men to pass time, and Valentin mocks Molina and his fantasies. But he also confesses to some envy that Molina should have all "the fun of telling" (15) and asks that he be allowed to "chime in once in a while too." Valentin's gesture displays his growing acceptance of Molina but is also important in suggesting that he is beginning to see how Molina's fantasy life may have just as much validity and resonance as his own attempts at hardheaded political realism.

Nothing ([1950] 1979b) by Henry Green has the former lovers Jane Weatherby and John Pomfret share the telling of a story about the making of a gramophone record, while John's current lover, Liz, humiliates herself by desperately trying to join in. This illustrates the fact that while oral narratives may always have inbuilt recipient design (Edwards and Potter 1992), the design may be as much to antagonize the audience (or part of the audience) as to provide them with what it is anticipated they will want to hear. Perhaps the most outrageously inventive example of collaborative storytelling occurs in Waugh's *Decline and Fall* ([1928] 1983), where news of Prendy's death is interspersed among the lines of a traditional hymn, "the recognized time for the exchange of gossip" (183) between his fellow prisoners. This demonstrates once again how novelists, particularly dialogue novelists, can be very resourceful in their deployment of the techniques at their disposal for creating drama and tension out of the speech of their characters.

Characters' narratives may expand upon what we already "know" about events from dramatized scenes or narrative reports. Alternatively, and perhaps less commonly, a character's account may offer a foretaste or teaser for what is likely to happen in the future. But even though a narrative account may be re-presenting events we have already been told about, how characters manipulate and distort those events may be significant and, in the case of a comic retelling, highly entertaining. Of course there is always the possibility, common in crime fiction especially, that a character's account of either his or her own actions or those of others may turn out to be inaccurate or deliberately misleading. But as attribution theory (Edwards and Potter 1992) has highlighted, when we remember and retell events we always attribute blame and provide motivation for the actions carried out by others, even where this is not overt or explicit. Moreover, if "accounts *of* actions are invariably, and at the same time, accounts *for* actions" (Edwards 1997, 8), then, according to Palmer (2007), we can glean a great deal of information about characters' mental states and their interrelations from even seemingly straightforward reports of events and actions.

Speech Events

In the dialogue novel, very little may be happening outside of the exchanges taking place between the characters, such that "dialogue here is not the threshold to action, it is the action itself" (Bakhtin 1984, 252). Dialogue novels are often explicitly organized around set-piece scenes where conversation is central to the ongoing action—for example, highly formalized and structured speech events such as the interview or the interrogation. In the latter case, what characters say and what they are doing while they speak are crucial in terms of the outcome of the "event" in which they are participating, that is, whether they get the job, give away crucial secrets, and so forth. In these instances, too, the behavior of participants is circumscribed and the power relations between them are inherently unbalanced, providing the most clear-cut examples of a "coercion to speak" (Fogel 1985) where every nuance and gesture is under scrutiny. Fogel also argues that where such scenes are repeated, they come to function as the dominant idea of dialogue perpetuated by that narrative, serving to normalize and sanction certain kinds of verbal behavior.

Isabel Ermida (2006) has examined the relationship between dialogue and power in Orwell's *Nineteen Eighty-Four* (1949), where "coercion" is both overt and covert, tainting even the most private and intimate of exchanges. Ermida concentrates on the overtly coercive interrogation of Winston by O'Brien, but also on the strategy of "talking by instalments" (105) that Julia and Winston adopt to try to avoid detection. To understand how these sets of interactions work, Ermida argues, we have to remember the specific situational factors that constrain what the characters are able to say and do, and that this particularly affects how polite tokens are used and understood. Ermida critiques existing theories of politeness and argues that in the world imagined by Orwell, politeness can be used as a weapon (e.g., by O'Brien), while it is precisely the absence of polite tokens that signals the intimacy between Winston and Julia.

In scenes where conversation is at the center of some kind of formally or informally organized "event," great importance may be placed on openings and closings, on how characters establish, or reestablish, their mutual relations, and on how the speech event is marked off as something unique, tied to that specific context. Consequently, we are reminded that the "action" in such scenes consists as much of the conversational work that may be going on beneath the surface as it has to do with what the characters are saying, or with the effects their words and exchanges may produce. However, the dialogue novelist may equally thrust readers into the midst of some kind of conversational event with little or no orientation, leaving them to work out the context, who is saying what to whom, and the relevance or purport (if any) of the talk.

An entire section of Evelyn Waugh's *Black Mischief* ([1932] 1986, 55–57) is given over to a tea party taking place at the British Legation.[1] The narrative framing of this scene contributes greatly to the impression that it is self-contained and helps create a sense of an intricately wrought symmetry and patterning. Speech here is accompanied by the ritualistic actions associated with the English tea party, but the comic refrain ("More tea, Bishop?") that punctuates and ends the scene is repeated with sufficient regularity to suggest that the hostess has more in mind here than simply tending to her guests. Indeed, the frequency with which the Bishop is offered tea during this short scene suggests that this is being employed as a strategy to divert his attention away from the other topics of conversation and to foreclose the possibility of his entering into the conversation as a full participant. The strategy bears out Toolan's (1987, 404) claim that "topic-suppression" may be important in the management of conversations, highlighting once again the need for a holistic, dynamic approach to the discourse context rather than a narrow focus on the individual utterances and intentions of speakers.

As we noted in chapter 2, genuine scenes of multi-party talk such as this one from *Black Mischief* are relatively rare in the novel. In terms of action, it is clear that when there are multiple participants, trying to convey to the reader everything that may be going on during a conversation may be impossible. This is especially true where you have "non-ratified participants" (Goffman 1981), bystanders, eavesdroppers, and the like who are co-present during a conversation without necessarily ever being invited or allowed to contribute to the ongoing talk. Nevertheless, as in the scene from Waugh's novel, we can often deduce from what the characters say to one another what they may be doing or how they may be reacting, even (as in the case of the Bishop) where they remain silent or are prevented from joining in a conversation.

Waugh teases the reader with hints about scandals involving some of the characters (e.g., Mrs. Walsh's domestic situation) while seemingly relegating large-scale events (the war in Azania) to the status of minor irritants. The satiric intent is evident here, as the workings of empire are held up for ridicule and the ineffectuality of the Legation members is cruelly exposed. But Waugh is also playing games with our narrative expectations, immersing us in the characters' eccentric preoccupations (antirrhinums, marmalade) as a way of ensuring that we appreciate the full absurdity of expecting these people to impose any order or meaning on the situation they are charged with trying to manage. It could be argued that Waugh and other novelists of this period[2] are displaying some impatience with the notion that the novel has to be driven by story events, especially where this might be understood to privilege certain kinds of action over others.

As this scene from Waugh's novel demonstrates, though conversational events may be presented as discrete, they often rely on knowledge gleaned from preceding or subsequent scenes and hence require vigilance on the part of the reader. Of course, Waugh is not above employing narrative red herrings, making us backtrack in order to try to discover who says what, so that any attempt to piece together events proves highly problematic. Moreover, though considerable narrative time may be given over to such conversations, they may do very little to advance the action or illuminate the characters, or it may be that the more interesting action is taking place on the fringes.

Rethinking the Scenic Approach

Most existing critical and theoretical accounts of fictional dialogue proceed by isolating specific scenes or events for analysis. Throughout this study, I have constantly been referring to "scenes" of talk as though these are somehow always clearly defined. In many ways the structure of novels invites this kind of approach, particularly where "scenes" take up whole chapters, are demarcated typographically, or are clearly "framed" by the narrator to build to some kind of climax or denouement. From the point of view of the critic, scenes offer a neat unit of analysis, but they also encourage close consideration of the immediate context of talk and how it is being organized and managed by the participants.

A key influence here is Goffman (1981, 130), who argued that conversation is "naturally bounded" by "ritual brackets" and who elsewhere (1959) devised an explicitly dramaturgical model of interaction. Although Goffman does allow for what he calls an "open state of talk" and for non-focused interactions, much of the language in which such analyses is steeped perpetuates the idea that utterances and the larger interactions of which they form a part are complete, fixed, and open to inspection rather than tentative, fluid, and open to interpretation. For example, in discourse analysis conversation may be analyzed in terms of "moves" (e.g., Toolan 1985), implying a sense of direction and planning to the exchanges. Conversation analysis, which claims to focus on conduct rather than intentions of speakers, is often in danger of imposing order and meaning on conversations by analyzing exchanges in terms of sequences, presupposing some relationship between utterances and their movement toward some kind of goal. And even Herman's (2006) "holistic approach" talks about "scenes of talk" as though these are easy to abstract from the surrounding discourse. Such work can result in a tendency to isolate stretches of talk from the surrounding discourse and to see conversation itself as something that is bounded and discrete rather than as something that is continuous with actions of various kinds or as something that may be fragmentary and incomplete, often profoundly frustrating and unsatisfying.

Recent work by Deborah Tannen (2006) has focused on intertextuality in interaction and demonstrated how difficult it can be to ever isolate stretches of talk as somehow coalescing around a single or discrete topic or event. Tannen demonstrates how topics may be recycled across conversations, even where they have seemingly been brought to a close. She also found that conversations are frequently reframed by participants, for example, where a conversation about who does the laundry may become a conversation about the current state of a couple's relationship. Finally, Tannen argued that conversations may be re-keyed where the tenor or tone changes, from a serious to a lighthearted or humorous tone, or vice versa.

Novelists, however, have always recognized these possibilities, and dialogue novelists in particular are often sensitive to the fact that characters do not always pick up on each other's utterances in sequence, or that conversations are never really "over" where participants may resume their talk and make overt or covert reference to previous conversations. Moreover, breakdowns in the organization and management of conversation often provide dramatic intensity, and comic capital may be derived from conversational mishaps, mishearings, and the kind of mayhem that may ensue when participants come from different cultures, generations, and classes and have different expectations of the encounters in which they are taking part. What has happened in a given conversation may therefore be a matter of interpretation as much for those who take part in it as for those who try to analyze its purport and significance.

The idea of using dialogue to deliberately slow the action down or to foreground the seemingly banal and inconsequential seems fundamental to many dialogue novels. This contradicts both Toolan's (1985) assertion that fictional dialogue is non-routine and Davis's (1987) claim that interactions in fiction are always related to some kind of overall design. Indeed, it is almost a badge of honor for the dialogue novelist to eschew actions or events of any kind of conventional magnitude or significance. In the novels of Ronald Firbank, events often appear completely unrelated, and the characters are less concerned with the authenticity of the stories they hear and relate or their outcomes, being far more concerned with the impact they create and the attention they accrue. If it is up to the reader to search for the relevance of utterances in dialogue novels (Iser 1974), then more often than not Firbank's novels leave us frustrated. Instead, Firbank's narrative technique creates for the reader the effect of flitting around between conversations that seems to be a prime occupation and goal for his characters. Evelyn Waugh ([1929] 1983, 58) acknowledged his debt to Firbank and commended the way Firbank took "the particles of his design" from "the fashionable chatter of his period." This points to the fact that Firbank does not construct his dialogue around some preconceived "design" but rather derives his "design," such as it is, from the "vapid and interminable" talk of his characters, resulting in novels that may be frustrating in terms of conventional notions of plot and character but which are uniquely suited to re-creating the spontaneity, chaos, and eccentricities of social chatter.

Henry Green often used the titles of his novels to ironically foreground their lack of plot and noteworthy "action." In *Party Going* ([1939] 1978), the ultimate irony is that the fogbound travelers seem incapable of "going" anywhere, either literally or metaphorically. V. S. Pritchett (1980, 118) said of Green that "human repetitiveness was a sort of poetry for him" and that he delights in inventing endless variations on a theme, especially within his characters' speech, rather than in necessarily moving along the "action" of his plots, thin as they often are. Green often creates scenes around the characters' conversations and refers to conversations as if they fall into convenient patterns: for example, a section in *Doting* ([1952] 1979a) opens with the framing comment that "Mrs. Middleton was having her third conversation with her husband on the subject of Annabel Paynton" (224). However, here Green seems to be deliberately drawing attention not only to the artifice of his own narrative structure but also to the way in which his characters approach their conversations with a particular strategy in mind; in the case of Mrs. Middleton, to deliberately adopt an attitude of "pained surprise, of grieving bewilderment."

"Booby Traps"

Like many other dialogue novelists (particularly Firbank, Wodehouse, and Waugh), Green employs the "booby trap" (Carens 1966), a device whereby seemingly inconsequential events or incidents are alluded to by the characters throughout the narrative, becoming ever more absurd and providing a kind of ironic commentary on the "action" of the main plots. In *Nothing* we are provided with intermittent updates on the fate of Arthur Morris and his toe, as the story is passed from character to character. According to Oddvar Holmesland (1986), Arthur's story encapsulates the mood of the novel, because he is reduced piece by piece to nothingness. At first, great humor is derived from Arthur's situation, with innuendoes suggesting some correspondence between Arthur's toe and his sexual organ, but the tone soon becomes more somber as we hear that Arthur's ankle has to be removed, later that he is dying, and finally that his death has already taken place, "offstage." Apart from the obvious black humor of such a device, it highlights the claustrophobia of the world of the characters, their love of the surreal and the absurd, and their need not only to pass on and share information and stories but also to add their own imprint to the telling.

A related device, also employed for humor, is to juxtapose conversational exchanges with some highly incongruous action. A memorable instance of this occurs in DeLillo's dialogue novel *Cosmopolis* (2004), when the protagonist, Eric Packer, conducts an erotic exchange with his chief of finance while having his asymmetrical prostate examined. In yet another variation, a narrator may present us with a report of a conversation only later to provide us with the "reveal" whereby we find out what was really going on while the conversation was being conducted. Waugh employs the telephone to this end in *A Handful of Dust*, where, after Brenda finishes sweet-talking her husband, Tony, the narrator reveals that she has all the time been playfully fending off her lover, John Beaver.

Such devices play on the ironic juxtapositioning of speech and action and bring to awareness the extent to which our interpretation of conversational exchanges depends upon context. In many dialogue novels, contextual details are at an absolute minimum, so the reader has to work hard to establish any kind of bearings in terms of the setting, what the characters look like, the time frame for the action, and so forth. This can mean that we become more and more immersed in the unfolding conversations between the characters, as we are aware that we have to rely so entirely on them for any kind of orientation. But as is evident with these various kinds of narrative "booby trap," we have to guard against relying too naively on the versions of events we are given and be alert to the ways in which context and timing affect our responses.

Checkpoint: Talking the Talk

Described by one reviewer as a "scummy little novel" (Wieseltier 2004), Nicholson Baker's *Checkpoint* (2004) caused controversy not just for its subject matter ("assassination porn" [Noah 2004]) but for its form, many questioning whether it should rightly be described as a play rather than a novel. In this regard, Baker seems to be taking up the challenge of fellow dialogue novelists in minimizing "action" to foreground talk, and especially the consequences of talk. Consisting entirely of dialogue laid out to appear much like a script, the "plot" centers on the efforts of Ben to dissuade his friend Jay from carrying out his threat to assassinate the U.S. president, George Bush. The novel plays on the "dividing line" (109) between thought and action, intention and performance, but also between fiction and reality, as Jay holds up the Bush administration's actions in Iraq as justification for what he proposes to do to the president. Much of the discussion taking place between the two men concerns what Jay would like to do to Bush, with Ben doing all he can to make Jay consider the implications of his proposed actions. Eventually, Ben persuades Jay to take out his anger on a cushion standing in for Bush, but the novel ends with Ben's panicked realization that Jay actually does have a gun, and so perhaps really is capable of carrying out the assassination.

The only explicit contextualizing information at the beginning of the novel comes in the form of a diary entry/letter head with the date (May 2004) and venue of the meeting (Adele Hotel and Suites, Washington DC). The rest we have to deduce from the dialogue. We soon learn that the conversation is being recorded by Jay, and his intention to assassinate the president is announced very early on in the meeting. The only interruption to the men's conversation occurs when room service arrives to deliver their lunch. This means that, true to Genette's (1980) concept of scene, the time it takes to read the novel approximates closely to the "action" taking place in the hotel room.

As with many dialogue novels, the reader has to attempt to reconstruct the context from the characters' sparse references to their environment, their shared past (the two are lifelong friends), and the events leading up to their meeting (Jay's summoning of Ben to the hotel room). As the two haven't seen each other for some time, they do engage in some catching up, providing us with information regarding their respective jobs, relationships, and so forth. For example, we learn that Jay has children whom he no longer sees, has been drifting between jobs, and has been through a "bad time." Occasionally, the characters provide us with narratives of past events, such as Jay's account of the antiwar march he goes on (17–22) and his narrative of the "chicken man" (59–60). More typically, the reader has to piece together from the dialogue the meaning of events referred to by the two men, and what these events might tell us about their relationship. For example, a reference to an accident involving a wheelbarrow (9–10) hints at tensions in the friendship but also suggests how close the two men are, as such a seemingly trivial incident clearly has great significance in terms of their mutual relations.

> JAY: I'm so sorry about that wheelbarrow, man.
> BEN: No no no.
> JAY: I felt bad, I just didn't see it in the dark.
> BEN: It's fine, it still works. It lists a little, that's all.
> JAY: Really sorry.

From this exchange we can work out that despite appearances, this incident has not yet laid to rest. Although we are given minimal cues, we can deduce that Jay caused some significant damage to this object, either through clumsiness or possibly through being incapacitated by drink. Although Jay opens with the speech act of apologizing, and reiterates his apology before initiating a topic shift, it is Ben who seems to be most keen to mitigate the damage ("it still works"; "that's all"). In terms of politeness theory (Brown and Levinson 1978), this could indicate that Ben is actually the more powerful party here, downplaying the damage (and potential threat to Jay's positive "face" wants)[3] to make Jay feel better. However, in the context of the novel as a whole it is clear that Ben is wary of Jay and anxious to avoid confrontation, suggesting that it is Jay who may in fact control the relationship. One of the ironies of the novel is that Ben is clearly the more knowledgeable (and rational) of the two, but he allows himself to be manipulated and controlled by Jay. This bears out Tannen's (1994) assertion that dominance is not inscribed *in* linguistic strategies but is played out differently in specific contexts.

As in Puig's *Kiss of the Spider Woman*, where the action focuses on the developing relationship between two prisoners, Valentin and Molina, Baker uses the confined space of the hotel room to gradually unfold to the reader the depths and complexities of the relationship between his protagonists. As in Puig's novel, too, the characters represent different ideological viewpoints as well as very different personalities, and this is conveyed not only through the opinions they express but also by how they conduct themselves in their conversations with one another. Ben appeases and flatters Jay ("You look good" [3]) and literally tries to talk him down from the action he proposes. But it transpires that Ben is in effect funding Jay's fantasies, as he is constantly offering to pay for everything and even supplies the tape on which the conversation is being recorded. Thus, although Jay is clearly the more unstable and dangerous of the two, much of Baker's satire seems to be reserved for the mealy-mouthed liberal and his inability to act and take responsibility. It is only at the end of the novel, when he finally realizes that Jay is capable of carrying out his threats, that Ben is stirred into action—mainly, it seems, because he is fearful that he will be implicated and seen as an accessory. Although Ben's language now becomes much more direct, issuing bald, on-the-record insults (Brown and Levinson 1978 ["you freak"; "you demented bum" (114)]) and commands ("get packing"), this only serves to highlight more forcefully how naive and ineffectual he has been in his handling of the situation thus far.

Baker's attempt to use these two characters to explore different ideological positions regarding Bush's so-called war on terror has been crudely misinterpreted by many critics, mainly because it seems to be assumed that Baker must agree with some or all of the views being expounded. But it is precisely the interplay between the opposing viewpoints that is facilitated the dialogue technique and seems so intrinsic to its effectiveness. Thus while at first it seems that we are being distanced from Jay, who has run from his responsibilities and whose fantasies of revenge on Bush seem so cartoonish, it emerges that Ben's support, financial and otherwise, has played no small part in bringing Jay to this point. Although it appears that Ben has succeeded in deflecting Jay from his proposed action, there is some ambiguity at the end of the novel as to exactly what is going to happen once the two men leave the hotel room. Baker deliberately exploits the openness of the dialogue technique, its game-like quality, to problematize the relationship between words and actions, intentions and outcomes, and to ensure that the debates that are initiated within the text continue far beyond it. The dialogue technique also serves to emphasize the irony that, while Jay complains about the corruption of the Bush administration, he is freely able to express not just his dissent but also his desire to remove the president by force, whether or not he truly intends to carry this out.

Conclusion

It can be difficult to sum up "what happens" in a novel where dialogue is foregrounded, because so much of what goes on seems to be "just talk." Yet once the reader becomes attuned to the fact that the more significant events and shifts in character relations may be taking place within and between their seemingly inconsequential or playful exchanges, this may provide more than sufficient drama and intensity.

As we have seen in this chapter, the dialogue novel relies heavily on the idea of the set-piece scene, where clashes and contests between speakers lead to some kind of climax or denouement. However, it has also been argued that the dialogue novel challenges our ability to cut up the verbal action into discrete events, and that this can radically disrupt our perception of causality and cohesion in the fictional world being represented. It can also lead to a questioning of the idea of dialogue, whereby talking things through is assumed to be productive of some kind of resolution and release. In the dialogue novel, characters do not necessarily engage in conversations as a way of resolving issues or working things through, and often their exchanges can be highly repetitive and full of frustrations and false starts for speakers and hearers alike.

We will see in the following chapter that the ratio of speech to action may vary considerably in different genres and that the volubility and preparedness of characters to verbalize their responses and emotions may be equally variable. This suggests that the relative value placed upon speech as opposed to action may be variable, too, for a wide variety of reasons, historical, social, and cultural.

This chapter has shown that foregrounding dialogue raises important questions pertaining to the idea of "plot" and "action" in narrative fiction. Dialogue novelists have shown us that drama and intensity may be found in the most mundane and routine of activities and that conversations may provide a forum and a setting wherein much can be achieved, both in terms of issues affecting the characters and in terms of their mutual relations. However, we have also seen how the notion of conversation as a bounded activity can be misleading and problematic and that what happens *during* a conversation may only be part of the story, as its reach may extend well beyond the moment. Thus, while dialogue can play an important role in creating a sense of cohesion between events and between the characters who find themselves caught up in those events, it can also highlight and reinforce the fact that sometimes those events cannot be pieced together, and sometimes all we are left with is fragments or a sense of dislocation and chaos.

5 : Framing

Introduction: Framing and Dialogue

In naturally occurring speech, participants may use prosodic and para-linguistic features such as changes in pitch, intonation, rhythm, and gestures to indicate where they are moving from one level of discourse to another—for example, when they are quoting someone else's words. The participants' stance toward the reported speech is often evident in the particular forms that this alignment takes, and it may be reinforced by more explicit and overt framing in the form of evaluative phrases. In prose fiction, typographical devices such as quotation marks, italics, paragraphing, and indentation serve to frame the speech of fictional characters, sometimes substituting for the prosodic and paralinguistic markers and betraying the narrator's attitude toward the speaker or what he or she is saying.

With regard to fictional dialogue, framing can refer both to the "gear shifting" (Page 1988) that takes place between diegetic levels within a narrative and to the ways in which participants in conversation communicate to one another the parameters and sets of expectations they take to be shaping and giving meaning to their contributions. The term *framing* is also used in cognitive psychology to refer to a "store of situational and contextual knowledge" (Jahn 2005a, 69) in the form of scripts or schemata that facilitate the processing and communication of certain conventionalized or stereotypical activities, situations, or experiences. In all three senses, the activity of framing may be perceived as delimiting, even restrictive, or as an ongoing process that is subject to negotiation, disruption, and revision. Particularly with regard to postmodern fiction, it has been argued that narratives often require that readers constantly reevaluate the various kinds of frame that appear to give shape or meaning to the action (Grishakova 2009). However, I will argue that the problematizing or disruption of frames may be more commonly a feature of novels in which dialogue is foregrounded, because there is an ever-present demand for the negotiation of the boundaries between showing and telling and the reachievement of shared contexts for the participants in the talk.

This chapter begins with a broad overview of some of the more prevalent and influential metaphors and theories of framing and assesses their implications for our understanding of how this activity works in relation to representing fictional dialogue. I go on to analyze a range of practices employed by authors, and specific scenes where the activity of framing is particularly noteworthy or innovative.

Metaphors of Framing

The metaphor of the frame usefully highlights the shifts in perspective that result from this process, but it also implies a controlling and enclosing activity in which the relationship between inset and frame is bounded and fixed. It borrows from the idea of a frame to a painting and is suggestive of fixed borders and levels within the narrative. The metaphor is usually accompanied by related metaphors of "territories" or ontological "realms" and the suggestion of a clear division between "outer" and "inner" worlds. While the extent to which framing is overt may vary considerably, the device typically serves to remind readers that the story world is separate from their own and draws attention to the act of telling and to the figure of the storyteller, thereby casting doubt on the extent to which any one telling will suffice. With novels where much of the narrative is given over to fictional dialogue, the movement between narrative levels—but equally the seeming absence of any overt framing—results in the reader's having to constantly reorient him- or herself and to negotiate between abrupt shifts of context, juxtapositioning, and hermeneutic gaps in the narrative.

Although critical analysis of framing as a literary device has been somewhat neglected, alternative conceptualizations for the frame abound, including orchestration, choreography, waiting in the wings, or compèring.[1] Nonetheless, each of these alternatives implies that there is intentionality and volition behind the activity and that the distribution of power is always unidirectional. Framing is thus associated with the establishment of hierarchies in discourse, whereby what is enclosed is somehow subordinate to the frame and where the metalanguage of the frame functions as a bearer or guarantor of the truth (MacCabe 1974).

Drawing on the language of computer programming, Marie-Laure

Ryan (2002b) has proposed that we replace the metaphor of the frame with that of the stack, facilitating an understanding of narrative as a multi-leveled and dynamic activity in which boundaries are there to be transgressed. Ryan's metaphor facilitates the conceptualization of narrative as accretion, avoiding the hierarchization that seems implicit in the concept of the frame. Ryan focuses her analysis on examples of metalepsis in narrative, where the reader's attention is drawn to the stacking and to the ways in which the various levels of the narrative become tangled or collapse into one another. Ryan's model is therefore better equipped to account for the experience of reading nonlinear narratives (discussed in chapter 8), and indeed for expressing how the activity of reading itself is not always a straightforward journey from A to B. But it might also be useful for highlighting the ways in which the "gear shifting" between narrative framing and fictional dialogue represents a much more complex and dynamic relationship between ontological realms than the metaphor of the frame has hitherto allowed, particularly in suggesting that these realms interact with rather than substitute for one another.

Theories of Framing

In the field of sociolinguistics, Erving Goffman's "frame theory" (1974) focuses on framing as a sense-making and social activity in everyday speech that allows distinctions to be drawn between ontological realms and different kinds of communicative practice. Here the metaphor of the threshold is utilized to convey the sense that participants actively signal the transition from one kind of frame to another, for example, where in mid-conversation a story may be initiated with a framing comment such as "Let me tell you about the time. . . ." Although Goffman's analysis is sensitive to the ways in which framing may be about controlling and manipulating interactions, he demonstrates how these frames are interactively managed and are constantly shifting as the demands of the situation or the roles adopted by participants shift. In particular, Goffman's theory demonstrates the inadequacy of fixed frames for speaker and hearer in conversation, allowing instead for a range of forms of participation for those involved in any given speech situation. Here, then, frames are understood not so much as marking off boundaries or separating the different levels of discourse as facilitating their interconnectedness and mutual dependence.

As developed by Gumperz (1982) and Tannen (1993), the notion of the frame has been explored both in relation to the kinds of discourse markers or "contextualization cues" employed in conversation and with specific reference to cross-cultural or intercultural communication, where agreement about the ways in which interactions are to be framed may prove problematic. Interactional sociolinguistics tries to move from a static to a dynamic notion of the frame, viewing context not as something external to speech but as something achieved and negotiated by participants in the course of their interactions. Influenced by ethnography and conversation analysis, the emphasis is on understanding how the management of talk—for example, how to begin and end a turn at talk or when to interrupt—frames the interaction in such a way as to promote mutual understanding. As the focus of study is on situated interactions rather than on stretches of talk that are isolated or abstracted from their contexts, the activity of framing is shown to be complex, with the potential for more than one frame and for conflicts and overlaps between frames in even the most seemingly structured and clearly defined encounters. Interactional sociolinguistics also emphasizes the importance of considering paralinguistic and prosodic markers of framing alongside the verbal, again reinforcing the characterization of the activity as dynamic and fundamental to the development of the speech activity in which the participants are engaged.

While much of the focus in theories of framing is on the role of the narrator in shaping and directing the reader's responses, Catherine Emmott's (1997) theory of contextual framing demonstrates how, in order to understand the process of reading a work of fiction, much more attention needs to be paid to the work of the reader in storing, recalling, and updating the information and impressions that the text gives up. In particular, Emmott is concerned with the ways in which readers build up a mental store of information about the current context, which is updated and, to borrow a metaphor from computing, "refreshed" as the reader's journey through the text progresses. Once again, therefore, the idea of framing is conceptualized as something that is subject to constant modification and which relies on the cognitive capacities and work of the reader in searching for continuity and coherence while also remaining open to the possibility of change. In relation to the reading of hypertext fiction (discussed in chapter 8), Emmott's theory is particularly useful in approaching the context of talk not as something that is fixed and universally agreed upon by participants, but as something that is subject to negotiation and revision, even to the point of reframing where new information or new interpretations of what is said come to light.

Framing and Dialogism

Mikhail Bakhtin's (1981, 1984) concepts of heteroglossia and polyphony in the novel demonstrated how difficult and perhaps inappropriate metaphors of containment are for a form in which multiplicity, variety, and interconnections of many different kinds are intrinsic. Moreover, his dialogic theory, and particularly his notion of double-voicedness in fictional discourse, suggests that it is possible to move beyond schematically insisting on the severance of frame and inset, toward recognizing the mutual interaction between them. Much of Bakhtin's work focuses on the various kinds of relations that may exist between the reporting context and the reported utterances: "With some of them we completely merge our own voice, forgetting whose they are; others, which we take as authoritative, we use to reinforce our own words; still others, finally, we populate with our own aspirations, alien or hostile to them" (1984, 195). Bakhtin's description of this process importantly highlights the ethical responsibilities that this relationship brings, depending on the use to which the words of others may be put and the ways in which they may be manipulated. The notion of double-voicedness further suggests that this is an ongoing process: "Someone else's words introduced into our own speech inevitably assumes a new (our own) interpretation and become subject to our evaluation of them" (195). Although Bakhtin's language may still imply a hierarchical connection ("subject to"), his theories celebrate the possibility of a kind of "gay relativity" (1968, 11) in which the relations between voices may allow for the possibility of subversion and the unseating of forms of authority and control in a constant and ongoing struggle.

Framing and Power

Many of the theories discussed so far challenge the static conception of the frame and the artificiality of the attempt to maintain clear distance and separation between the levels and boundaries of the text. In recent studies of the frame, the relationship between frame and inset is conceived of as a kind of dialectic (Frow 2002) in which it is suggested that influence, hierarchy, and power may not be unidirectional and that the process of framing allows for ongoing modifications and mutual interrelations. At the same time, it would be dangerous to engage in a kind of idealization of the possibility of mutual interplay if this were to result in neglecting the extent to which the structuring mechanisms of the text help reinforce and consolidate both internal and external power relations.

Although this study focuses on scenes of dialogue and novels where framing appears to be at a minimum, it is important to acknowledge that what makes fictional dialogue so fascinating is precisely this tension between its seeming "freedoms" and openness on the one hand and an awareness of the ways in which it is being shaped and ordered for our benefit on the other. Sternberg's (1982b) emphasis on approaching dialogue as "quotation" makes this point, shifting the focus away from represented speech as some kind of "copy" of a putative "original" speech situation and toward exploring "the mechanisms of mutual value assignments" (Jahn 2005b, 479) that exist between quoters and quotees. We must also guard against seeming to invest dialogue with idealistic qualities of freedom and openness, and thereby presenting any framing activity as unwarranted "interference."

Analysis: Varieties of Framing in the Novel

From the "Free Run" to the "Suspended Quotation"

Understood as part of the narrative strategy and structure of a text, the framing of fictional dialogue is primarily a matter of orientation and contextualization, locating the reported speech in terms of who is speaking, where the speaker is, when the exchanges take place, and so forth. In cases where dialogue is given a "free run," framing is minimal and unobtrusive, perhaps consisting solely of chapter or section breaks, the use of quotation marks, or the increase in white margins that visually signal a shift to the direct reporting of the characters' exchanges. However, it is important to guard against the fallacy that the characters' interactions somehow preexist their representation or to look at scenes of dialogue as if they exist in isolation from the surrounding text.

A wide range of novelists have employed the technique of launching the reader directly into the midst of an ongoing conversation with minimal narrative support, typically at the beginning of a chapter or section. The sense of disorientation that may ensue is often alleviated by the fact that the novelist creates a sense of a familiar routine for the reader, as in Joyce's teacher/pupil exchange near the beginning of *Ulysses* ([1922], 1986, 30) or Adam's interrogation at the hands of the customs officer in chapter 2 of *Vile Bodies* ([1930] 1987) by Evelyn Waugh. As mentioned in chapter 1, novelists have also experimented with the device of representing exchanges between their characters as if they were part of a dramatic script, such that any identifiable narrative voice appears to be temporarily absent. When this occurs in the midst of a novel using more conventional devices for the representation of speech, the effect may be one of defamiliarization, isolating the "scene" being represented, and drawing attention to the fact that it is being reproduced for us, as is the case with the conversation between Renton and the psychiatrist from *Trainspotting* discussed previously, where Renton's total contempt for the situation is abundantly evident from the way in which it is depicted.

In a novel such as Gaddis's *JR* ([1975] 2003), where the absence of framing is more sustained and uncompromising, the role of the narrator might be described as ethereal, or alternatively as somewhat cold and machine-like (Johnston 1998). Gaddis, like Joyce before him, erodes the hierarchical boundaries between the narrative discourse and the voices of the characters, especially by foregrounding the artificiality of the tags occasionally used to locate speakers and by blurring the transitions between scenes, much as scenes from a film may fade into one another. Both Gaddis and Joyce play with the technique of merging voices and having fragments of speech echoing across scenes, and both self-consciously use musical metaphors and effects to foreground the sounds and rhythms of what is being said as much as the supposed meaning. This is most evident in the Sirens section of *Ulysses*, where the utterances of Miss Douce and Miss Kennedy are enveloped by the narrator's lyrical and rhythmically balanced interventions ("She poured in a teacup tea, then back in the teapot tea") and overlaid with the impressions and sensations of those present, particularly Leopold Bloom. In Gaddis's *JR*, a novel of more than seven hundred pages, there are no resting places for the reader in the form of chapter or even section breaks, and the narrator provides little or no orientation for the reader, who has to rely entirely on recognizing the speech habits of the characters to discern where one conversation ends and another begins. With both writers, the reader needs to guard against a "lack of understanding of narrational stance" (French 1978, 2), particularly with regard to the use of irony, demonstrating how dangerous it can be to examine individual voices in isolation from the surrounding discourse. But whereas Joyce's novel experiments with echoing and flow, weaving the voices into a "unified fabric" (French 1978, 2), Gaddis's technique is described more as "stammer and flow" (Johnston 1998, 157) and is often described as "daunting" (Moore 1989), even by those who admire him.

With the device of the "suspended quotation" (Lambert 1981), the relationship between the frame and the inset speech is radically different, so that narrative description and evaluation may appear to take precedence over the utterances of characters. In contrast to the "free run," where the activity of framing almost appears to be absorbed or incorporated into the dialogue, here framing is much more overt and even playful, particularly where the narrator exploits the suspension for comic effect, as Lambert demonstrates is so often the case in the novels of Dickens. As we will see, the extent and tone of this framing activity may depend greatly upon the distance between the surrounding narrative discourse and the speech of the characters and on whether the narrative voice is clearly distinct from that of the characters. But as Dentith reminds us, "It is impossible to imagine a novelist who does not sort the words of his or her characters into some sort of hierarchy of significance" (1995, 45), even where he or she appears content to remain in the wings and allow the characters to dominate the stage.

It is precisely this relationship that distinguishes fictional dialogue from dramatic dialogue or a script. Thus even where there is very little observable difference between the layout of dialogue in a novel such as Nicholson Baker's *Checkpoint* (2004) and a play script, the reader's response to dialogue in prose fiction remains quite distinct. Dramatic dialogue is written to be performed, such that speakability and audibility are of the utmost importance. Action, gesture, and setting all contribute to supporting the dialogue in terms of engaging the audience, and play texts are structured into acts and scenes, facilitating changes in location and shifts in time and providing the audience with breaks from the drama. The structure of a novel, organized into chapters and sections, helps shape our expectations about the trajectory of the action and our relationship with the characters. Here, then, we might say that the reader's very experience of the text is being framed by the expectations generated by aspects of medium and genre.

The Frame as "Interference"

Traditionally, where characters' utterances deal with sensitive or taboo subjects, norms of politeness and decorum may mean that intervention is necessary to censor certain words or phrases, often to be replaced by asterisks or other textual markers of omission. Novelists may exploit this situation for the purposes of innuendo or for comic capital. For example, P. G. Wodehouse frequently derives great entertainment from his orthographic experiments in papering over his characters' verbal indiscretions, as in the following account of one of Sir Gregory Parsloe's frequent outbursts: "though —— is admittedly strong stuff, he had gone even farther than his companion, labelling Gally in his mind as a ***** and a !!!!!!!" (*Pigs Have Wings* [1952] 1957, 42).

Framing is also employed in the novel to translate or gloss a character's words where it is assumed that the dialect or variety spoken may be unfamiliar to the reader. Wodehouse regularly intervenes to translate the impenetrable expressions of his rural characters, such as Pirbright the pig man from *Heavy Weather* ([1933] 1988, 473): "Gur! . . . is Shropshire for 'You come along with me and I'll shut you up somewhere while I go and inform his lordship of what has occurred.'" While this could appear patronizing, the joke here is as much at the narrator's expense, as the wordy alternatives stand in awkward relief next to the expressions they are meant to illuminate.

For some novelists, the desire to foreground and flaunt their narrative "interference" seems irresistible. Thus in the novels of Dickens or Wodehouse it may appear that the narrator revels in coming center stage and stealing a little of the limelight from his comic creations. Elsewhere, the interference may be less about flamboyant display than about control and manipulation. John Mullan (2003) complains that D. H. Lawrence is far too heavy-handed in framing his characters' speech, "as if turning up the volume of the talk," and contrasts this with the practice of Graham Greene, whose narrator "wants to retreat to let his characters' emotions come to life."

Many writers have been guarded and even suspicious of the various ways in which narrators may interfere with the speech of characters and of devices that appear to authenticate or privilege that speech. In chapter 1, reference was made to James Joyce's disdain for quotation marks, and others have followed his practice of using dashes instead as a way of blurring the boundaries between frame and inset and of defamiliarizing the process by which speech is represented in fictional texts.

The dialogue novelist Henry Green objected to writers who insisted on acting like Greek choruses in their works, and his narrators frequently use modal expressions ("perhaps"; "if you will") to head off the possibility of the reader becoming overly reliant on the framing discourse. Green was also fond of teasing the reader with half-heard utterances, often displaying a casual disregard for accuracy and precision: "Julia said something or other in reply" (*Party Going* [1939] 1978, 421). As a consequence of his own deafness, Green was particularly sensitive to the ways in which dialogue could be misheard, often willfully, and his novels demonstrate the dangers of taking what people say at face value, and of assuming that the meaning of what we think is being said remains stable or can be fixed for any length of time. Instead we have ambiguity and deception, a blurring of boundaries between the public and the private, and an understanding that even those caught up in a speech situation may only have a vague or confused sense of the implications of what is taking place between them.

Ironically, therefore, though formally Green seems to foreground and privilege dialogue, the positioning of the reader in relation to what is represented demands a level of alertness to how the narrator shows his hand. This is most evident where seemingly innocuous contextualizing comments by the narrator take on a different meaning when considered alongside the utterances they frame. Although Green expressed his frustration with the ways in which speech tags hold up the dialogue "as if a husband and wife were alone in the living room, and a voice came out of the corner of the ceiling to tell them what both were like, or what the other felt" (1992, 139), he evidently enjoyed developing his own trademark tags ("temporized"; "wailed"), simultaneously managing both to suggest how the words are uttered and to convey that the narrator's colorful characterization of this may be highly speculative.

Postmodern Playfulness

In postmodern fiction, the perspective offered to the reader may be less stable and certain; in fact, it may appear that "the frame is there to be jostled, bent, or broken altogether" (B. Richardson 2002, 330). The boundaries between frame and inset may become blurred and ontological realms may be transgressed, resulting in what Ryan (2002b) has termed "level contamination." In such writing, the authorial or narratorial responsibility we might conventionally expect of the frame may be abrogated in favor of playfulness or uncertainty. The effect goes against Frow's (2002) notion of the frame as easing the reader into the fictional world and is closer to his characterization of the activity as forcing us to "see" the frame in such a way as "to account for the culturally determined *vraisemblance* by which the conventions determining the reception of the work are naturalized, become second nature" (337).

In *Kiss of the Spider Woman* ([1976] 1991), Manuel Puig opts for the Joycean dash rather than quotation marks and appears to eschew any kind of narrative contextualization of the dialogue other than section and line breaks between utterances. We do not even learn the characters' names until these are used in the exchanges between them, and it is solely through the dialogue that we discover their situation (they are sharing a prison cell) and learn anything of their "crimes." However, as the action of the novel moves outside the prison cell, Puig opts for the defamiliarizing devices of the dramatic script (246–50) and the official report (chapter 15).

Perhaps more mischievously, and at first somewhat perplexingly, Puig introduces a series of footnotes into the narrative which at times threaten to completely overwhelm the dialogue. The footnotes take the form of mock scholarly accounts of various theories of sexuality as well as turgid expansions on the plots of the movies with which Molina entertains Valentin. Rather than illuminating or harmonizing with the dialogue, therefore, the footnotes act as a kind of jarring note, distracting and distancing us from the characters' interactions even as they begin to show signs of responding and relating to one another. Puig's use of footnotes follows a tradition that goes back to the earliest novels, but it is perhaps more striking because of the absence of any other overt framing of the dialogue and because the appearance of the footnotes seems so random and whimsical.

Framing and Narrative Voice

In Puig's novel the "gear shifting" between the voices of the characters and the style and tone of the "official" or "authoritative" sources can seem quite abrupt and obtrusive. It is pertinent therefore to consider the relationship between the various voices heard in a text, ranging from the kind of distance evident in Puig's text, to novels where the voices of the narrator and the characters may be virtually indistinguishable from one another. In *Paula Spencer* ([2006] 2007), Roddy Doyle's follow-up to *The Woman Who Walked into Doors* ([1996] 1998), the title character narrates in dialect, and the dialogue is only marked off from the surrounding discourse by dashes, such that the distance between them is minimal and they appear to blend into one another. However, in *Trainspotting* by Irvine Welsh, first-person vernacular narrators interchange with a third-person narrator employing Standard English, challenging the reader's preconceptions both about the character narrators and about the relationship between Standard English and the Scots dialect. In the chapters narrated in Scots the reader does not have to engage in the same kind of "gear shifting" as in the chapters narrated in Standard English, but the effect of switching is to remind the reader of the tensions and gaps existing between the different varieties of speech and the implications of this in terms of their relative status.

Framing thus raises fundamental questions pertaining not only to whose voices we hear in a narrative but with how those voices are filtered through to us. Forster's narrator in *Howards End* ([1910] 1986) notoriously announces that "We are not concerned with the very poor" (58), and the narrator barely conceals his disdain for the likes of Jacky and her "experiments in the difficult and tiring art of conversation" (64). But narrators are rarely this brutal in their honesty. Instead, the convention is that we assume that a narrator has total recall, has full access to everything that may have been said in a conversation, and is so disposed so as to represent what was said truthfully and accurately. It may therefore appear ridiculous to talk of the rights of "paper beings" (Barthes 1977) or to be anxious about accuracy and truthfulness when there is no originary source for the exchanges being depicted. But as with any aspect of the narrative, it is germane to examine the choices that are being made in terms of how the framing of those exchanges may affect the reader's response. It is also important to remember that even where clear hierarchies seem to exist between the voices in a text, the relationship between them may be dialogic in Bakhtin's (1981) sense, potentially leading to all sorts of dislocations and displacements.

Frames within Frames

Another interesting variant of framing is where an embedded or inset narrator frames the dialogue within his or her own narrative, contributing to a kind of Russian doll or "stacking" (Ryan 2002b) effect in terms of the narrative layers. Once again, this technique may alert the reader to the ways in which framing might influence or even distort the dialogue, particularly if the narrator admits to uncertainty, hesitancy, or another such factor influencing his or her ability to represent the utterances of others, or where a given narrator is retelling a story passed on from another source. In Puig's novel, Molina's recounting of the plots of the B-movies mainly relies on reporting speech indirectly, and Molina makes no attempt to disguise the extent to which his own response to the films and to the characters colors his narrative. Indeed, the intensity and heightened involvement of his narrative style help to engage Valentin (and the reader), despite the contrived nature of most of the action he recounts.

In the novels of Ronald Firbank, the utterances and sayings of various characters are constantly circulating among the closely knit social sets to which they belong. Frequently, listeners only catch a fragment of what is being said, resulting in all sorts of misunderstandings and misapprehensions. With the "babel of voices" technique (discussed in chapter 3), the wresting of utterances from their original contexts and the playful or malicious uses to which we see these utterances being put radically unsettle the notion of the frame as something solid, stable and reliable.

The narrator's introduction to the climactic scene from *Vainglory* ([1915] 1998, chapter 22)—"There came a babel of voices"—displays no inclination to explain or guide the reader in terms of what is to follow, as though the action speaks for itself. We do get some contextual information, namely, that the exchanges take place "on the lawn and in the lighted loggia" and that "the total town" is present. From then on, however, we are left to work out for ourselves who exactly says what to whom from the fragments that we are offered. The effect of this is to give the reader the impression of being offered privileged access to the social group and the secrets and scandals that circulate between them.

Among the seemingly frenzied exchanges are a number of utterances that pass on information secondhand. In particular, at the end of the babel we catch a fragment of a narrative seemingly recounting a couple's financial difficulties: "'Let us sell the house, dear,' she said, 'but keep the car! We can drive round and round the park in it at night. And it looks so charming for the day'" (204). We know that this is a report of someone else's utterance because it is framed by a double set of quotation marks and by the inclusion of the speech tag "she said," and we can deduce that the individuals involved are in an intimate relationship because of the use of the vocative "dear." Moreover, the utterance appears to display a certain desperation on the part of the unnamed "she" who is mentioned, as after the initial concession ("Let us sell the house") she appears to resort to pleading her case for holding onto the car.

We can deduce from previous hints in the babel that the fragment alludes to the financial strains affecting the relationship between the Pets, but the focus is clearly on Mrs. Pet's attempt to retrieve some semblance of dignity from the situation. The utterance is an example of what Tannen (1989) calls "constructed dialogue," where a speaker is purporting to (re)construct what someone else has said but also has to draw the listener in by means of exclamations ("keep the car!") and repetition ("round and round") to heighten the sense of drama. However, we cannot be sure whether the speaker intends to evoke sympathy for Mrs. Pet or to mock her histrionics, and we never find out who is recounting Mrs. Pet's words. Indeed, as is so often the case in Firbank's novels, the reader can never feel fully confident in the authority or reliability of any of the speakers in passing on stories and snippets of information to one another. Instead, Firbank's technique foregrounds and seems to celebrate these speakers' predilection for distortion, exaggeration, and melodrama, leaving little room for sympathy for those who may be affected by the rumors and the innuendoes.

Earlier, I discussed the techniques employed by Joyce and Gaddis for creating a flow between scenes rather than relying on conventional chapter or section breaks to mark off conversations as discrete entities. In Firbank's novels it is impossible at times to detect where one conversation begins and another ends, as the narrator creates the effect of moving between or dipping in and out of conversations, for example, by the frequent use of the continuous tense ("was telling," *Vainglory* 1915, 96). Moreover, it becomes difficult to tell with any certainty whether the snippets of information and gossip being circulated have been acquired second- or thirdhand or have even been completely fabricated by the speaker. The embedded framing of speech therefore overlays and disperses the responsibility for the reporting in such a way that the tracking down of sources and the location of contexts for utterances becomes nonsensical, and the truthfulness and even the meaningfulness of the exchanges become secondary to the drama and the intensity they may generate.

Framing and the Reader

If we consider the framing of fictional dialogue as a kind of "meta-inter-action" (Mazzon 2009) that takes place between narrator and reader, we must allow that this will directly affect how the reader responds to the interactions between characters depicted within the context of the story world. But as Humphrey Carpenter (1990, 234) has observed, while it is more common for a narrator to share a joke with the reader at the expense of one or other of the fictional characters, it is possible that the narrator may collude with his or her characters so that "it is the reader who tends to be excluded." Here, then, the narrator may regard the whole business of framing with a certain irony and may even take liberties with the per-ceived norms regarding the relationship between frame and inset. Equal-ly, the reader may choose to disregard or at least question the framing of scenes of dialogue where that runs contrary to his or her response to the interplay between the characters and its potential significance.

With "behaviorist narratives" (Palmer 2004) the narrative frame is restricted to primarily external details that provide only minimal orien-tation for the reader. Here the narrator does not just withdraw but refus-es to intervene to clarify or explain what is being said, leaving the reader to negotiate potential interpretations of the scenes depicted. In the scene from Waugh's *A Handful of Dust* ([1934] 1987) discussed in chapter 4, Brenda Last's reaction to the news of her son's death is affecting precisely because of how the narrative manages to convey the chaos of the scene and the confusion of Brenda's emotions. The episode remains both pow-erful and difficult because the narrator offers no explanation or judgment of Brenda's response, but appears content to merely coldly record what is said. Waugh is boldly prepared to leave the reader feeling uncomfort-able and even confused, and in so doing he demonstrates how effective the interplay between narrative discourse and fictional dialogue can be in evoking the depths and complexities of the unspoken and the unsayable. In Emmott's (1997) terms, the scene requires constant reframing on the part of the reader, and its effects linger to cast a long shadow over the rest of the novel. Narrative framing therefore seems to require acute sensitivity on the part of the author in terms of getting the balance right between direct-ing the reader and allowing the reader to become immersed and engaged with the characters and the various situations and dilemmas they face.

Conclusion

This chapter has demonstrated how important the framing of fictional dialogue is not only in understanding the effects produced but also in understanding how the different levels and voices within a narrative interpenetrate and react to one another. While the tendency in the past was to isolate frame and inset and to characterize the frame as something that is static and unchanging, recent theories have allowed for a rearticulation of the relationship between frame and dialogue so as to encompass the possibility of an ongoing interaction in which the balance of power may be less defined. We have seen how novelists have played with and in some instances openly revolted against the idea that the utterances of their characters must be subordinate to and contained within a narrative frame that is invested with authority and purports to offer the reassurance of some kind of control. But we have also seen that framing may be understood as involving the active participation of the reader and thus as something that is part of an ongoing process subject to constant updating, which is vital for understanding why reading and rereading scenes of dialogue can be endlessly rewarding. In the next section I will explore dialogue in the context of genre and examine how new modes of communication and representation have further affected the relations between narrative discourse and fictional dialogue.

PART III | *Genre and Medium*

6 : Dialogue and Genre

Toward a Generic Approach to Dialogue

As we have seen, an important contribution to the study of fictional dialogue has been offered by approaches that explicitly evaluate representations of speech with reference to linguistic models of conversation (Leech and Short 1981; Toolan 1985). Although such studies often focus on specific formal or institutionalized activity types or conversational genres, drawing on the work of discourse analysts (Sinclair and Coulthard 1977; Burton 1980), little or no consideration has been given to date to the ways in which different fictional genres may inscribe as "natural" certain patterns and forms of talk. Kozloff's (2000) study of filmic dialogue shows how productive such an approach may be, as she examines the verbal patterns that characterize the melodrama, the screwball comedy, the Western, and the gangster movie, arguing that through repetition "these verbal patterns became part of our expectations of 'generic verisimilitude'" (138). Far from suggesting that all representations are formulaic, this approach demonstrates that we cannot continue to speak of "verisimilitude" as a given but must examine more fully how different genres present us not only with distinctive, sometimes exotic idioms but with alternative models of interaction and communication.

In previous chapters the term "dialogue novel" has been used to group together novels from different periods and by different writers that share the characteristic that the narrative is conveyed almost entirely by dialogue alone. We have also seen that many of the novels and novelists that foreground and experiment with dialogue may be located broadly within a comic tradition. Page (1988) and Chapman (1994) have shown that the written representation of dialect owes a lot to comic writing, but we can also identify clearly how types of speech—such as rapid-fire repartee and banter—and devices such as the use of punch lines and the booby trap (Carens 1966) owe a great deal to joke structures and the language of humor (Nash 1985). Comic writers are adept at exploiting misunderstandings and seeming failures of communication, and they are not afraid to immerse themselves in the routine and the banal. It seems possible to argue, therefore, that dialogue is a defining feature of some genres more than others and that a tradition of experimenting with speech and conversation emerges within particular genres, leading perhaps to certain genre-specific conventions or forms of representation.

Dialogue in Hard-Boiled Crime Fiction

This chapter will focus specifically on the dialogue found in hard-boiled crime fiction of the American variety, because although this is widely held to be a defining feature of the genre, it has received very little in-depth analysis. A fascination with capturing the argot of the criminal underclass can be traced back to the earliest origins of fictional writing (Burke 1993). In the twentieth century, writers of crime fiction were with almost tedious regularity lauded for their artistry with dialogue, based on little more than a vague reference to their superior "ear" for recording speech, creating the impression that they simply transcribe and record preexisting linguistic habits and patterns of speech. When it comes to analyzing the dialogue, the tendency is to focus on vocabulary and idiom rather than on the underlying patterns and structures of the talk. The former approach results all too often in the mere listing of distinctive turns of phrase rather than any exploration of the implications of their use or their function within the wider discourse. Closer analysis of the dynamics of the talk may indeed lead us to revise a simplistic assessment of its "realism": it is curious that no matter how heated exchanges between characters may become, or how much they are concerned with exerting their power, they never seem to interrupt one another or talk across one another.

Coupe and Ogden (1992, xi) describe the language of hard-boiled crime fiction as "mean, slangy, witty and tough," though in many cases the "wit" of the characters is distinctly thin. Clearly, this language is a world away from the kind of language typical of the "Mayhem Parva" school of detective fiction (Watson 1971), where criminals politely submit to the questioning that in turn leads to the discovery of the truth and the restoration of order. This is not to say that such writing is without interest from the point of view of analyzing dialogue, particularly as so much depends on deductive reasoning and characters overhearing and deciphering fragments of conversations. But hard-boiled crime fiction holds a particular fascination in terms of its dialogue, not only for its closeness to the ground but because its foregrounding of deviance, its transgressions of countless norms, can be so refreshing. Indeed, Ken Worpole (1983, 35) has claimed that "it was in American fiction that many British working class readers . . . found . . . an unpatronising portrayal of working class experience and speech which wasn't to be found in British popular fiction of the period."

While hard-boiled fiction is often associated with extreme violence, actual physical harm may be fairly limited, and much of the "action" is taken up instead with the characters' intricate planning of their crimes, negotiating deals with the forces of law and order, or reflecting on their past crimes. This is why dialogue is so important to the genre, as we see the pressures facing both criminals and cops, pressures exerted by their superiors and by their social circumstances but also by the constant fear of being betrayed or double crossed. This is also a world in which characters are unusually sensitive and even paranoid about what they say and how it will be interpreted, as the possibility of surveillance, of official and unwarranted "overhearing" of their exchanges, is ever present. These pressures and sensitivities result in forms of talk where evasion and euphemism become habitual and where listeners have to work at deciphering the meaning of what is being said or risk the consequences. Yet suspicion about talking too much is matched by a compulsion to talk and the attempt to assert oneself, such that these fictions help to expose the complex, often contradictory motivations underlying conversational interaction.

Gangster movies are often said to be especially "noisy" in comparison with other genres, and the same might also be said of hard-boiled fiction. Kozloff (2000, 205) also argues that the dialogue in these movies contains a lot of "rambling repetition," and we see this feature, too, in hard-boiled fiction, where characters need to buy time to think and reassess their strategy. As well as boasting an extensive vocabulary for the description of weapons and what they can do, another distinctive feature of the language of this genre is the liberal use of obscenities. Nick Lacey (2000) reminds us that the cinema lagged behind print novels in this respect because of censorship issues, and it was not until Quentin Tarantino that a filmmaker immersed us in this kind of language in the way hard-boiled writers had been doing for some time. Tarantino also learned from these writers that obscenities could fulfill a number of discursive functions—for example, acting as markers of solidarity as much as displays of aggression—and that orchestrating obscenities could produce scenes of an almost operatic quality. We should not underestimate the ability of hard-boiled writers to continue to probe the boundaries of taste and decency, and the genre has long been plagued by accusations of racism and sexism.

Page (1988) notes that slang and jargon can quickly become dated, losing its appeal, so it is unlikely that the success of these novels rests purely on their ability to capture the idiom of a particular time and place. Dialogue in crime fiction is about much more than offering the reader the vicarious thrill of catching a glimpse of the darker side of society. Owen Gleiberman (quoted by Dawson 1995, 73–74) suggests that, at its best, such writing may tap into the frustrations we all have from time to time with the social norms and polite conventions that govern our interactions: "In a civilized world where people have to watch their tongues on the job, in the classroom, even perhaps when speaking to their loved ones, there's something primal and liberating about characters who can let it all hang out, whose ids come bursting forth in white hot chunks of verbal shrapnel."

The Friends of Eddie Coyle and *Get Shorty*

George V. Higgins's *The Friends of Eddie Coyle* is seen by many as a classic of the genre, despite Higgins's antipathy for the "hard-boiled" label. Notable for its foregrounding of dialogue, the novel tells the story of small-time crook and sometime informer Eddie "Fingers" Coyle, weighed down by his "responsibilities" and ultimately betrayed and dispatched by his "friends." Higgins's novel, first published in 1970, reflects contemporary anxieties about crime but also about police corruption and surveillance of private conversations.[1] Providing a disturbing critique of the American dream, *The Friends of Eddie Coyle* powerfully depicts a world where it seems that everything may be bought and sold and where characters are driven by necessity and fear. In this world, conversation may occasionally afford an opportunity to unburden oneself, but more commonly it is merely a way to set up a deal or get some business done: there is little sense here of any desire to listen to and interact with others beyond extracting information from them.

Elmore Leonard has openly acknowledged his debt to Higgins, in terms of both technique and subject matter. Both writers have in turn been compared with Hemingway, highlighting the extent to which their narratives foreground and experiment with dialogue. Moreover, both writers show us how "ordinary" criminals are in many ways, and both portray criminality as a matter of accident and contingency rather than as a distinctive mind-set. Both Higgins and Leonard have sought to distance themselves from the so-called Hammett-Chandler line, most evident in the way they construct their fictions as ensemble pieces rather than focusing on the lone figure of the detective or the private eye. Leonard in particular has become known for his experimentation with point of view, often surprising the reader with an unexpected shift to the perspective of a seemingly minor or marginalized character.

First published in 1990, *Get Shorty* is one of Leonard's most knowing fictions, playing with our preconceptions of the genre and with issues of representation through its cross-cutting of the criminal underworld with the movie business. The plot follows onetime "shylock" Chili Palmer as he arrives in "tinsel town" on a twin mission to track down a fraudster and a "slow pay." Chili finds that his ability to negotiate and to improvise, honed in his criminal dealings, serve him in good stead for getting on in the movie business, as he pitches to stars and studios and helps deal with some dubious "investors." Leonard's novel is much lighter in tone than Higgins's, as it is clear that Chili derives great joy from his verbal dealings with others. As I will argue, Leonard's novel is influenced by both the comic tradition and by the postmodern, demonstrating how genres and the boundaries between them are becoming increasingly blurred.

While both novels were adapted successfully to the screen,[2] continuing an association that goes back to the earliest examples of the genre, *Get Shorty* in particular raises interesting issues to do with "verisimilitude," foregrounding as it does the extent to which movie dialogue both influences and is influenced by "real" speech. Therefore, instead of measuring the effectiveness of fictional dialogue solely according to how far it mirrors everyday interactions, we should consider how far it plays with our conceptions of what is "recognizable," whether that is taken from "life" or from other novels, the screen, and so forth.

The "Coercion to Speak"

As was suggested earlier, hard-boiled crime fiction presents us with a world where truths are contingent and where hearing and talking constitutes work that carries very real dangers as well as rewards. More specifically, hard-boiled crime fiction may be said to exemplify what Fogel (1985) calls the "coercion to speak," discussed in chapter 2. Fogel's analysis of scenes of dialogue where speech is extracted or forced from a participant, and where a whole exchange may be made to happen by some individual or organization, highlights the need to pay heed to the "larger, governing shapes which make dialogue happen or not happen at all" (195).

Crime fiction is ripe for this kind of analysis, since conversations rarely just "happen" but are carefully set up and are often explicitly economic as much as interpersonal transactions. Force and pressure are exerted on participants not only within the context of that exchange but as a result of their obligations and duties to others, whether that is to the family, a criminal gang, or, in the case of the cops, their colleagues and superiors, the institution of the law, and the concept of justice to which they are subservient. Thus when Higgins's novel ends with Jackie Brown's lawyer asking despairingly, "Is there any end to this shit? Does anything ever change in this racket?" (216), it drives home how all of the characters are caught up in the system that oppresses them. These pressures and stresses are never far from the surface in these fictions, and they help shape the form that the interactions take. As Higgins (1991, 116) puts it, "Most communication depends on our ability to understand what is actually meant by the things that are actually said. What is said is usually a deliberate substitution for what is actually meant. This is especially so when the talker is under some kind of stress, and is fighting it while at the same time trying to conceal it."

Fogel's (1985) model of dialogue suggests that such feelings of "stress" are by no means confined to the kind of extreme situations we find in crime novels; instead, they are something we can all identify with as users of language, because conversation is about the exercise of power, and because linguistic exchanges do not take place in a vacuum but are shaped and constrained by the "larger, governing shapes" of any given society. Like Foucault (1978), Fogel does not conceive of coercion and power as something that is possessed or even exercised by one party alone, and he does take into consideration the role of the listener, allowing that in certain cases of overhearing there may be an element of coercion. But a "coercion to listen" may be just as prevalent as a coercion to speak in many if not all instances of conversational interaction. In crime fiction this manifests itself clearly because hearing and listening are duties carried out for reward or favor: Foley instructs Deetzer in *The Friends of Eddie Coyle* to "go out and see what you can hear" (65). Thus we have some idea of the work that informers must do in collecting, selecting, and evaluating what they hear and passing it on to the relevant party, and we are also aware of how much is at stake for them if they are discovered.

Characters in crime fiction often acknowledge the work they have to do in getting at the meaning of what is said, where that may be left deliberately ambiguous or vague. Meaning is therefore portrayed not just as a matter of speaker intention but as reliant on the listener's powers of deduction and interpretation. Later on in *The Friends of Eddie Coyle*, Foley confides to his colleague his doubts about another informer: "Half the stuff I get from him is stuff I get by listening to what he says, he doesn't know what he's telling me" (100). But this kind of talk is not confined to those, like the detective, whose job requires them to pay minute attention to detail: because so much is at stake for all of the characters in these fictions, they are constantly working over and analyzing what they hear.

Fogel's (1985) study is an attempt to challenge what he sees as the simplistic equation of novelistic dialogue with fun and freedom, and in *The Friends of Eddie Coyle*, at least, there is little sense of talking as anything other than a chore and a way of conducting business. When it comes to pleasure, talk is discouraged: annoyed by his girlfriend's behavior, Scalisi asks Eddie wearily, "You ever get laid without a lot of goddamned *talk*?" (130). However, a weakness of Fogel's theory is that in focusing on coercion, it downplays the subversive potential of dialogue, particularly as celebrated in the comic tradition. Leonard's writing blurs the boundaries between comic writing and crime fiction, openly flirting with comic conventions and rhythms, such as the one-liner or the punch line. Thus whereas in Higgins's novel the characters most often appear to be acting and speaking out of necessity rather than choice, in Leonard's novel Chili Palmer in particular seems to revel in the opportunity to engage in verbal play. Furthermore, it affords Chili a degree of social mobility and respect denied most of Higgins's characters. Leonard's novel gives us a glimpse of the glamorous world to which Chili aspires, whereas Higgins's characters inhabit a much seedier world that is closer to the classic hard-boiled model, living out the contradictions of their time, casualties of a capitalist system which breeds envy and greed (Lacey 2000).

In both novels, if characters are constrained to talk they also see talk as a release, as is evident in the way they continually tell stories and, as an important bond, constantly match each other's words. Kozloff (2000) has claimed that in gangster films characters are promiscuous and unrestrained with their language, so talkativeness is as much a weakness as it is a weapon. Although talk in crime fiction may also at any time spill over into violence, while it teeters on the edge, the sense of energy, of irresponsibility, of excess, is thrilling. Indeed, it might be argued that in Leonard's writing in particular the dialogue is carnivalesque in Bakhtin's (1968) sense of the word, delighting in the language of the marketplace, overthrowing all kinds of taboos, and creating an environment where the language of officialdom is not so much mocked as completely sidelined. However, as with the carnival spirit, this sense of freedom is only possible within certain boundaries, and if the characters do deploy speech and stories against others, they also have to learn how to manage and control this potentially dangerous weapon: in *Get Shorty*, Chili Palmer's motto is, "Don't talk when you don't have to" (6).

Tuning In to Hard-Boiled Talk

The role of the reader in this type of fiction is quite different from that in classic detective fiction. Just as Kozloff (2000) found with gangster films, the reader of hard-boiled fiction is often placed in the position of being "outside" the world represented, not as a detached or privileged observer, as is the case in the whodunit, but more as someone who cannot always catch or follow everything that is being said. In the novels of Higgins and Leonard, few contextual cues are given to the reader either in terms of where and when the action is taking place or in terms of who is speaking. In Higgins's novel, for example, speech tags are kept to an absolute minimum and seem to be deliberately obscure, referring to Eddie in an exchange in chapter 3 simply as the "stocky man" and offering even less of an insight into his interlocutor, who is referred to only as "the second man." In *Get Shorty*, the early chapters do offer some biographical information about Chili, but it comes only after the dialogue has already hinted at the difficulties of his marriage. Whereas Kozloff sees this trait as potentially alienating, it is rather the case that we are drawn into the worlds of the characters because, as Higgins observes, "Reading is a participatory sport" (1991, 82) in which we have to play our full part and in which we must experience the shortcomings as well as the skills of the other participants.

The more we read, the more we become attuned to the language and the codes used by the characters, but just like those characters, we cannot escape the necessity to listen hard to what is being said. In *Get Shorty* the characters provide us with metalinguistic commentaries that serve the function of glossing what is said, as when Harry and Chili discuss the ins and outs of what it means to "option" a script (70). Yet such a device does not appear in any way strange or stilted, because it is an inevitable consequence of the clash of cultures and linguistic registers between the criminals and those involved in the movie business. Leonard's dialogue also has the characters reacting to what is being said, often coming back to a comment made earlier in a conversation, or picking up on something that is insinuated or suggested, to catch the other off guard. For example, after Chili has run his idea for a movie past Harry, he is surprised when Karen turns the conversation to the question of how he broke into the house, "getting back to it" (45) by asking him directly, "How did you know Harry was here?" This is a potent reminder that a lot hangs on what is said and how it is interpreted for these characters, making them highly sensitive and even obsessive about the minutiae of their exchanges.

Conversations in both of these novels take a lot for granted, so that even where characters may be meeting for the first time, they seem to assume some shared knowledge. A striking feature of the style of these two novels is the extent to which characters share a propensity for euphemisms and for vagueness. In *The Friends of Eddie Coyle* the word "friends" is used repeatedly, becoming increasingly ambiguous and taking on a sinister edge as we gradually realize it refers to criminal associates rather than social acquaintances. Much of the language used to describe violent acts is similarly euphemistic, acting as a code whereby such criminal acts can be openly discussed with impunity. Inevitably, such language lends itself to comic misunderstandings or mix-ups, but this is also a world in which loose talk can be very costly: in *The Friends of Eddie Coyle*, Scalisi's gang are finally undone when his girlfriend takes revenge for his sharing of sexual confidences with Eddie by informing on him. Ironically, whereas overhearing and informing is solicited and paid for elsewhere in the novel, this information is given freely and voluntarily.

Despite the dangers involved, the characters play with ambiguity and vagueness, seemingly assuming that their interlocutors will be able to decipher the meaning behind what they say. At times it almost seems as though the characters are engaged in some kind of game to see who can be most vague:

> "... I was talking to Dillon the other day at the place and I was saying to him, has somebody got something in with them...."
>
> "I heard something about Dillon that I didn't like," the second man said.
>
> "I know it," the stocky man said. "I heard that too." (*The Friends of Eddie Coyle*, 18)

While these utterances appear to flout Grice's ([1963] 1975) maxims by being deliberately vague and uninformative, in the context of this exchange there is no indication that either party is frustrated or annoyed by this; indeed, they seem to match and echo each other's words in terms of their vagueness. Moreover, such exchanges cannot be taken as indicating any kind of linguistic deficiency on the part of the characters, as soon after these exchanges we are provided with ample evidence of their potential for verbal dexterity, as "the second man" refers to a mutual acquaintance as being "as tight as a popcorn fart when he's on a job" (19). What this demonstrates is the importance of always placing utterances—and even longer exchanges between characters—within the wider context in which they appear, rather than judging them according to some kind of template or model of conversational behavior that cannot take into account the way in which exchanges are locally managed and understood.

This becomes more difficult when, as so often occurs, conversations are repeated out of context and reported secondhand by characters in whom we can have very little confidence. Just as the characters always have to be on their guard and consider the possibility that what they are saying is being overheard, so too must the reader be vigilant. In *The Friends of Eddie Coyle* the reader is often thrust into conversations not knowing whether the participants are criminals or cops. With conversations taking place between members of the criminal fraternity, interesting power dynamics and hierarchies emerge, sometimes based on age (as with Eddie's conversations with Jackie Brown) or class (Jackie Brown's conversations with the student radicals), sometimes based on who is "friends" with whom (Dillon's conversation with "the man" in chapter 26). Conversations taking place between cops and informants also have an interesting dynamic, one in which information is power and vagueness is a way of negotiating what is at stake and who is in control of the interaction. Conversations of this kind are characterized by their reliance on hypotheticals ("If . . ."; "Suppose . . .") as the characters sound each other out and seek to establish what is on offer. Significant, too, is knowing who has called a meeting and who decides when it is over; although it is often the informers who hold the conversational floor (in chapter 6, Dillon virtually takes up the entire chapter with his monologues), it seems that their storytelling and verbosity is almost a badge of commitment, concealing the fact that actually they are revealing very little of any significance.

Talk and Solidarity

In both *The Friends of Eddie Coyle* and *Get Shorty*, language is an important means of conveying and constructing a sense of solidarity in conversation. Sometimes a bond may be established through the subject matter, for example, sharing knowledge about weaponry (in *Friends*) or movies (*Get Shorty*). Terms of address may also help build solidarity, and the significance of names is spelled out early on in *The Friends of Eddie Coyle* in an exchange between Eddie and Jackie Brown, where it emerges that revealing one's name to an associate is a sign of trust and a kind of badge of honor.

But it is stories and the telling of stories that most obviously perform the function of bridging divides and helping forge alliances. In both novels, characters relate stories of past crimes and experiences as a way of gaining respect or asserting authority over others. In *Get Shorty* the enmity between Bo Catlett and Chili Palmer is temporarily suspended as their enthusiasm for the movies gets the better of them and they engage in reconstructing the plot of the doomed "Mr. Lovejoy." Here, as is often the case, collaborative storytelling is motivated by some kind of power play. Thus in *The Friends of Eddie Coyle* (chapter 11), Foley encourages Dillon to reveal more and more by recapping ("Okay . . . Eddie's making a lot of calls"), providing encouraging back channel communication ("Uh huh"),[3] and asking questions and offering supportive reinforcement ("It's good to have friends"). But it is often left deliberately ambiguous as to who is really controlling these exchanges and how far their apparent enthusiasm for their storytelling is exaggerated or contrived for the purposes of manipulating the other party.

As we have seen, the characters' tales of violence and the threat of violence that their words carry may often be more chilling than the fairly limited, almost mundane acts of violence in which they participate. In *The Friends of Eddie Coyle* the bank robbers are scrupulously polite in their dealings with their hostages, and Eddie is actually asleep when he is executed. In *Get Shorty*, Chili is amused by the preconceptions Harry and others have of the "shylock," demonstrating that the mere threat of violence is more than enough in most situations. When violence does erupt it has a slapstick quality, such as when Bear rigs Bo's balcony to copy a scene from a movie, leading to the latter's fatal fall. Acts of violence are therefore portrayed as either anticlimactic, almost routine, or purely random. They are not dwelled on or gloried in, and they seem incidental to the main business, which is the characters' jostling for position through their verbal interchanges.

Ordinary People?

Writing of Higgins's influence on him as a writer, Leonard reveals that he came to realize that "criminals can appear to be ordinary people and have some of the same concerns as the rest of us" (2000, vi). Thus neither writer is particularly concerned about probing the criminal mind, and while their characters occasionally display flashes of virtuosity in their speech, many of the conversations are banal. In *The Friends of Eddie Coyle*, chapter 27 begins with Foley and Waters discussing how to make a cheese sandwich, and it is only midway through the chapter that they get around to talking about Eddie, whose fate the reader is anxious to learn about. Such writing guards against becoming clichéd or stereotypical by demonstrating how crime, and the detection of crime, often arises out of the banal and the seemingly inconsequential.[4]

It is important to remember, of course, that the appearance of ordinariness here is carefully crafted and that both the placement of the scene and the utter absorption of the conversationalists in their topic contribute to its impact on the reader, who is anxious to hear of Eddie's fate. For all its apparent realism, therefore, the dialogue in these novels is highly stylized, the rhythm and timing of utterances carefully stage-managed to create distinct, almost self-contained set-piece scenes. A favorite technique is to end a scene with some kind of reversal, surprising the reader with a change of tone or a punch line that undercuts what has gone before: when Eddie makes the call to Foley informing on Jackie Brown, perhaps the most telling indication of the tension he is under comes when he turns to the woman in the queue for the telephone to tell her, "Fuck you, lady . . . and the horse you rode in on" (108). Alternatively, a scene may end on some kind of coda that picks up on a thread or a theme discussed earlier. In *The Friends of Eddie Coyle*, chapter 13 concludes with Jackie Brown warning "the kid" who has just delivered his guns to "lay off them fucking eggs" (95), taking us back to where the scene started, with the kid complaining that because he had such a long wait he has eaten three plates of eggs. This device not only provides a neat conclusion to the scene but also demonstrates Jackie Brown's desire to assert himself over this "kid," something his youth and inexperience often make impossible.

Filmic Motifs and Point of View in *Get Shorty*

Leonard takes this stylization a stage further as he appears to construct his narratives almost like scenes from a film, with shifts in point of view, fading in and out of scenes, and comic punch lines and cliffhangers. In *Get Shorty* the narrative constantly plays with the boundary between script and narrative, most explicitly in the scenes where sections of dialogue are recorded using conventions more appropriate to a film script than a novel (115–17, 196–201, 288–91). Throughout *Get Shorty* the boundaries between fiction and reality are constantly being blurred, with "real life" movie stars such as "Bobby De Niro" being discussed alongside the fictional "Michael Weir." The characters discuss scripts and whether the characters in them would actually say these things, as though Leonard is asking his reader to do the same with his fictional constructs. When Harry Zimm first encounters Chili he is uncertain as to whether the conversation has been scripted by Karen, and throughout the novel the dialogue has the quality of the "already said" (Eco 1984). When Chili meets Michael, they discuss the latter's performance in *The Cyclone*, a movie about organized crime set in Brooklyn (174–80). Michael's discussion of his method and his analysis of the Brooklyn accent offer an interesting insight into issues pertaining to representation and impersonation that have implications for Leonard's own method in the novel in trying to evoke not just the sounds but the "attitude" of the likes of Chili. It also allows us to see that whereas Chili may be seduced by the movies, the world he inhabits is ironically just as glamorous to those whose conception of "reality" has become dislocated and distorted.

One of the distinctive features of Leonard's style is his manipulation of point of view, and in *Get Shorty* many of the scenes are filtered through the "camera eye" of Karen Flores, once again blurring the boundaries between prose fiction and script/film. In chapter 4, Karen eavesdrops on the conversation taking place between Chili and Harry that the reader has been made privy to in the previous chapter. Karen can only pick up fragments of the conversation and only hears Harry's side, so she is forced to try to reconstruct what is going on by analyzing every nuance of what she can hear and drawing on her knowledge of Harry's character. The device allows Leonard to provide the reader with more of Karen's own backstory, as some of the chapter is taken up with her flashback to her earlier relationship with Harry. It also demonstrates how her overhearing "coerces" her into becoming involved in what unfolds between the two men. But one of the more interesting aspects of the technique is the way it offers us another insight into the dynamics of the relationship developing between Chili and Harry. Thus, whereas at the beginning of the chapter Karen is anxious for Harry, by the end of the scene she is able to locate the exchanges more comfortably within the schema of the movie pitch she recognizes from the "familiar words" she overhears ("What's it about?").

Chili Palmer's Verbal Dexterity

If the characters appear remarkably attuned to the minutiae of conversational interaction, this is most apparent in the portrayal of Chili Palmer. Although Chili seems at times to be starstruck, he is shown to be highly skilled at setting up and stage-managing the scenes in which he conducts his business. For example, in chapter 10 Chili helps Harry Zimm prepare for a meeting with his "investors," going so far as to groom Harry in what to say and do as well as rearrange the room to make sure he remains in control of the interaction. After the meeting is over, Chili even conducts a post mortem, analyzing and reflecting on what happened. This scene demonstrates once again the fact that "players" in the criminal world are not so different from "players" in any other environment, but it also forces us to reflect on the extent to which "real life" imitates art as well as vice versa.

Through the character of Chili, Leonard seems intent on challenging the reader's preconceptions. Offering us an insight into his modus operandi, we see that Chili is able to exploit the resources of language to great effect. Rather than issue threats, Chili offers suggestions, and he confuses his interlocutors by backtracking to something they mentioned earlier, ensuring that he maintains control over their exchanges. Thus Chili's skill extends far beyond merely having a way with words: he employs strategy and cunning. This impression is reinforced by the narrator in the minimal framing of the dialogue he contributes, for example, describing how Chili "caught the tone" (46) of the conversation and noting his analysis of the contributions of others ("Harry was staying with it").

For the reader, this highlights the extent to which Chili is alert and sensitive to the organization and dynamics of the interactions in which he plays a part. Chili's desire to manipulate and control exchanges reaches a comic climax when he attempts to coach Michael Weir to play the part of a shylock, with hilarious consequences. Indeed, Karen is so impressed by Chili's verbal performances that we are told at one point that she "wished she could write some of it down" (219). Chili is set up in the novel with some fittingly inept stooges, running rings around Leo the dry cleaner and Ray Bones the mafia hard man, producing some superb comic set pieces. But this device is never allowed to become predictable, and Chili is just as likely to keep surprising the reader as to hoodwink his adversaries.

Conclusion

While this analysis has highlighted some important differences in context, ideology, and technique between the two novels, it has been productive to focus on dialogue within a specific genre. The usefulness of this approach is twofold. On the one hand, an analysis of the dialogue may cause us to revisit our assumptions and preconceptions about the genre. For example, while the analysis has demonstrated that the genre may still be concerned with giving voice to a sense of alienation from modern society, in many ways the dialogue also counteracts this by showing that solidarity is still possible even where betrayal and double-dealing are commonplace, and that the desire to communicate through storytelling and through the exchange of banter is still strong. In Higgins's fiction this may primarily be a means of staving off that sense of alienation, of adapting to and making the best of the conditions available. But in *Get Shorty* the possibility of something more fulfilling is held out, suggesting that it is possible to use language not just to impose one's will on other people, or for some kind of ulterior motive, but to break free from the confines of environment and background and take pleasure in the games people play.

At the same time, focusing the analysis in this way can help to underline the importance of relating dialogue to a specific context and to specific reader competencies. While it is vital to recognize how representations of speech reflect changing cultural conditions and practices, it is also useful, therefore, to consider dialogue across and within different genres. Such an approach could be extended to examining dialogue in other genres— for example, science fiction or romantic fiction—in order to identify the prevailing models and norms of interaction that these genres subscribe to and help inscribe. Even with postmodern fiction, where the boundaries between genres are so often blurred, there is scope for investigating how writers experiment with generic conventions and expectations as well as how characters knowingly play with these in their spoken interactions.

7 The Alibi of Interaction
Dialogue and New Technologies

The Emergence and Impact of New Communication Technologies

Writing in 1930, Evelyn Waugh remarked upon the "infinitely expanding means of communication" available to his contemporaries, but he expressed concern that this might also entail "an infinitely receding substance of the communicable" (40). A sense of anxiety and bewilderment in the face of the emergence of new communication technologies and mass media forms is evident in much of the writing of this period, leading to what Brantlinger (1983, 34–35) calls "negative classicism." But it is far too simplistic to suggest that this was the only reaction, and Waugh's own writing provides ample evidence to suggest that writers were fascinated with and excited by the possibilities that these new forms opened up, both in terms of their narrative potential and their impact on "the communicable."

This chapter will explore how novelists in the twentieth and twenty-first centuries have reacted to the emergence of new technologies such as the telephone, radio, television, and computers, all of which mediate spoken interaction. I will analyze the innovative ways in which novelists remediate (Bolter and Grusin 2000) these new forms, and also consider the extent to which the "logic of remediation" is emancipatory or reactionary. I will also argue that novels representing these new technologies offer valuable insights into their cultural impact. Although I will briefly discuss mass communication forms such as telegraph and film, I will concentrate primarily on technologies that have come to be absorbed into the domestic routines of the home. The main emphasis will also be on technologies associated with "secondary orality" (Ong 1982) rather than literacy, where speech is transmitted or reproduced, or where characters talk to, or talk around, various technological objects. However, I will argue that maintaining a dichotomy between orality and literacy becomes much more problematic with the emergence of computer-mediated communication such as e-mail or chat rooms.

Vincent Miller (2008) has claimed that web-based technologies increasingly focus on phatic communion, where the emphasis is not so much about passing on content or information as about maintaining some kind of social network. Of course, it is easy to question how new any of this is—for example, by pointing to representations of social milieu in which gossip and rumor take precedence (as in the scenes from Firbank's novels discussed in previous chapters). Moreover, as Miller goes on to explore, the compulsion for some kind of intimacy goes hand-in-hand with self-disclosure as a kind of quid pro quo whereby mutual trust is gained and maintained. Miller links his analysis of phatic communion in online interactions with recent work on the individual in late modernity, and particularly with Anthony Giddens's (1992) theory of the self as something that is actively constructed as part of an ongoing "reflexive project." A key argument to emerge from my analysis of literary representations of online forms of communication is that as much as they provide new opportunities and possibilities, they also offer an "alibi of interaction" whereby, under the guise of reaching out to others, participants may pursue a "selfish agenda" (Wardaugh 1985, 56), making use of the resources at their disposal to facilitate but also camouflage introspection and communion with the self.

It is tempting to try and place responses to new technologies within the available literary-historical frameworks of Modernism and Postmodernism and to oversimplify them as "negative" (Modernism) or "positive" (Postmodernism). This approach is unsatisfactory for many reasons, not the least of which is the fact that it is often writers who are on the margins of, or even openly antipathetic to, these movements, who are most likely to engage with these new technologies in their fictions.[1] Another temptation is to see new technologies as increasingly determining the ways in which we communicate with one another, rather than as emerging in response to social trends and needs that are themselves the products of wider and more deeply rooted historical and economic factors. Raymond Williams's ([1974] 1990) influential study demonstrated that it was no coincidence that new technologies such as radio and television emerged alongside one another, as they were explicitly developed to bring the world "out there" into the home, while the technologies of the telegraph and the telephone reflected the demand for greater speed in communication. Nevertheless, the idea that technologies are neutral and merely respond to, rather than shape, our forms of communication is equally dangerous, potentially blinding us to the ways in which certain norms and practices come to seem natural or inevitable. An important question this chapter seeks to answer is the extent to which new technologies help redefine prevailing notions and scripts for what counts as "communication" or more specifically "interaction," as attitudes and practices change to accommodate or to counteract their impact.

Fictional representations of new communication technologies frequently present them as both "problem and promise" (Simmons 1997), with the characters' responses to these technologies often displaying a high degree of reflexivity. Postmodern fiction, it is true, focuses more keenly on issues of mediation and the manipulation of the "real," while in the fictions of the early decades of the twentieth century there is less need for novelists to defamiliarize new technologies, as they can assume that they are still strange and unfamiliar to most readers. Undoubtedly, the novel remediates (Bolter and Grusin 2000) new media in part because they pose a threat to its cultural centrality, but for novelists fascinated by the texture of speech and the structures of social interaction, an intrinsic delight is to be found in the opportunities for formal and graphic experimentation that result. Telegrams and e-mails are relatively easy to remediate, as both rely on writing more than speech, but representing telephone conversations, television shows, or radio broadcasts within a piece of prose fiction can be much more challenging. Consequently, both novelist and reader are forced to reflect on the merits and shortcomings of these technologies as forms of communication. Thus a delight in formal innovation encourages hypermediacy (Bolter and Grusin 2000) and reflexivity about the specific medium or channel of communication in question. Moreover, if they are to be anything more than stylistic experiments, such remediations need to immerse the reader in the specific social and cultural conditions in which these technologies are produced and consumed.

It is no coincidence that experimentation with the representation of speech and interaction in the early decades of the twentieth century came about at the same time as the emergence of several key new technologies and the "talk explosion" (Kacandes 2001, 2) they helped precipitate. Thus, just as the telegraph and the telephone privileged the idea of immediacy and economy in communication, so too were novelists such as Heming-way, Waugh, and Green experimenting with a "telegraphic" style (Waugh [1929] 1990) in their narratives, most notably by stripping back the speech of their characters and exploring the implications of communicating at a distance for their characters' interrelations. Similarly, just as radio and later television brought voices from all over the world into people's homes, so it was that the early-twentieth-century novel became increasingly focused on providing a sense of variety and reach in the voices it featured (Blake 1981). This is not to imply a simple causal pattern here, but rather to suggest that the "privileging of interaction" (Kacandes 2001, 14) during the period was both more widespread and more significant than has previously been understood.

Kozloff (2000) has written of the way in which films continued to revisit the transition from silence to sound long after the technology to produce sound films was developed, and it therefore seems reasonable to assume that the novel, too, would respond to the emergence of the "talkies" in some fashion.[2] John Mepham (1997) suggests as much when he claims that film opened up new possibilities for the representation of speech and led the way for the novel to follow. Kozloff's (2000) analysis of the "polylogue" in film provides one such example, where the resources of the visual/aural medium are exploited in a manner that is considerably more difficult to replicate in prose fiction. Yet while much has been written about the ways in which novelists have been influenced by cinematic techniques such as the flashback and montage, less attention has been paid to how techniques such as the "long shot" may be remediated in prose fiction, for example, to create the effect of multi-party talk as background, indiscriminate noise, or a "babel of voices."[3] Similarly, though a lot of emphasis has been placed on the way contemporary novels represent the blurring of the boundaries between the mediated and the "real" that television seems to facilitate, less focus has been placed on concepts such as that of television "flow" (Williams [1974] 1990) and how it might influence novelistic technique and the representation of characters' interactions. This chapter will therefore focus specifically on scenes of verbal interaction where the characters' talk in some way responds to or is shaped by the technological changes taking place around them.

Both linguists and media theorists are rightly suspicious of a naive effects-based approach in which a single factor, in this case technology, is isolated and removed from all the other factors (increased informality, social mobility, the impact of two world wars, etc.) that contribute to change. But novels are full of characters who mimic what they hear at the movies (Susie, Colonel Plum's secretary, speaks "in a voice she had learned at the cinema" in Waugh's *Put Out More Flags* ([1942] 1982, 201) or on their television screens (Chauncey Gardiner in Kosinsky's *Being There* [(1970) 1997], and Willie Mink in DeLillo's *White Noise* [(1984) 1986]), or incorporate the register of computers into their everyday speech (e.g., Karla's "I crashed myself" in Douglas Coupland's *Microserfs* [(1995) 1996, 101]). While such mimicry is more often than not for the purposes of parody or satire, some novels openly celebrate the way in which language is constantly being stretched and manipulated for creative and playful purposes. Thus while the novel is pulled in the direction of foregrounding speech/orality because of these emerging new forms, it is also the case that this very fascination with the texture of language, its shapes and sounds, arises out a desire to play with character speech that is the driving force for many of these fictions.

Telephone Conversations

In the early decades of the twentieth century, novelists began to experiment with the telephone conversation, not only as a plot device but also as typifying many of the changes in communicative and social practices to which they were anxious to respond. Thus while the telephone helped speed up contact between individuals, it was regarded with distrust for eroding social boundaries (you couldn't tell who might be calling you) and for intruding on people's privacy. Waugh claimed that he was one of the first novelists to experiment with telephone conversations in his novels.[4] In the tradition of stage farces, Waugh exploits the potential of telephone conversations in terms of plotting and deception, and like many of his contemporaries, he draws much of his humor from the continued awkwardness his characters feel at having to converse via this "instrument."[5] The telephone is shown to be indispensable to the lifestyle of the Bright Young Things immortalized in Waugh's early comic novels, with their endless partying and inability to fix on anything for very long, and Waugh is especially alert to the ways in which new technologies may divide the generations.

In one of his most famous scenes, Waugh devotes an entire chapter of *Vile Bodies* ([1930] 1987) to two telephone conversations taking place between Adam Symes and his erstwhile girlfriend Nina (chapter 11).[6] The dialogue is presented almost entirely without narrative intervention, conflating the sense of haste with which first Adam calls off the wedding, then Nina announces she is engaged to someone else. However, there is irony at the characters' expense and their repetition of the phrase "I see" when it is clear that they can neither "see" each other literally nor "see" in the sense of understanding what the other is trying to say. The scene skillfully evokes the sense of emotional and physical distance between the characters, but it also hints at the fact that though they seem to prefer this form of communication as a way to avoid anything too "intense," occasionally their party masks slip to hint at their inner fragility.

Waugh clearly revels in the opportunity for stylistic play that the telephone conversation provides. The phrase "I see" recurs throughout the scene, acting as a kind of coda to the exchanges, and the mirroring of the two conversations provides a pleasing sense of symmetry. In addition, the scene is arranged in such a way as to highlight the characters' echoing and matching of each other's contributions ("Is that all?" "Yes, that's all"), such that it takes on a rhythm of its own, where each phrase and contribution is neatly balanced, suggesting that despite what the characters may be saying to one another on the surface, the bond between them remains strong. This closeness is also evident in the way they anticipate what the other is about to say and how they may be feeling: it is Nina, not Adam, who reconstructs the story of what has happened to scupper their wedding plans, and both display sensitivity to how the other is feeling ("I'm afraid not"; "You'll be furious") even if their actions seem precipitate and cruel.

David Lodge's *Nice Work* (1989 [1988], 310) reflects the author's fascination with the telephone as one of his characters, a post-structuralist lecturer, muses about the feasibility of a thesis on "telephonic communication and affective alienation in modern fiction, with special reference to Evelyn Waugh, Ford Madox Ford, Henry Green. . . ." But it seems that this alienation effect is far from confined to the period when the technology first emerged, and writers since Waugh's time have returned to the device often to explore and foreground awkwardness and artificiality in their characters' interactions.[7] Although in many novels telephone conversations have become mere "stage business," it seems that despite the ubiquity and familiarity of this form of communication—and the emergence of mobile communication technologies, the Internet, and so forth—the ability to speak to one another across vast distances while not being physically co-present continues to fascinate and to frustrate.

Nicholson Baker's *Vox* ([1992] 1994) offers perhaps the most provocative use of the telephone conversation as a narrative device to date. The novel is composed entirely of dialogue in the guise of a single long conversation taking place between a man and a woman brought together by a mutual interest in phone sex, who reveal their fantasies but also some of their fears and anxieties as they work toward achieving simultaneous orgasms. Baker's novel draws on a long history associating the telephone with sex,[8] and it certainly heightens the eroticism for the participants, who have to describe their surroundings, their actions, and what they look like to each other but who also have to rely on their imagination to project themselves into the other's world. In the absence of a visual link, aural cues and echoes become more and more important, and the characters rely on their matching of each other's words and stories to negotiate just how far they can go. Baker's representation of the telephone conversation is highly reflexive, as the characters refer to the "power" of the telephone and to the fact that "different rules" (92) apply. Rather than inhibiting their intimacy, the telephone appears to liberate the two characters, but they also acknowledge their predisposition to the anonymity and intensity of this kind of encounter, as one admits to being "a compulsive confessor" (100).

Such representations seem to suggest that power and gender relations between participants in telephone conversations may be much more fluid or unstable because they are physically separate and cannot see where the other is or what they are doing. In terms of narrative, the device of the telephone conversation is ideal for creating an almost hermetically sealed dyadic unit in which the characters' relationship can be probed and exposed and in which the reader is placed in the position of an overhearer, given intimate access to the characters' most private and intense exchanges. Indeed, Lodge hypothesizes that "there is a sense in which all dialogue in prose fiction is like telephonic dialogue, because (unlike drama) it must make do without the physical presence of the speakers" (1992, 172). Although the "rules" place constraints on the characters in Gricean ([1963] 1975) terms to be maximally relevant (Relevance), to provide enough information (Quantity), and to avoid obscurity (Manner), the pressure to make themselves understood can prompt them to disclose or confess, and to discover more about themselves than they would in a face-to-face encounter.

Broadcast Talk: Radio and Television

Writing of the "larger role for speech" in the English novel at the beginning of the twentieth century, Norman Page (1988) suggests that this process may have been "abetted by the new aural culture of broadcasting." In particular, radio drama, driven by the need for distinctiveness and memorability in its play of voices (S. J. Douglas 1999), is likely have had at least as much of an impact on novelistic dialogue as the advent of the "talkies." Although media theory has tended to concentrate on the impact of television to the neglect of radio, critics are beginning to appreciate radio's unique contribution to cultural life. For example, Paddy Scannell (1996) has argued that radio played an important part in bringing into people's homes accents, dialects, and languages that they might otherwise never encounter, offering scope for the breaking down of class and even cultural barriers.

Yet despite radio's "distinct power to forge group ties" (S. J. Douglas 1999, 327), when the technology was new it could have much the same alienating effect as the telephone. In Waugh's *Put Out More Flags* ([1942] 1982, 120), set during the Second World War, the admittedly fragile Angela Lyne is made even more anxious by the noises emanating from her radio, where "Tirelessly, all over the world, voices were speaking in their own and in foreign tongues." Similarly, in Waugh's semi-autobiographical *The Ordeal of Gilbert Pinfold* ([1957] 1988), the eponymous hero is driven mad by his inability to tell whether the voices that torment him come from the radio or are the product of his delusions. Angela Lyne hears her voices while bathing, Pinfold while on board ship, suggesting a darker side to the seeming virtues of radio's portability and accessibility. Moreover, these representations demonstrate the unique capacity of what McLuhan called "the tribal drum" (1964, 263–64) to get inside people's heads in a powerful but also potentially frightening fashion and to expose divisions as much as it may forge ties between peoples.

Even toward the end of the twentieth century, suspicion and uncertainty about this form of broadcast media linger on in novelistic accounts. DeLillo's *White Noise* ([1984] 1986) features just as many references to radio as to television, though it is always the latter that is mentioned in discussions of the work of this "poet laureate of the media age" (Weinstein 1993, 301). This may be because DeLillo seems to deliberately set out to merge the two media in the reader's mind rather than keep them distinct, as both are anthropomorphized to have a will of their own. At various points both television and radio cut into and across the Gladney family's conversations as if to encourage some kind of "para-social interaction" (Horton and Wohl 1957),[9] and together they form what Weinstein (1993, 303) calls a "choral narrative" in which the environment speaks as much as the protagonists. DeLillo seems fascinated by the capacity of broadcast media to bring news, public information, drama, and storytelling into the home, blurring the boundaries between private and public spheres. He also seems fascinated by the way in which television and radio take on an informal, familiar register when addressing their audiences and with how they become absorbed into domestic routines, so that listening to the radio or "watching" television takes place alongside other activities such as reading a newspaper or doing the household chores.

The sounds and voices emanating from their radios and television screens follow DeLillo's characters wherever they go in their home, providing the background to even their most intimate and private exchanges. In the scene where Jack and his wife, Babette, discuss her affair with Willie Mink, the radio comes on unexpectedly, but it is only when the conversation is over that Babette finally switches it off, "killing the voices" (202). Babette is hooked on confessional talk radio and even claims at one point that "talk is radio" (264), displaying once again how these mediated conversations insinuate themselves into but also help shape the family's interactions. Radio is what the family listens to when they are traveling, providing them with some continuity with what they are familiar with from "home." Thus while radio functions to bring the world "out there" into the home, as Williams ([1974] 1990) claimed, it also seems to represent a connection with "home" when the family has to go and face "out there."

New communication and broadcast technologies have always been accused of either somehow preventing us from talking to one another or of degrading the quality of our communications so that we substitute the phony (para-social) for the "real," the banal for the deep and meaningful. But as suggested earlier, it may be instead that they provide us with an "alibi of interaction" whereby through maintaining a facade of connecting with other people, however remotely, we find a way of externalizing our thoughts, confronting our private fantasies and fears. The "white noise" produced by such technologies may therefore afford a space wherein interiority is camouflaged and given limited sanction. In DeLillo's novel, Jack says, "I turned off the radio, not to help me think but to keep me from thinking" (126), powerfully evoking the complex relationship with ourselves that these technologies can mediate. Susan J. Douglas (1999, 22) suggests something very similar by claiming that radio ensures we are "taken out of ourselves . . . yet paradoxically hurled into our innermost thoughts." Writing of DeLillo's novel, Mark Osteen (2000) argues that television muffles as well as amplifies its audience's spiritual yearnings, so that while such technologies do comfort and distract, it is important to recognize that they *can* also amplify those yearnings.

Cognitive approaches (e.g., Palmer 2004) have shown us that speech and thought are not separate realms so much as permeable boundaries, forcing us to reassess the conceptualization of thought as something that takes place as some kind of willed activity in solitude and silence. Rather than blame new technologies for changing how we think and relate to one another, therefore, we should consider whether they present us with questions about cognition and social interaction that we have yet to fully address.

Whatever figures we accept about the number of hours per day people spend watching television, and however narrowly we define what constitutes "watching television," there is a relative paucity of novelistic representations of fictional characters sitting in front of, talking about, or talking to their television screens. The advent of the telegraph, the telephone, radio, and cinema prompted a much more instantaneous reaction, as novelists appeared more anxious to explore the implications of these new forms of communication and to mock their absurdities. McHale's (1992) contention that cinema was the cultural dominant of the Modernist era, while television is the cultural dominant of the Postmodern, highlights the fact that we have had to wait a while for the novel to fully wake up to television as a cultural phenomenon. Indeed, as Volker Hummel suggests, by the time novelists such as DeLillo turned their attention to television culture, it had become necessary to defamiliarize what had become so ubiquitous and overfamiliar to their readership.

Of course, television's lack of cultural respectability may help explain this neglect, as may the fact that television artifacts are so ephemeral, ensuring that references to them date quickly. Just as with the earlier technological advances, novelists' most common response to television has been either satirical (Kosinsky's *Being There*) or at best ambivalent (DeLillo's *White Noise*, Pynchon's *Vineland* [1990]). Similarly, novelists who consciously set out to explore the popular cultural reference points by which their characters map their lives are more likely to embrace television as a cultural phenomenon. And just as in the 1920s and 1930s, it is primarily with and through dialogue that these novelists probe and play with the possibilities that the televisual medium brings.

In the novels of Kosinsky, DeLillo, and Pynchon there is a strong emphasis on the way everyday language and behavior is memetic[10] of what we see and hear on our television screens, and all seem to deliver a rather bleak vision of how this process will affect the intellectual and cultural lives of their protagonists, potentially turning them into half-alive morons (the Thanatoids in *Vineland*) or making it impossible for them to distinguish what is mediated from what is real. Although these novels are far too sophisticated to indulge in a simplistic "media effects" model, they do not appear to offer the possibility of either an active audience or of a kind of television that is self-reflexive and ironic. Perhaps this is because, as David Foster Wallace (1993) maintains, television's determination to be ironic about itself, to engage in self-parody, means that it is more difficult for writers to use irony or parody in representing television in their fictions.

Television studies has come a long way from the "hypodermic syringe" version of the television viewer as passive consumer. The contemporary "dialogic" view of television culture (e.g., Fiske 1987) proposes an "active viewer" who goes far beyond just "decoding" what is broadcast to relating television output to their own social experiences and providing oppositional responses (Hall 1980) to dominant readings. Several studies (e.g., Hobson 1980) have provided evidence that viewers discuss and debate the content of television shows and the direction of their plots, such that the viewing experience spills over the physical boundaries of the show into their everyday lives and verbal interactions. Meanwhile, ethnographic research by David Morley (1986) and Tania Modleski (1983) has provided evidence of what viewers *do* while watching television, and showed how viewing habits, preferences and responses may be gendered. And the concept of para-social interaction (Horton and Wohl 1957) illustrates the extent to which viewers interact not only around their television sets but also with them.

In addition to researching how we talk about television, media and cultural theorists have analyzed what kind of talk is privileged and preferred on our screens. For example, Andrew Tolson (1991) has demonstrated how television serves to institutionalize certain variants of "conversation." He also reminds us that while talk on television always carries an element of performance, it produces a high degree of reflexivity, to the point where talk about talk comes center stage. For many television critics, a key issue is whether foregrounding certain kinds of talk on television can be empowering for groups whose voices are not heard or not listened to in mainstream culture.[11]

A question that remains unanswered is whether television provokes and facilitates such discourses or merely provides a very visible public forum whereby they can come out into the open. Similarly, we do not yet know how far patterns of communication and discursive models represented on television influence or spill over into everyday interactions, although some preliminary research on this has been conducted on the reworking and recycling of radio discourse in everyday talk (Spitulnik 1997). Of course, it is necessary to avoid overgeneralizing and to recognize that different television genres invite different "reading relations" (Fiske 1987). Nevertheless, we might speculate, as Thomas de Zengotita (2005) does, that television seduces us with "the irresistible flattery that goes with being incessantly addressed" or presents us with the illusion of a "talking cure" (Shattuc 1997), whereby confession is always therapeutic and cathartic, never leaving us vulnerable or exploited.

Linguists, meanwhile, have rarely gone beyond describing the "language of television," and we are still waiting for someone to rise to Hudson's (1980, 171) challenge to analyze "the effect of the mass media on people's speech." Beyond occasional studies (e.g., Stuart-Smith and Timmins 2004) of the effects of specific TV shows or personalities on attitudes toward accent, very little research has been conducted into the likely implications for language of an activity so many of us spend so much of our time doing. Alla Tovares's (2006) study of the interpenetration of public and private spheres in gossip about a television show has gone some way to opening up discussion about how television may function as a resource within conversational interaction for the raising of difficult or sensitive issues. Moreover, Tovares found that conversations about television shows were seen as continuations of ongoing interactions rather than as new topics somehow outside of or irrelevant to the private sphere, and were used by participants as a way of inviting others to share the conversational floor. The use of public voices in this way is therefore seen as potentially positive in facilitating interactions that might not otherwise be possible. More recently, Kay Richardson (2010) has provided a sociolinguistic account of television dramatic dialogue, not only focusing on the kinds of talk featured on all kinds of TV shows but also exploring the contexts of production and reception in which these representations are found. Such work also demonstrates that much is to be gained from looking at dialogue in different discourse contexts such as literature, television, and film not as distinct or exclusive of one another but as sharing mutual influences and traditions.

American postmodern fiction focuses on the ubiquity of television and the extent to which it defines our reality. Many critics have noted that such novels raise important epistemological questions; for example, Philip Simmons (1997, 168) claims that *Vineland* "captures the way in which . . . television has been absorbed into the everyday rhythms of speech and thought." In *Being There*, *Vineland*, and *White Noise* the characters seemingly cannot conceive of events and even their own subjectivities unless they are mediated for them, and many of their interactions with others take place in the context of television, whether that is literally in front of the TV screen or shaped and defined by their understanding of what constitutes interaction in the terms defined by what they watch. Wallace (1993) even contends that the American novel has been tainted for many by the generation of "tinny"-eared young writers whose experience of verbal interaction leads them to "structure commercial-length conversations around the sorts of questions myopic car-crash witnesses ask each other" (168).

British and European television represents a slightly different viewing context for the novelist for a number of reasons. Representations of television viewing often associate the activity with the working classes or use it as a shorthand for cultural impoverishment,[12] but they are far from the "cultural scapegoat" (Fitzpatrick 2006, 50) they seem to be in much American fiction. Digitalization and satellite technology have had a huge impact both on the way people watch television and in the output made available to them, some arguing that this will lead to the emergence of new, diverse niche audiences. People no longer watch television as a family, because most households have multiple TV sets, and changes in working habits mean that the home is no longer likely to be exclusively a haven for men and a workplace for women as observed by Morley (1986). In popular culture, nostalgia for simpler, more "innocent" times is often signified by shared references to cult shows or children's TV,[13] and the rituals of television viewing predating recent technological advances. Such a response can be heard and seen in films, TV shows, and popular music, and also, as I will argue, in contemporary fiction.

Roddy Doyle's *The Woman Who Walked into Doors* ([1996] 1998) recounts the story of Paula Spencer, an alcoholic and victim of domestic violence, in her own words. Doyle refuses to sentimentalize Paula's situation, and much of the dark humor in the novel comes from the blunt, nononsense language she employs in recounting the beatings and hardships she has faced. At first glance, television figures in the novel as a source of escape from the daily grind but also as a way of forging bonds with others. While the novel reflects primarily on the viewing habits and preoccupations of a particular cultural moment (spanning shows from the 1970s to the early 1990s), nevertheless it offers some interesting insights into the place of television in the home and its penetration into the language and conversations of its audiences.

Paula reveals how, in an attempt to get closer to her boss, "I watch Coronation Street now—I tape it—because Marie watches it and we can talk about it" (108). Such references seem to suggest that the kind of television you watch functions as a kind of "cultural capital" (Bourdieu 1986) by means of which imbalances in power are enacted and reasserted. However, studies (e.g., Geraghty 1991) have shown that soap operas such as *Coronation Street* provide female audiences with openings to conversations and discussions that often confront cultural stereotypes and taboos. Moreover, soaps are said to provide women with a "masculine-free zone" (Fiske 1987) and even a means to resist and defy the patriarchal system that works to deny and repress female pleasures.

Doyle explores more fully the complexities of female viewers and their interrelationships in a scene (111–12) where Paula and her daughters (and her young son, Jack) sit down together to watch an episode of the American show *Baywatch*. A program notorious for its pneumatic women running around in skimpy swimwear, Doyle seems to employ it in this scene to show up the intergenerational conflict between the women in the Spencer household. The scene is presented almost entirely unmediated, with Doyle minimizing the narrative intrusion further by preferring dashes to quotation marks. Paula initiates the discussion, provoking her daughters by attacking the show, but although there is more than a hint of bitterness here, it also betrays her desperation to have some kind of connection with them, as she admits that "I just say it—or something like it—to get them going." The women focus exclusively on the physical appearance of the screen actors, and the source of the conflict comes from the fact that the younger girls refuse to acknowledge that these women are fake, preferring to subscribe to the fantasy that "it's the swimming" that gives them their impossible physiques.

Of course, the significance of this scene comes from the fact that we know that Paula is a victim of domestic violence and of the myths of a patriarchal culture that oppresses women of all ages, backgrounds, and physical shapes. Her daughters come across as assertive and prepared to defend their views, but they also seem to have internalized the male gaze, as they measure themselves as inadequate against the impossible standards set ("They're gorgeous"). Although at first Paula seems frustrated by her daughters' refusal to see through this, we soon realize that she has another, more selfish source of frustration—she is merely counting the minutes until she can dispatch her son to bed and drink herself into a stupor. Thus Doyle demonstrates how talk about and around television can act as a kind of camouflage under which some of the tensions within the family can be aired.

Later in the novel, Doyle returns to the rituals of television viewing to expose further the tensions simmering beneath the surface of family life. In a flashback to the first time Paula takes Charlo home to meet her parents (117–18), watching television is presented as a ritual over which the patriarch, Paula's father, presides. At first the representation seems fairly benign, as Doyle plays with nostalgic references to popular British TV shows from the 1970s with knowing references to characters such as "Bernie the Bolt." Through Paula's narration, Doyle shows how television is "enmeshed in people's memories of the stages of their days and their lives" (S. J. Douglas 1999, 32). But it soon transpires that there is a desperation underlying the family's, and especially the father's, need to perform this ritual.

Initially, talking about television seems to perform a phatic function, as Paula's father invites Charlo to join with the family in their enjoyment of one of their favorite shows, the popular quiz show *The Golden Shot*. Introductions of this kind are often tense encounters, and although Mr. Spencer's questions function as "other-oriented tokens" (Laver 1981), displaying concern for Charlo's interests, because they are usually reserved for persons of higher status speaking to their social inferiors, they in effect serve to put Charlo in his place. Under the very public "coercion to speak" (Fogel 1985) of Mr. Spencer's insistent questions, Charlo reluctantly joins in, but his approbation for the show and its host is so lukewarm ("He's alright") that Paula's father soon becomes suspicious. It quickly becomes clear that talking about television, far from deflecting the tension, merely forms the backdrop to a contest wherein Mr. O'Leary tries to reassert his authority in the face of this challenge from the young newcomer. It also emerges that Mr. O'Leary is more interested in watching Charlo than *The Golden Shot* ("Daddy looked at Charlo looking at the telly"), and the conversation becomes a kind of verbal duel (McDowell 1985) between the two men, with Paula looking on admiringly at Charlo's performance ("It was a brilliant answer; it shut Daddy up"). What makes Charlo such a frustrating adversary for Mr. O'Leary is that his responses are unpredictable. When Mr. O'Leary tries to mitigate Charlo's face-threatening acts (Brown and Levinson 1978) by allowing that the show may after all be "all a cod," Charlo rejects his efforts by seeming to come to the show's defense ("The prizes are real").

What Doyle does so successfully here is demonstrate how power relations within the home are maintained and asserted not necessarily always in violent or overt displays, but through manipulation of the most ordinary and banal of domestic activities. The scene also reveals women's complicity in this process, as Mammy engages in para-social interaction with the TV set ("Left a bit") and tries to draw the men's attention back to the show. Daddy responds by offering Charlo another opportunity to redeem himself, switching to a discussion of "Catweezil,"[14] another popular show from the period about a time-traveling magician. As well as giving Charlo the possibility of a fresh start, Mr. O'Leary also implicitly invites Charlo to stay on by reassuring him that the show is "on after this." The family's viewing is thus represented as a kind of "flow" (Williams [1974] 1990) wherein the choice of show is less significant than the mere fact of their watching television together. Another act of mitigation is apparent in Mr. O'Leary's admission that "the reception could be better," as he appears to be taking a step backward in the confrontation by putting himself down (at least by association). However, Charlo refuses to be drawn in, replying with blunt monosyllables ("No") and committing more face-threatening acts by overtly attacking the family favorite ("I think it's stupid"). The tense standoff between the men escalates as Charlo continues with his insults while Mr. O'Leary resorts to repeating the mantra that punctuates the exchanges, "We like it," and which weighs like a heavy hand on the entire scene.

The show is now forgotten—"The contestant in The Golden Shot won a car but no one said anything"—and Paula is left to reflect on the fact that "there was never a hope" of the two men getting along. Although she acknowledges that the tension could just as easily have been triggered by anything else, it is clear that watching television is an important site for contestation within the home. As Morley's (1986) research showed, males tend to take control not just of what is watched on TV but how it is watched, and having lost his contest with Charlo, Mr. O'Leary turns his attention to his wife (119). His reminder that "Catweezil's on now" has the illocutionary force of a command to his wife to come and watch the show, and though she resists, looking back on the scene Paula recognizes that this was all part of his attempt to bully his family, and that "That was why he liked Catweezil, because it wasn't fuckin' funny. Charlo was right; it was brutal." The sadness for Paula is that she realizes too late that "him and my father were very alike," that the rebellious Charlo will soon be presiding over his own domestic regime where petty disputes escalate into conflict and brutality.

The episode is multi-layered, the nostalgia and comedy sitting uneasily alongside our bleak recognition of where all this is heading for Paula and her family. At first the scene appears self-contained, with the dialogue building to its climax with exquisite comic timing. But in adding a kind of epilogue to the scene, Doyle demonstrates how the grievances and niggles of family life can resurface at any moment, with the resulting aggression usually being turned against the weakest or most vulnerable. For Paula, the scene illuminates the poverty of her mother's life:

"She didn't do anything except sit in front of the telly and watch the programs that he put on and say yes and no when he spoke to her" (120). At the same time, she realizes how much her father has changed from the man who at least tried to engage with his children to someone who just "stopped" (121) and gave up.

Doyle is sensitive to the fact that television is woven into the fabric of these people's daily lives, both reflecting and shaping the ways in which they relate to those around them. Thus television is seen as providing an illusion of togetherness (they are physically co-present) while providing an alibi for non-communication, inattention, and the deflection of the conversation away from matters too directly affecting the family. Mr. O'Leary's insistent repetition of the collective "we" highlights the fact that he is increasingly desperate in his attempts to hold together the show of "being a family." Instead of quizzing Charlo about his prospects or his suitability as Paula's boyfriend, Mr. O'Leary asks him about TV shows. Similarly, in the earlier scene from the novel, Paula tries to connect with her children through discussing their favorite show, but they reject her efforts, and she cannot sustain them because her craving for alcohol is so strong. For brief moments, maybe, the family can unite around the television to laugh at, deride, or adore their favorite characters, and the shows they watch provide them with subject matter for discussion and some sense of shared pleasure. However, Doyle skillfully demonstrates how talk about and talk around television is not hermetically sealed from the rest of family life but is instead often a means by which underlying tensions and frustrations are brought to light.

What television talk thus facilitates is a kind of multi-party talk whereby under the guise of reacting to or commenting on what is unfolding on screen, another layer of discourse may be unfolding between the viewers. In Doyle's novel these viewers are far from passive, and they have learned to incorporate television not only into their daily rituals but also into their conversations and interactions with one another. Talking around television thus appears to constitute a distinctive activity type or conversational genre that participants quickly master and manipulate. For example, there is a strong preference for talk to be confined to commercial breaks, and in Gricean ([1963] 1975) terms to be relevant to what is being watched (observing the maxim of Relevance) and to be brief enough not to disrupt the viewing (observing the maxim of Quantity). There is also add-ed pressure on participants to time and shape their contributions and to be sensitive to the viewing needs of others. Furthermore, as the ethnographic research strongly suggests, there may be gendered differences in the way participants interact around television, where men are found to prefer to watch in complete silence, whereas women are accustomed to building their viewing into their domestic routines and to talking during and over the television.

More broadly, such television talk shows us that verbal interaction need not always be composed of discrete, dyadic, bounded exchanges but may rather be fragmentary, disrupted, interruptible, and part of the "flow" of everyday life within which all sorts of other activities, including verbal activities, take place. David Herman (2006, 84) calls this a "Copernican revolution" in our understanding of discourse, as talk is seen as "inextricably embedded in activities" rather than a mere "backdrop for speech." Moreover, talk around television offers a model of conversation where utterances may not always be directed at their intended recipients but may be deflected around and via both on- and offscreen acts and personages. Writing such as Doyle's, by engaging with rather than being dismissive of such talk, shows just how much may be revealed about people's hopes and desires, anxieties and frustrations, when their attention is seemingly diverted or deflected by the images and voices thrown out by a box in the corner.

Virtual Interactions: Computer-Mediated Communication

Novelistic representations of virtual interactions (namely, human-computer interactions and communication between persons facilitated by a computer, e.g., chat rooms, e-mail, etc.) again present us with what at first seems strange and alienating, and again a primary response has been to satirize the unfamiliar.[15] While virtual interactions are usually conducted through a graphic interface, I discuss them here because they occupy a territory somewhere between speech and writing.

In David Lodge's *Small World* ([1984] 1985), set in the world of academia, the hapless conference bore, Robin Dempsey, finds himself outcast to the wilderness of the fictional Darlington University. Increasingly lonely and embittered, Dempsey finds comfort in ELIZA,[16] a program designed "to enable computers to talk" (154). But the conception of "talk" that this allows is severely restricted: "The conversations had to be of a contextually specific type, with well-defined rules and goals, in which the computer could take an essentially questioning and prompting role, programmed with a repertoire of possible responses to cues likely to appear in the context" (154).

Lodge sets out the exchanges between Dempsey and ELIZA like conventional fictional dialogue, defamiliarized only by the fact that the contributions are all capitalized, presumably to remind the reader that these exchanges are typed rather than spoken. Despite the extreme functionality of ELIZA's input, Dempsey soon develops a dependency on this interaction, liberated by the fact that he is talking to a machine who can neither remember nor pass judgment on anything he actually says. During the course of the novel, Lodge provides us with tantalizing snippets of these conversations and hints at their increasing intimacy and intensity. At one point, one of Dempsey's colleagues, Josh Collins, warns him that he may be "overdoing it" with ELIZA, reminding him that "That thing . . . Can't really talk, you know. It can't actually *think*" (243). But Dempsey brushes off Collins's warnings and we see his contributions descending into a kind of maniacal rant, prompting ELIZA to finally crack and tell him to "SHOOT YOURSELF." Collins's part in setting Dempsey up is thereby exposed, but we are never told the extent of his involvement, leaving some ambiguity about ELIZA's powers.

This device hilariously exposes Dempsey and shows the depths to which he has sunk, but Lodge is also poking fun at the exaggerated (at the time) claims being made for the sophistication of computer programs and people's willingness to believe in a "ghost in the machine" when it comes to the possibility of externalizing their own desires and fantasies. What Lodge touches on here is the freedom that comes from what Moran and Hawisher (1998, 90) call the "uncommitted intimacy" of virtual interactions, so for Dempsey the appeal is that he can voice all his frustrations and anxieties without having to give anything in return and without having to deal with any of the constraints or the messiness of face-to-face encounters. ELIZA's function here is similar to that of Bakhtin's "super-addressee," whose "absolutely just responsive understanding is presumed, either in some metaphysical distance or in distant historical time" (1986, 126). She provides the perfect alibi of interaction, with all the trappings of the confessional but without a confessor who can judge or even remember one's confessions. For Bakhtin the different ideological forms that the superaddressee may take are all expressions of something that is intrinsic to human language, that is, the need to be heard and to seek responsive understanding. But the superaddressee offers all of this at a distance, providing a simulation of human interaction without the attendant stresses and tensions.

Many theorists of new technologies have tried to account for the ways in which seemingly impoverished interactions of this kind can somehow free the user to engage in introspection and to explore regions of the self hitherto dormant. For example, Sherry Turkle (1995) hypothesizes a "second self" that is conjured up via the computer screen, possible only because while it alleviates loneliness and a sense of isolation, it can make no demands in return. Meanwhile, S. J. Douglas (1999, 14) uses the metaphor of the "fig leaf" to convey how, for men in particular, such interactions provide an outlet for their emotions and needs that they can defend and justify to themselves because of its associations with "technology" and the "scientific." Perhaps most radical of all is Donna Haraway's concept of the cyborg (1991), in which the potential of new technologies to help us transcend the limits of human biology creates the possibility of post-gender, even posthuman worlds and discourses. Of course, such responses can seem impossibly utopian, and it is vital to remember that not everyone is going to have access to these technologies, let alone be liberated by them. But the idea of creating and playing with virtual selves and realities clearly has important implications for the interactions we find online and for understanding the specific rules of engagement, or norms of politeness and exchange, that may apply.

Microserfs ([1995] 1996) by Douglas Coupland immerses us in the world and language of a group of (mainly male) coders working for Microsoft. The novel takes the form of a journal kept by one of the coders, Dan, but the narrative also incorporates e-mails and a chat room encounter as well as scenes where the various characters engage in what they call "face talk." In this world, therefore, it is almost as though face-to-face interaction is a novelty, and the boundaries between "face time" and the time spent on screen are increasingly blurred.

Although e-mail exchanges may be best understood in the context of the epistolary tradition, Page sets the precedent for including them in discussions of fictional dialogue on the basis that they constitute a kind of "talking on paper" (1988, 49). Many linguists (e.g., Baron 2000; Crystal

2001) have argued that e-mails occupy a place somewhere between speech and writing, and they certainly substitute for "face time" for Dan and Abe. Dan describes himself as an "email addict" (21), and his messages range from the banal to the philosophical and are often highly reflexive. Dan claims that "the cool thing with email is that when you send it, there's no possibility of connecting with the person on the other end" (21–22), suggesting once again that the sender is somehow liberated. Both Dan's and Abe's e-mails are often highly introspective and expressive of what Jones called the novel's "metaphysical angst" (1995, 54). But Dan also recognizes that "our email correspondence has given us an intimacy that face-to-face contact never would have" (210), and the e-mails are full of involvement strategies (Chafe 1982) such as posing and answering questions, abbreviations, and the use of the present tense, as if drawing the receiver into the sender's immediate context. What this suggests is that there is a highly complex set of motivations at work here, as in the ELIZA exchanges from Lodge's novel. Interaction relies on the belief—or at least hope—that there is someone or something "at the other end" who is listening and responding to what is being said. But it may be liberating not to know too much about that entity, how and when it may respond, and to maintain both physical and emotional distance.

The compulsion to disclose and to share is presented as being very powerful, especially for these individuals who find "face time" so challenging. But there is a very real sense in which this process is portrayed as being potentially full of risks, both in terms of imposing on the recipient and in terms of opening up feelings and emotions that can then no longer remain hidden. An increasingly anxious Abe tells Dan, "Sometimes I feel kind of lost. There. I've revealed too much. I'm going to send you this before I can stop myself" (305). Here it is almost as though Abe is relinquishing responsibility for his feelings by almost literally sending them on to Dan, and both seem to shape their relationship around the medium through which they communicate.

E-mails in *Microserfs*, like Dempsey's interaction with ELIZA in *Small World*, function as a latter-day version of the confessional, bearing out Foucault's (1978, 59) claim that "we have . . . become a singularly confessing society." Foucault goes on to contend that the confessional places strict demands on confessors, coercing them to find and reveal hidden truths which they then must take responsibility for, but also that the form confession takes, reliving and re-presenting one's experiences or failings, unearths certain "truths" hitherto hidden from one's self. The act of externalizing one's thoughts in written e-mails and making them communicable to some distant other facilitates this process. But the distribution of power is much more complex than even Foucault seems to allow, because *Microserfs* portrays the act of confessing as an imposition as much as it is a release, placing a burden on the listener/receiver not only of carrying around someone else's angst but also of not being able to share that with another. What is expressed in the novel is the profound need to keep trying out new forms of communication, not as a means of escaping reality, or oneself, but as a way of destabilizing and offsetting the familiar and the routine.

Conclusion

We have seen in this chapter that a major response to what Kathleen Fitzpatrick calls the "anxiety of obsolescence" (2006) is to satirize new technologies and highlight their limitations. There is also plenty of evidence to support Fitzpatrick's claim that this anxiety may be felt more keenly by those who are most threatened by change, namely, "beset white manhood" (2006, 233). At the same time, the analysis has shown that foregrounding and engaging with the discourses produced by these technologies can be productive not only of stylistic tours de force, memorable plot lines, and scenes of high comedy but also of important and timely questions to do with the nature of communication and the power dynamics between interactants. For example, the anonymity and distance that characterize these different discourses may be liberating, but they also serve to highlight the extent to which we project certain expectations and demands onto one another. It is all the better if that other cannot answer back, judge us, or take the attention away from ourselves, offering us the illusion of ultimate control. But more than this, the examples discussed here suggest that interactions in these new and unfamiliar guises can force us to contemplate the complex relations existing between what we conceptualize as our inner, thinking selves and the selves we project in our public commerce with others, suggesting that any equivalence between silence and contemplation, or between noise and vacuity, is far too simplistic.

8 Stuck in a Loop?
Dialogue in Hypertext Fiction

Hypertext Fiction and Interactivity: Issues and Debates

Hypertext fiction has provoked much debate since the appearance of the first examples in the late 1980s. Much of this debate has been focused on questions regarding the status of these fictions and their implications for the experience of writing and reading. Where close analysis of the form has been attempted (e.g., Jane Yellowlees Douglas's [1994] readings of Michael Joyce's *afternoon, a story*), it has mainly consisted of an attempt to "make sense" of the narrative, untangling the strands of the plot, and searching for some kind of closure. While this approach has offered valuable insights into the narrative structures of these fictions and into the mechanics of the interfaces they employ, few insights are provided into specific aspects of their style. Recently, an attempt has been made to close this gap by "second wave" hypertext theorists (Ensslin 2007; Bell 2010), but even here no attention has explicitly been paid to the role of dialogue in this kind of fiction.

Hypertext fiction has come a long way since the earliest examples, most notably in exploring the possibilities of creating a multimedia artifact in which sounds and images accompany the written text.[1] However, this chapter will focus on the use of dialogue in two early hypertext fictions. Both Michael Joyce's *afternoon, a story* (first published in 1987) and Jane Yellowlees Douglas's *I Have Said Nothing* (1994) have achieved near-canonical status, having been excerpted in print in the Norton anthology of postmodern American fiction (Geyh 1997). As is often the case with hypertext fictions, the writers, Jane Yellowlees Douglas and Michael Joyce, also happen to be two of the foremost theorists of the form, and the sense of mutual influence is unavoidable. The aims of this chapter are twofold: to explore the functions of dialogue in these fictions, and the extent to which the representations are innovative; and to examine whether we need to reassess our models for understanding the functions and forms of fictional dialogue as we have begun to apply them to the print novel.

Critics such as Marie-Laure Ryan (2002a) argue that now that the hype about hypertext fiction has died down, we are left with the sobering fact that outside of university departments and a fairly small group of writers and theorists, these fictions are not widely read or talked about. Questions have been raised about the quality of the writing, and skepticism has been expressed about the more overblown claims made for the form. In particular, the claim that such fictions offer the reader an interactive experience has been exposed as both hollow and naively literal (e.g., Miall 1999). But this debate has led to a fascinating examination of exactly what we mean by interaction, which has important implications for the study of exchanges that take place within the story world as well as between reader and writer, hitherto the main focus. As we have seen, existing studies of dialogue-as-interaction (Leech and Short 1981; Toolan 1985, 1987) tend to focus on set-piece scenes and conversational routines or rituals, but the very idea that we can isolate and fix on a "conversation" as some kind of event becomes much more problematic in hypertext fiction as the context and even the content of what is said is much more mutable.

Nevertheless, when we approach dialogue in hypertext fictions it is instructive to acknowledge the long history of experimentation with the technique in the print novel, raising important issues concerning the forms and functions of narrative and their ideological implications. Michael Joyce frequently acknowledges, both in his nonfictional writing and in the intertextual references within his novels, his debt to writers such as James Joyce ("the Greater Joyce"), Samuel Beckett, and Gertrude Stein. I will argue that some of the techniques employed in hypertext fiction are recognizable from print novels, but this is not to say, as critics of hypertext fictions tend to do, that there is nothing new here. Rather, it is to assert that the representation of speech, too often dismissed or ignored as merely providing color and variety in a text, is crucial to our understanding and experience of that text, whether it be in print or hypertext form, and that experimentation with the device may provoke far-reaching questions about the forms and functions of narrative fiction.

What hypertext fiction can do that the print novel cannot is to unmoor scraps and fragments of dialogue from any notion of a fixed context or a set sequence, creating the effect for the reader of being "stuck in a loop" where the "same" utterances recur but mean something quite different at each recurrence because of where and when they are encountered. This experience can prove frustrating if we approach the dialogue with the expectation that it will miraculously illuminate some absolute truths about the characters or the situations in which they find themselves. But if we give ourselves up to the experience of revisiting and revising what we think we know and what we think we hear and see, then we can appreciate the unique pleasures that this endless "loop" can offer as we weigh up different possibilities and interpretations without seeking to reduce or resolve them. As Yellowlees Douglas puts it, hypertext "propels us from the straitened 'either/or' world that print has come to represent and into a universe where the 'and/and/and' is always possible" (1998, 155).

In order to try to understand how we as readers might be open to such pleasures, it is important to consider the cultural and technological climate in which such fictions take their place. New communication technologies such as cell phones and the Internet mean that we have become habituated to the notions of talking to disembodied voices, receiving instantaneous feedback to exchanges taking place across huge distances, and combining holding a conversation with other activities. We also tend to become inured to the potential downsides and limitations of these advances—for example, not really knowing to whom we are talking, being expected to participate in constant chatter, or having conversations disrupted by technological failures. In such an environment, being "stuck in a loop" becomes infinitely preferable to being "out of the loop"; maintaining contact becomes an end in itself, and the speed and sheer quantity of exchanges become a kind of badge of honor in themselves. The kinds of interactions that hypertext fictions present may therefore be reflective of wider changes in communicative practices while also posing a radical challenge to the prevailing idea of dialogue we have from the print novel.

I Have Said Nothing and afternoon, a story

The hypertext fictions I have chosen for analysis feature scenes of character interaction crucial to the central action, and these scenes raise important questions to do with the importance of sequencing and context for fictional dialogue. Both are products of the Eastgate stable of writers, and both use the Storyspace "writing environment" with some slight variations. Both also feature plot lines identified by Moulthrop (1995) as central to many hypertext fictions—namely, automobile accidents and their aftermath—highlighting for Moulthrop not only the centrality of the trope of the "accident" in the reading of these fictions but also the ways in which they foreground the concept of "breakdown." Joyce's *afternoon, a story* concerns itself with the narrator, Peter's, quest to discover what has happened to his ex-wife and son, whom he believes may have been in an accident. In Yellowlees Douglas's *I Have Said Nothing* the narrator tries to make sense of events surrounding the deaths of two of her brother's girlfriends in automobile accidents. In both fictions, the reader is left in some uncertainty about the causes of the accidents and the time lines and causal sequences in which events occur.

Like many other hypertext fictions (e.g., Shelley Jackson's *Patchwork Girl* [1995]), the narratives are told mainly in the first person. Particularly in the case of Yellowlees Douglas's story, the narrative retains a speech-like quality, with the narrator directly addressing the reader and employing an informal, often colloquial register. Most of *I Have Said Nothing* is narrated from the same perspective, though embedded within this are other narratives, such as the girlfriends' experiences of their accidents. In *afternoon, a story* we have Peter's version of events, but depending on which pathway the reader follows we may also encounter the points of view of other characters involved in events, including Lolly, Peter's employer's wife and therapist; Nausicaa, the co-worker with whom Peter and possibly his employer are having an affair; and Lisa, Peter's ex-wife. Such a technique opens up the possibility that events and conversations may be remembered differently depending on whose perspective we have, but as I will argue, we may equally be presented with different versions from within the same narrative perspective. In both of these fictions, therefore, the narrative frames within which the scenes of dialogue are located offer the reader no guarantee of certainty or even reliability—or any possibility of an escape from the "loop"—but demand an active involvement.

Conventions and Forms of Talk in Hypertext Fiction

Before embarking on the analysis, I was interested to discover whether the representation of speech would in any way be influenced by conventions of online talk. *afternoon, a story* bore some traces of online talk, most obviously in the use of angle brackets rather than quotation marks, a device familiar from online chat rooms. This technique may be a conscious allusion by Michael Joyce to "the Greater Joyce," who, as has previously been mentioned, described quotation marks as an "eyesore" and preferred less-obtrusive dashes as markers of speech. However, the technique in *afternoon, a story* is not entirely consistent: for no discernible reason, when Peter attempts to communicate via Datacom with the emergency services, quotation marks are used for the exchanges. In *I Have Said Nothing* the more conventional quotation marks are used, but speech is occasionally left unmarked, again for no discernible reason. It is interesting to speculate, therefore, whether this technique marks a rejection of the formalizing of conventions for the representation of speech that took place with the rise of the realist novel noted by Mepham (1997), and a return to the freer practices of the early novel, as noted by Page (1988), Fludernik (1996), and others.

For the most part, however, the conventions for representation developed in the print novel are adhered to quite closely. The layout of utterances is much as in the print novel, and hesitations, overlaps, and interruptions are minimal in both texts, although marks of omission are sometimes used to indicate an utterance tailing off or being left unfinished. An interesting exception occurs at the beginning of *afternoon, a story* with an interjection from Peter's unnamed interlocutor <as if it were yesterday?> [begin],[2] conveying the impression that Peter's attempt to tell the story is faltering and in need of constant prompting or reinforcement.

Both fictions display some degree of heteroglossia (Bakhtin 1981) in that they represent a variety of different speech styles and accents. In the print novel such representations serve an important function in bringing characters to life, especially those whose role in the narrative may be fairly minimal. In *I Have Said Nothing*, the speech of one of the emergency service personnel who attends to one of the fatalities is marked by italics and deviant spelling ("Shit, she's *daid*"), and the speech of the narrator and many of the characters in this fiction may be described as a kind of youth slang. In *afternoon, a story*, reference is made to Lolly's southern accent, to the British accent of Peter's son's assistant headmaster, and to the Irish accent of Desmond, the current partner of Peter's ex-wife. However, these representations are less about trying to offer the reader a faithful rendering of how the characters speak than they are about conveying the randomness of their connections with one another and their sense of displacement. Moreover, they tell us less about where these characters come from than about the attitudes of others toward them. For example, Peter's resentment toward Desmond and his suspicion that Desmond is deliberately cultivating his Irish persona is hinted at when he describes Desmond as speaking "like a hornpipe Irishman" [Desmond].[3] In this respect, the narrator offers the reader little real help in terms of firmly locating the action (although some place names are referred to) or the social world inhabited by the characters. Similarly, no specific reference is made to the time in which the action takes place, but references to new technologies (Datacom in *afternoon, a story*), films, writers, and so forth may offer some clues as to the general time frame.

In terms of the forms of talk or speech genres represented, most of the dialogue consists of dyadic exchanges, mainly face-to-face (e.g., Wert and Peter's verbal dueling [McDowell 1985] in *afternoon, a story*), with some interesting technologically mediated versions of this—the critically ill father of Luke's dead girlfriend having to write down his contributions to a conversation in *I Have Said Nothing* [Yet he knows], or Peter using a Datacom service in *afternoon, a story* [no, I say]. In both these instances, the effect seems to be one of exacerbating the difficulties the characters experience in trying to communicate with one another.

Many of the conversations in these fictions offer the reader some sense of recognizable conversational routines (Coulmas 1981) or scripts (Schank and Abelson 1977). Telephone conversations perform key expository functions in both fictions, notably, conversations between the narrator and her brother in *I Have Said Nothing* and between Peter and his son's assistant headmaster in *afternoon, a story*. These conversations contribute to the impression that characters' relations in both stories are rather distant and faltering, but also that they may need the physical distance afforded by telephone in order to express themselves and come to terms with what has happened. In this sense, at least, it seems that new technologies are not always a hindrance to communication. In both fictions it is as though the characters find talking to one another often difficult but somehow therapeutic, as though it is only by talking things through that they are able to come to terms with the traumatic events in which they are caught up. This aspect of their talk becomes most obvious in *afternoon, a story*, where, as Yellowlees Douglas has identified (1994), Peter's therapy session with Lolly is crucial in providing a sense of closure to the narrative. However, there is also a very real sense in which the scripts that the characters have available to them may be found inadequate when it comes to trying to understand the traumatic events in which they are caught up.

Speech tags in both fictions are fairly minimalistic, most commonly present tense ("she says," "he says"). As a result, the process of representation appears much more tentative, as though the narrator is not so much recording what has been said as replaying and even reworking utterances. Only occasionally do speech tags go beyond this to perform the function of stage directions (Page 1988), adding descriptive or paralinguistic commentary. In some instances we also get the narrator's commentary on and evaluation of exchanges. In *afternoon, a story*, Peter's varying accounts of his conversation with Wert feature framing comments that reveal his feelings toward his employer, as in the lexia [a bet] where he refers to Wert laughing "preposterously."

Dialogue and Context

While neither of these fictions is radically experimental in terms of the formal devices used for the representation of speech, both invite us to rethink the kinds of assumptions we can make about the characters based on what they say, because of the specific ways in which the speech is framed. Moreover, both seem to deliberately eschew some of the techniques available for contextualizing their characters' utterances. Speech tags are occasionally omitted altogether, forcing the reader to try to work out who is saying what from idiosyncratic speech patterns or tics or from contextual cues. This experience of being immersed in a conversation that is already under way and of trying to match up utterances that appear fragmentary or disconnected is familiar to us from the print novel, but it is also recognizable to anyone who has entered an online chat room. In hypertext fiction, the disorientation is compounded by the fact that we cannot read backward (or even forward) in the text to try and help us locate the utterances, as what comes before and after very much depends on the path that the reading takes. In *afternoon, a story* we are presented with the following unmediated exchanges from the lexia [bimmie]:

> <I'm afraid I still don't know.>
> <It's . . . >
> <Don't encourage her, really! She drives one and doesn't know! That's Lolly all over, the dirt-poor, Suthrin' gal, jes an ole redneck, ain't never had no shoes, ate hush puppies and channel cat. Her father had a limousine! And Faulkner rode in it!>

<It's a BMW. A trendy term for it.>

<It's no coincidence—she says—the chronicles of the Yuppie. It's all a cry for Momma and the Binkie . . . The conceit in naming the rational one Spock was never lost on this generation. We grow old without ancestors and we are unwilling to become them.>

To make any sense of such exchanges, we must rely on pronouns and terms of reference in order, as Catherine Emmott (1997) puts it, to "reactivate" a previously encountered fictional context. From the proprietorial way in which Lolly is referred to here, we can infer that one of the speakers is her husband, Wert, and that he is talking about her, in the third person, in her presence, to a third party, presumably Peter. Reference is made elsewhere in *afternoon, a story* to an incident linking Lolly's family to the novelist William Faulkner [Faulkner], but here Wert recycles the story for the sole purpose of humiliating his wife. Not only does he make fun of her southern accent, but he also ignores her contributions and cuts across Peter's attempt to help Lolly out. Although initially disorientating, therefore, the lexia may offer us important insights into key relationships in the novel, namely, the relationship between Peter and his employer and between Wert and Lolly. Peter's effort to intervene on Lolly's behalf also hints at a possible relationship between them. The fact that the reader has to work out these possible interrelations and consider not only the characters' individual contributions but how they respond to and interact with others again invites a more active involvement.

However, all this deductive work is complicated by the fact that what precedes and follows the dialogue may change depending on the reading, meaning that the context within which we interpret these utterances may be very different. In Emmott's (1997) terms, it is difficult to know exactly which context we should "reactivate." For example, in one reading of the novel, Peter and Wert are having affairs with the same woman, Nausicaa, while in another Wert is having an affair with Peter's wife, so Wert's arrogance and belittling of his wife might be as much directed at Peter as at Lolly and may indeed betray his underlying insecurity. Similarly, the very notion of Peter engaging in banter about a car takes on a darker significance in the light of his quest to discover the truth about an automobile accident he may have witnessed, and the lexia [bimmie] may be encountered at different stages of, and even different versions of, this quest, depending on the pathways the reader chooses. To borrow a metaphor from computing, it seems as though context is something that is constantly being "refreshed" rather than reactivated in the course of reading these fictions, not in the sense of wiping out or overriding previous versions but of allowing us to explore ever different sets of dynamics and their possible outcomes.

In both fictions, conversations are often represented within a given lexia, meaning that whenever we access that lexia the conversation will follow the same trajectory. However, one of the key distinguishing claims of hypertext fiction is that "our choices change the nature of what we read" (M. Joyce 1995, 581), and thus it is perfectly possible for readers to opt out of such a reading by clicking on a yield word that takes them into a different lexia. As has already been said, it is also the case that what precedes and follows a given lexia is determined by the particular pathway the reader has taken, so although in the default readings the trajectory will remain constant, if the reader chooses to explore the many possible links it will change from reading to reading.

This facility to play around with our sense of sequence and context constitutes hypertext fiction's most striking disruption of the idea of dialogue prevailing in the print novel. In some instances, conversations unfold over a series of lexias rather than within a single lexia. Consequently, if readers opt out of the default reading, they may not immediately discover a character's response to a particular utterance, or they may encounter several alternative responses. Thus we have a heightened sense of what Bakhtin (1986) calls the "addressivity" of the utterances, because while they anticipate some kind of answering voice, that anticipation may be prolonged and even ultimately frustrated. For example, in *I Have Said Nothing* the lexia [What?], in which the narrator's brother, Luke, revisits the events surrounding the death of his girlfriend, Jules, ends with the line "What he said is this:" leading the reader to anticipate that in the next lexia we are going to get some kind of report of what Luke actually said. However, in the same lexia we are told that Luke "can't seem to get the narrative order of events quite right," preparing us for the possibility that this report may be far from straightforward.

There are five possible links from this lexia, only one of which purports to directly represent what Luke says. [Drew] consists of direct speech in which the narrator's brother refers to a scene from the film *Deliverance* and breaks down as he reminisces about his intimate relations with Sherry in the morgue. This insight into Luke's world reinforces our impression of him as a morally ambiguous character. Clicking on a different link leads to an indirect report of the brother's memories of the events surrounding the death of his girlfriend, Sherry [She hadn't], in which Sherry's culpability for the accident that kills her is hinted at. Taking these pathways suggests that the deaths of his girlfriends are inextricably linked in Luke's mind and that maybe he revisits Sherry's death as a way of trying to come to terms with or, alternatively, avoiding having to deal with what happens to Jules. Another possible next lexia [She always] begins with a reflection on the quality of Jules's voice, though it is left ambiguous as to whether this is from the point of view of the narrator or her brother. Once again, unproblematic sympathy for the characters is forestalled by an admission that "There's no reason for you to believe this particular version more than any other." A fourth possible link leads to a lexia comprising a blank space followed by the narrator's reflections on the difficulties of recording these events [Get it down], while another link leads to a quotation from Heraclitus reflecting on the concept of order [random sweepings], in this case offering the reader nothing, it seems, of what the brother may or may not have gone on to say. The latter three lexias all therefore focus on the difficulties of placing these events—and, crucially, what may or may not have been said—in some kind of narrative structure, a difficulty faced by the narrator as much as by her brother. Once we become aware of these alternatives, it is not simply a matter of choosing one over the other but of trying to juggle the different possibilities, and to revisit what we thought we knew about the characters and the events in which they were involved.

Hypertext Dialogue and the "Talking Cure"

This may leave us feeling "stuck in a loop" in the sense that there appears to be no way of resolving these alternatives. But as was suggested earlier, the work that we are required to do as readers may also be richly rewarding, as the characters and the circumstances in which they find themselves emerge as being far more complex than they at first appear. For example, the narrator's telephone conversations with her brother in *I Have Said Nothing* prompt the gradual disclosure of his feelings of guilt and responsibility about the deaths of his girlfriends, challenging the impression we get of him elsewhere as shallow and insensitive. What this seems to suggest is a privileging of dialogue, understood as a kind of "talking through" of perplexing or traumatic events, whereby the process of engaging in dialogue is as important as any truths or revelations it may unearth. Particularly significant in this respect is the prevalence of therapeutic discourse in *afternoon, a story*. As was said earlier, in Yellowlees Douglas's reading of Joyce's *afternoon, a story* (1994) the conversation that takes place between Peter and Lolly, following the pattern of a therapy session, is said to be crucial in allowing the reader to arrive at some sense of closure, as Peter is made to confront and finally acknowledge his involvement in the accident in which his ex-wife and son are killed. But as Yellowlees Douglas allows, this conversation is only ever accessed in some readings of the novel, and what she never adequately addresses is why she assumes this reading is "fuller" or more satisfying than any other.

As we saw in chapter 2, many media theorists (Shattuc 1997) and linguists (Cameron 2000) have identified this notion of the "talking cure" as holding particular sway in contemporary Western culture and have begun to question its hegemonic hold. It does seem as though some scenes of dialogue in these fictions tantalizingly offer the possibility of grasping the "truth" of what has been happening to the characters or insights into their true natures, wrested from them as they question and interact with one another. It might be argued, furthermore, given the evangelizing about interactivity that often accompanies discussions of hypertext forms, that this in turn offers a kind of validation and reinforcement for the experience of interacting with the text in which the reader seems to be engaged.

Reflexivity and Anxiety in Hypertext Dialogue

However, in both *afternoon, a story* and *I Have Said Nothing*, the narrators display considerable anxiety about the act of "saying" anything, and both fictions are full of metadiscoursal comments that bring into question both the ability of the characters to work through the issues facing them and our impulse to take their disclosures at face value. *afternoon, a story* begins (in some readings) with Peter telling us "I want to say I may have seen my son die this morning" [I want to say]. The intriguing choice of lexis here conveys Peter's lack of certainty about what "may" have happened. But perhaps more interestingly, in expressing his "want" to "say" this, to share his story with others, the suggestion is that although this is going to be a painful effort for Peter, he anticipates that it will somehow do him some "good." Similarly, in *I Have Said Nothing* the narrator's reflections on her brother's inability to articulate himself [eight years later], are bound up with her increasing unease and distaste for his involvement in his girlfriends' deaths, as though somehow his holding back is a sign of moral culpability.

Yet if the need to speak out is portrayed as compelling, and ultimately cathartic, the speakers in these fictions seem equally to fear the unpredictable consequences of trying to say what they mean. The title of *I Have Said Nothing* is taken from a quotation from St. Augustine, suggesting that whereas *afternoon, a story* models itself on therapeutic discourse, Yellowlees Douglas's fiction draws on the tradition of the confessional: "I have done nothing but wish to speak: if I have spoken, I have not said what I wished to say."

Thus while the "wish" to speak may be perceived as somehow good for one's soul, here it is something that the speaker has to apologize for or excuse ("I have done nothing"), and is accompanied by the realization that far from providing relief, it may be deeply frustrating and unsatisfying. Anxiety about *how* to speak is foregrounded in both these fictions, and seems to reflect, in part at least, not just the pain of not being able to express oneself, but the fear of being misunderstood. In this sense, then, the anxiety is not simply inwardly directed, but is a response to the characters' continued efforts to try and engage with others and feel that they belong to, or participate in, some recognizable shared social context. The reader's experience of trying to situate the characters' utterances therefore echoes the characters' own ongoing search for a context in which their attempts at communication will become meaningful. For example, in his conversation with the assistant headmaster at his son's school in *afternoon, a story*, Peter muses on the "delicacies of parent-school interactions with the non-custodial parent," while in his session with Lolly she asks him <Is this how you think you should speak . . . with a therapist?> [obligations], and in the lexia [we read] he ponders <How do I speak authentically?>. Particularly for Peter, it seems, the "coercion to speak" (Fogel 1985) and to conform to what others expect and demand of him may be oppressive. Nevertheless, it may be the case that speaking "authentically" is not something we always have a prepared script for, but rather something that requires flexibility and even creativity, as the following exchange between Peter and Wert from the lexia [Do people] suggests:

<Do people really talk that way?>
<I don't know> Wert says. <You are the poet.>

In *I Have Said Nothing*, this anxiety about expressing oneself is more explicitly extended to the composition and writing of the story, as the reader constantly comes up against the lexia telling us "That was all she wrote"[4] and is made privy to the narrator's feelings of unease about recording this material and turning it into fiction.

Shifting Contexts and the Problem of "Sequence" in a Scene from *afternoon, a story*

The structure and sequencing of conversations in these fictions compound this sense of the difficulty of "saying" anything. Fragments of conversations resurface across lexias and utterances are repeated in different contexts, so whenever we think we may have grasped what the characters are trying to say to one another, we have to think again. The more we read these fictions, the more we become aware that exchanges between characters can take different paths and produce very different sets of character relations and bifurcations of the plot. Yellowlees Douglas's readings of the exchanges that take place between Peter and his employer, Wert (1994), expose perhaps most clearly the ways in which, far from offering us elucidation or a sense of resolution, scenes of dialogue may leave us stuck in a seemingly endless loop.

Different versions of exactly what Wert and Peter say to one another and how and when they say it have far-reaching implications for our understanding of both the relationships between the central characters and what may or may not have happened to the narrator's ex-wife and child. What remains true of all these different readings is that Wert is Peter's employer and that their personal lives are entangled in some way. Beyond such fragments, what the characters know about each other and about those who are close to them is uncertain, as is the question of how this conversation relates to the accident involving Peter's ex-wife and child.

As Yellowlees Douglas discovered, the structure of *afternoon, a story* means that readers only encounter certain lexias in a particular sequence, and she estimates that the lexia [asks], featuring the lunchtime conversation, crops up in four specific contexts, determined by the choices the reader makes. The content of the lexia, she claims, is identical each time it is encountered:

> He asks slowly, savoring the question, dragging it out devilishly, meeting my eyes.
> <How . . . would you feel if I slept with your ex-wife?>
> It is foolish. She detests young men.

In one narrative strand, the lexia is placed within a version of the conversation in which Wert appears incredibly immature and is in playful mood, teasing Peter. In another possible narrative strand, Wert asks his question to distract Peter from his anxiety about the accident. In a third strand, the lexia occurs in the context of Peter's affair with a co-worker, Nausicaa, and Peter interprets Wert's question as a display of jealousy. Yellowlees Douglas also found that the conversation reappears after a narrative strand representing Nausicaa's point of view, in which we discover that she is sleeping with both Peter and Wert, so that Wert's question is not all it appears on the surface and may be as much about his relationship with Nausicaa as it is about his possible involvement with Lisa, Peter's ex-wife.

Finally, Yellowlees Douglas found that readers might come across this lexia after they discover that Wert and Lisa have been spotted together by Peter, though he isn't certain that they are having an affair. Read in this context, Yellowlees Douglas argues, Wert's question becomes a "real" one, that is, what speech act theorists call the felicity conditions (Levinson 1983) which would make it a "real" question are in place, and it alters our perception of the accident Peter thinks he has witnessed: in one version of these events, Peter sees Lisa and Andy riding in Wert's truck and loses control, so it becomes much more plausible that he was not only involved in causing the accident but that he *meant* to cause it.

Depending on how we arrive at this conversation, Wert can appear brash and obnoxious or insecure and even threatened by Peter. Similarly, Peter can appear fretful and ill at ease, evasive, or even manipulative. Not only does it become difficult to arrive at an understanding or evaluation of the characters based on what they say, or to decide who is in control of the exchange and who gains from it, but it also becomes difficult to hold onto any sense that we can trust or believe anything that we are told the characters may or may not have said. All we have are different possible versions of what may have taken place and what may be true of the relationships between the characters, and once we are made aware of the possibility of seeing (and hearing) things differently whenever and however we revisit the lexia, it is always going to be charged with these alternatives, none of which can be totally discounted or set aside. Different interpretations of this lunchtime conversation, therefore, are not just about unearthing its nuances or analyzing the subtle power plays between the characters, but necessitate our asking, How did we arrive at this scene, and where might it take us?

Yellowlees Douglas does not focus specifically in her discussion on the implications of Wert's reiteration of his question in a later lexia [He, he says] or Peter's response to Wert's question <As if I were your father> [as if], access to which once again depends on the path we take. Within the lexia [asks] we are told what Peter is thinking, but the fact that his verbalized response is recorded in a separate lexia, and that we don't in turn see Wert's response to this, means that the conversation that takes place between them is fragmented. More significantly, perhaps, Yellowlees Douglas's account of this scene does not mention the lexia [Werther 4], in which Werther's question and Peter's response are both represented. This conversation takes place in a completely different setting: the reception area where the two men work as opposed to the diner where the lexia [asks] takes place. This change in setting has potentially significant consequences for our interpretation of what is said and for our sense of what kind of conversational script we may be following. Given that Werther is Peter's employer, the fact that they are no longer on "neutral" territory and that their conversation takes place in the presence of a colleague, Mrs. Porter, instead of the waitress in the diner, makes Wert's question appear even more loaded.

Yellowlees Douglas's analysis locates the exchanges within narrative strands, though it is never made clear exactly what is meant by this or how they may be revisited. She does not seem to allow for other ways of navigating the text, whereby the reader clicks on yield words or browses links and follows them. In a sense, of course, to do so is to open up endless new possibilities, making the possibility of an exhaustive or definitive account of the scene even more remote. At some point that same lunchtime, Wert muses about the possible effects of his allergy to walnut pollen [yesterday]. This utterance also appears in the lexia [yesterday 2], and once again the relationship between the utterance and the rest of the lunchtime conversation is complex: in some readings the comment about walnut pollen precedes Wert's question about Peter's ex-wife, while in others it follows it. In the former instance it could be interpreted almost as a phatic token (Laver 1975), preparing the ground for Wert's attempt to unsettle Peter, while if the comment comes after Wert's question it could be interpreted as an attempt to change the topic and perhaps to recompense for his rather embarrassing directness.

Wert's comment about the walnut pollen seems to come out of nowhere, and this is a characteristic feature of the representation of speech in both *afternoon, a story* and *I Have Said Nothing*. Characters' utterances often appear deliberately ambiguous or opaque, sometimes appearing to be directed at no one in particular and left hanging in midair with no sign of any response. Both fictions, but especially *afternoon, a story*, have a dream-like, surreal quality: the events that take place and the characters we encounter often appear quite bizarre.

Furthermore, scenes of dialogue often seem to produce startlingly frank exchanges between the characters, with antagonisms and tensions surfacing with little warning or preparation: in *I Have Said Nothing*, Luke suddenly and rather shockingly turns his anger on his sister, telling her, "I wish to Christ it'd been you. Why the fuck wasn't it you instead?" [You sit, you think]. Indeed, in this respect it seems that dialogue almost plays the function of a shock tactic, reminding the reader that nothing can be taken for granted.

Conclusion: What Can We Learn from Hypertext Dialogue?

The disruption of a sense of sequence to exchanges in the scene from *afternoon, a story* makes it difficult to argue with any certainty what the characters' strategies are or to decipher how far a character is responding to something that has been said or, instead, is initiating an exchange or topic shift. Therefore it is difficult to rely completely on existing models for analyzing fictional dialogue, or even to talk of these encounters as conversations, where it seems we cannot identify with any certainty the ways in which the talk is being organized and managed. In turn, it seems we must recognize that, as Cuddy-Keane (1996, 156) has claimed, "In the poetics of conversation . . . the very first principle is that the discussion is 'always to be continued.'" Such a realization has far-reaching implications for how we approach the analysis of fictional dialogue, as it becomes much more difficult to locate and refer to exchanges as something constant or fixed if it is possible to replay and revisit those exchanges differently. Indeed, by freeing up fictional dialogue from being tied to a particular context and having utterances and fragments of utterances resurfacing in unexpected, unpredictable ways, hypertext fiction seems to offer new and exciting possibilities for the dialogizing of the novel, in Bakhtin's (1981) terms.

As is true with so many aspects of hypertext fiction, it is not so much *what* we encounter that seems new or different as *how* we get there, and how every seeming point of arrival marks another possible departure. Thus even where exchanges between characters remain stable and constant across successive readings of the hypertext fiction, our interpretation of such scenes is constantly subject to disruption and to seeming inconsistencies. From the print novel we may be familiar with the notion that conversations may be misremembered, or remembered differently according to circumstances, and are also familiar with being presented with fragments of a conversation that may leave its meaning and its outcome vague or ambiguous. Reading a hypertext fiction, the reader has to choose which version of the conversation to follow, and these choices shape our perceptions of what may have taken place and to whom it occurred.

As we have seen, dialogue in hypertext fiction follows many of the conventions we are familiar with from the print novel; it continues to exploit the illusion that when we are given direct access to the utterances of characters, we get an authentic insight into their world. In addition, the hypertext fictions analyzed here appear to perpetuate an idea or ideal of dialogue as a way to work through issues or problems and even as a way of uncovering difficult "truths" that might otherwise remain hidden. However, the characters' desire to do so is perhaps more symptomatic of what sociologists call "narrative wreckage" (Frank 1995), since their efforts to make sense of who they are and what has happened to them are continuously breaking down or colliding with inconsistencies that smash apart any attempt at order and closure. This means that their narratives, and their efforts to recover and work through what was done and what was said, are also stuck in a perpetual loop.

For the reader, what makes the possibility of ever getting out of this loop so remote is that the ground beneath is constantly shifting. If, as Yellowlees Douglas (1998, 158) has claimed, "hypertext can show us that context is everything," then it also seems to show us that context is mutable and ever-shifting. Print novelists have experimented with the technique of immersing the reader in a scene of dialogue with little or no contextual framing, and as readers we may revisit a scene or a particular utterance and interpret it differently on rereading. In hypertext fiction, however, the point is that the context may be different depending on our reading, so it is not possible to arrive at a reading where all of these different versions may be reconciled or in which any one version is privileged over possible others.

This analysis of two hypertext fictions has shown that new technologies do not necessarily entail wholly new forms or techniques for the representation of speech. Indeed, in some ways the representations offer a reinforcing, reassuring view of dialogue as a way of talking through difficult experiences and uncovering hidden depths and truths. However, we have seen that hypertext fictions do disrupt our notion of dialogue as something that is fixed and stable, and that instead exchanges between characters may resurface and be replayed, unsettling any attempt to petrify those exchanges or the power relations they enact. Jay Bolter (2001, 136) has argued that "hypertext fiction often seems to attempt to take back what has been said and replace it with something better." In this sense, hypertext fiction is perhaps able to convey the sense that conversations are not simply events or contests that, once complete, are pushed aside and forgotten. Instead, we are left with differing versions of how the conversation may have been played out, offering the possibility of endlessly revisiting the exchanges and the relations between characters. Thus just as hypertext fictions challenge our notion that a story exists independently of its telling, so too we may need to revise and reappraise our concept of dialogue as a sequence of exchanges ordered and managed so as to produce some kind of closure for the characters and for the reader. And just as we come to accept that stories do not always have to lead anywhere, so we may need to approach fictional dialogue not only with a view to expecting answers to questions or the unearthing of hidden truths, freeing us up to enjoy and immerse ourselves in the subtle intricacies and nuances that emerge when we take pleasure in being stuck in a loop.

Conclusion

One of my prime motivations for writing this book was to provoke a discussion of fictional dialogue that goes beyond describing the extent to which it is or is not realistic or that simply views the dialogue as a transparent portal into the minds of the characters and the worlds they inhabit. I hope I have demonstrated that there is much more to be said about fictional dialogue, more than I have been able to do justice to in this study.

As I have shown, rather than just provide descriptions of speech styles, we can begin to analyze the interactions that take place between fictional characters in terms of power dynamics and in terms of situating these exchanges within specific social and historical contexts. We have the tools we need to provide this kind of analysis, thanks to the efforts of linguists and ethnographers of communication, and thanks, too, to the work of stylisticians in demonstrating the applicability of these models to fictional speech situations. However, it is important to go further than merely acknowledging that power is displayed in scenes of conversational interaction or analyzing that display in unidirectional terms, as tends to be the case, for example, with speech act theory. Instead, we need to accept that power, in Foucault's (1978) terms, is not necessarily "held" by any one participant but exists only as it is exercised and put into action, so that the distribution of power is constantly shifting, sometimes within as well as between utterances.

At the same time, this study has shown how theories of dialogue based on the work of Mikhail Bakhtin allow us to understand how heteroglossia and polyphony help define the modern novel, and how the very concept of dialogue carries with it certain ethical and political norms and ideas that require careful scrutiny. In particular, I have been concerned to challenge the notion of dialogue as an ideal or normative idea that circumscribes certain patterns and standards for conversational behavior and which perpetuates the myth that such behavior is always equitable and sensitive to the needs of the other.

Another important strand of my argument has been the need to approach dialogue not just as a series of intentional statements uttered by autonomous individuals but as something that can only be understood in the context of how utterances are taken up and responded to by others. In scenes where characters misunderstand one another, willfully in the novels of Green and Compton-Burnett, focusing on responses and reactions in conversation becomes ever more necessary. But this is also a feature of scenes of intimacy, as I demonstrated in my discussion of Roth's *Deception*, where the intensity of exchanges depends upon recording every small gesture and reaction. Influential in this regard is Goffman's (1981) view of conversational interaction as an ongoing process in which participation extends beyond the static roles of speaker and hearer to include all those who might be touched by and affected by the way in which interactions circulate and reemerge across time and place. My argument is that such a notion of dialogue offers the reader an active role, not just in deciphering the puzzles presented by cryptic or elliptical conversations, or even imagining what goes on in the fictional minds of the characters, but in fully participating in the experience such a form of representation seems uniquely to offer.

The focus on the twentieth and twenty-first centuries was in part the result of practical considerations, but it is also my contention that this period radically opens up the novel to ever more diverse forms of talk, not just in terms of accents and dialects, but also in terms of speech genres and technologically mediated communication. To this end, while the focus throughout has been on literary representations, I have argued that much is to be gained from engaging with developments in popular culture and the emergence of new media and new communication technologies, ranging from the telephone and the radio at the beginning of the twentieth century to the huge impact of computer technologies that continue to present us with new ways of connecting and networking with one another.

Suggestions for Further Research

This study has necessarily been limited both in terms of the range of authors and texts discussed and in terms of the approaches it has been possible to consider. A glaring omission is perhaps the analysis of dialogue in the context of gender, particularly since feminist linguistics has proved this to be such a fascinating and important area of study. Such an approach might take the form of exploring how conversations and the assumptions of participants may be influenced by gender, for example, in scenes between intimate partners, such as those from *Deception* and *Carpenter's Gothic* discussed previously, or scenes taking place within the context of the family, as in Compton-Burnett's *Brothers and Sisters*. It would also be productive to explore whether there are substantive differences to be found in the ways in which all-female or all-male conversations have been represented. For example, novels such as Graham Swift's *Last Orders* (discussed in the appendix), or Irvine Welsh's *Trainspotting* frequently foreground scenes of groups of men (from very different age groups) in interaction with one another, while the genre of "chick lit" might offer similarly fruitful material for analysis in terms of the patterns and preoccupations of all-female talk.

Similarly, while some attempt has been made here to locate the analysis of dialogue within specific historical and cultural contexts, much work remains to be done on how notions of what constitutes "conversation" and "dialogue" may be variable across cultures—and across different epochs of the same culture. Most of my examples have been taken from anglophone literature, and many of these could be said to be representative of an even narrower cultural sphere in terms of class, race, and gender. I recognize, therefore, the need to engage with the work of writers for whom the practices and norms of conversational interaction may be somewhat different, particularly as one of my concerns in this study has been to challenge and critique linguistic and ethnographic universals. In particular, Carole Edelsky's ([1981] 1993) challenge to the "one-at-a-time" norm of conversational interaction (discussed in chapter 2) might be explored in relation to the literatures of the Caribbean, as studies such as Patricia Mohammed's (2002) have demonstrated that overlapping speech and group talk are viewed very differently there than they are in European cultures.

While this study touches on some of the theories and concepts arising out of the field of cognitive narratology, there is clearly much more scope here, too, for developing a theory of dialogue that goes beyond the intentions and verbalized thoughts of characters toward understanding how "external" and "internal" interpenetrate and combine on so many different levels. In particular, an analysis of fictional dialogue that adopts a holistic approach and embraces Palmer's (2004) notion of the "social mind in action" could open up new possibilities and new understandings of both the speech situations and the kinds of interrelationships made possible within them.

I have suggested in my analysis that it can be productive to approach fictional dialogue from the perspective of genre, but again the extent to which I have been able to explore specific generic differences and concerns has been limited. There is scope for much more work in this area, particularly with regard to accounting for the prevalence of dialogue in some genres more than others. Kay Young's (2001) work on romantic comedy has already established the importance of dialogue for this type of narrative, but such an approach could equally be extended to genres such as science fiction, where all sorts of interesting possibilities present themselves in terms of interactions between humans and nonhumans or between characters from different worlds and different epochs.

One of the difficulties of writing this kind of book is that ever more interesting examples present themselves, making it impossible to ever approximate an exhaustive account of the various experiments with dialogue that exist in the novel. The almost overwhelming scope of the project is ever more real because I have attempted to include in my analysis examples shaped by the "information multiplicity" (Johnston 1998) of the latter decades of the twentieth century forward and to explore the implications of newly emerging computer-based writing such as hypertext fiction. As new genres and new modes of storytelling emerge on the World Wide Web, and as online interactions and social networking become dominant modes of communication, the need to constantly reevaluate and reexamine our basic terms and assumptions becomes ever more pressing.

In my analysis I have touched upon issues to do with the rhythm and timing of conversational exchanges, and I have also pointed to the importance of taking into account prosodic and paralinguistic features of the dialogue. While fields such as linguistics and translation studies may offer valuable insights into the latter, discussions of rhythm and timing in conversation tend to be highly impressionistic, and yet the pace and orchestration of exchanges are so intrinsic to the effect achieved that they really are deserving of much more precise and detailed examination. This is especially true of comic fiction, where the notion of comic timing has been woefully neglected, but it might equally be true of genres such as the thriller, where the ramping up of tension is crucial and often exquisitely designed.

Closing Remarks

In my preface I outlined how and why I first became fascinated by fictional dialogue more than twenty years ago. This fascination has not diminished, and I am more certain than ever that this is a field of study where we still have much to learn, both about fictional dialogue as a narrative technique and about what it tells us about our ability to communicate with one another within specific environments and sets of social conditions. In particular, I hope I have demonstrated that the idea of dialogue can embrace a wider spectrum of experiences than has hitherto been the case, to include feelings of exclusion, isolation, and frustration at not being heard. I also hope that we can expand the ways in which we measure participation in dialogue to include overhearers, silent witnesses, and those who manipulate and willfully misunderstand.

Appendix

Last Orders: *An Analysis of a Chapter from Graham Swift's Novel*

Note: where "aint" appears in quotation below, I follow the practice of the novel in omitting the apostrophe.

For reasons of space and practicality, in previous chapters it has not always been possible to offer exhaustive analyses of lengthy extracts taken from the novels under discussion. I have also argued against the "scenic" approach, in which an analysis focuses on a chapter or section of a novel as though it were freestanding and unconnected to the surrounding narrative. However, it is important to offer a demonstration of how the arguments put forward in this book might inform a detailed analysis, as well as how the incorporation of tools and terms from linguistics relates to the theoretical claims I have been making. Thus in what follows I focus on an example of what Goffman (1981, 131) calls a "nicely bounded social encounter" while also recognizing, as he does, the problem of "blithely" labeling such encounters as autonomous.

Graham Swift's *Last Orders* traces the journey of a group of men who come together to carry out the last wishes of a London butcher, Jack Dodds, leading them along a circuitous route from the city to the sea where they finally scatter Jack's ashes. Described as "polyphonic" (Bernard 1997) in its style, the chapters are mainly focalized through the perspectives of the various male characters, though occasionally the voices of the female characters break through. In addition to opening up the text to different perspectives, the foregrounding of the vernacular ensures that the novel is heteroglossic in the Bakhtinian sense (see introduction). For Emma Parker (2003), the novel is predominantly an exploration of male spaces and an incisive exploration of the twin crises of masculinity and Englishness experienced by the central group of men. This sense of crisis or decline is highlighted by the narrative structure of the novel, which intersperses scenes set in the present with those taken from the characters' past. Chapter titles use both character names and the names of the various places the men pass through on their journey, and the style of the novel remains close to the oral, foregrounding the vernacular in a manner very reminiscent of Bakhtin's (1984, 8) notion of skaz: "a technique or mode of narration that imitates the oral speech of an individualized narrator." Moreover, within many of the chapters narrated by these individualized narrators, conversational exchanges and the reporting of others' words are prominent.

Despite Daniel Lea's (2005) claim that *Last Orders* is made up of a "refreshingly artless collocation of voices," I will argue that the chapters devoted to the conversations of the men are both artful and compelling in their presentation of the tensions and constraints underlying the men's mutual relations. Indeed, taking *Last Orders* as his case study for exploring the role of dialogue in fiction, John Mullan (2003) argues that Swift's novel is "charged with things that cannot be said" and sees "clamming up" as one of its defining features. This points to the fact that as the novel unfolds we discover more and more about the characters and the secrets and traumas they have been trying to keep hidden. Thus like Philip Roth's *Deception*, discussed in chapter 2, Swift's novel provides ample evidence that pared-down dialogue can sustain scenes of heightened emotion and can draw in the reader to feel an intense involvement with the lives of the characters. Reflecting many of the issues I took up in chapter 1, Mullan recognizes that Swift's is a highly stylized representation, unrecognizable, he suggests, to any student of actual conversation because of the way in which it maintains a sense of "decorum" throughout, never descending too far into hesitation, nonsense, or obscenity. Mullan also highlights the importance of the reporting clauses (discussed in chapters 1 and 5), noting Swift's preference for the self-consciously "reticent" and arguing that the constant repetition of "he says" helps to establish the novel's rhythm while reinforcing the impression of orality.

Although *Last Orders* is structured around discrete chapters that center on a specific character or place, the effect is often one of dipping in and out of an ongoing conversation. This is underlined by the use of the present-tense reporting clauses and helps to consolidate our sense of the central group of characters as people whose lives have been bound up with each other's for many years. Thus, while the chapters are often scenic, they are not formulaic in the sense that the openings and closings are more fuzzy than finite, and also in the sense that the echoes and continuities between them are crucial to the cumulative effect of the increase in tension and emotion that the novel creates. As with *Deception*, the men's conversations hint at subsequent revelations, and the sense that some of them know more about these events than others adds to the tension and the expectation that their relationships with one another may be about to shift irrevocably.

The chapter "Blackheath" offers a snapshot of the characters on their car journey and makes skillful play of their confinement in an enclosed space. An example of what I have called multi-party talk, the chapter presents the characters away from their usual meeting place, the pub, and although it appears that they are on some kind of mission, the chapter opens with Vic questioning the itinerary and, by implication, the purpose of their journey. The suggestion is that we are arriving in the midst of the characters' talk, albeit at a point where a new topic shift is being initiated, as Vic brings the men back to the reasons for Jack's "last orders" regarding where his ashes should be scattered. This triggers a series of competitive utterances in which Vince, Lenny, and Ray wrangle over who knows Jack and his life's story best, resulting in an uncomfortable silence that is only disrupted when Lenny makes the first of several references to Vince's attempts to elevate himself beyond the man who brought him up ("From a meat van to a Merc, eh?").

"Blackheath" presents the reader with something approaching Genette's (1980) concept of the scene (discussed in chapter 4), where story time is roughly equivalent to discourse time; indeed, it is almost as though the reader is sitting alongside the men, reacting to every nuance and gesture. As was also discussed in chapter 4, Swift focuses as much on characters' reactions as on their actions, such as they are, especially as the reader becomes more attuned to the specific points of tension to which they seem relentlessly to return. The slow pace of the action and the sparseness of the utterances also encourage the reader to ponder what lies beneath the surface of the male banter and to question how far what we are witnessing is an exercise in evasion or even "topic suppression" (Toolan 1985; also discussed in chapter 4). Swift's dialogue, then, is truly dialogic in the Bakhtinian (1981) sense of the word (outlined in the introduction), as each speaker responds to but also anticipates what the other may say, and each utterance remains open to constant reinterpretation and revision.

In earlier chapters in this volume, the analysis focused on moments of crisis or tension in conversations between couples or families (such as those taking place in *Carpenter's Gothic* and *Brothers and Sisters* that I analyzed in chapter 3). The bonds that tie the group of men in Swift's novel are of a different order, and it is more unusual to find this kind of intensity in conversations between friends and acquaintances. Yet the chapter "Blackheath" does invite the reader to share the intersubjective world of the men, and through the dialogue technique we become sensitized to their verbal mannerisms and their habitual way of dealing with one another. In particular, Swift's technique helps create the sense of continuing consciousness in Palmer's (2004) sense (see the introduction and chapter 3), as we are acutely aware that the surface banter barely conceals the men's long-held grievances and antagonisms. At the same time, the power of Swift's writing comes from his ability to hint at the resentment but also the mutual dependence of the men, and it is evocative and sometimes excruciating precisely because they all help to prop up the barriers that make their attempts at communication so problematic. Once again, therefore, Swift's writing demonstrates the richness of the dialogue technique, moving us away from static conceptions of character toward an understanding of how a different "self" may emerge in interaction with others (as discussed in chapter 3), even where those others may think they know all there is to know about each other.

Particularly significant, and frequently commented on in the narrative framing of the dialogue, is the fact that Vince, Jack's adopted son, who is driving the car, uses his driving mirror throughout to keep an eye on his fellow travelers while wearing shades so that they cannot see his eyes or read his emotions. In an earlier chapter ("Old Kent Road") we are told that Vic sits alongside Vince with the other two men, Lenny and

Ray, in the back. This seating arrangement means that Lenny and Ray are able to communicate privately ("Lenny gives me a glance"), despite Vince's attempts to monitor proceedings via his mirror. Earlier chapters also help establish the importance Vince places upon status, particularly his pride in the car he is driving, and show him using his position of control to tease and torment his passengers.

Throughout the novel, Swift shows great sensitivity toward the paralinguistic accompaniments to speech (discussed in chapter 1), as when we are told that "Vic's hands move a little over the box" containing Jack's ashes as though to protect them in the context of an exchange where Lenny and Vince wrangle over whether or not Jack can still see what is going on. Indeed, the accounts of the characters' reactions and responses ("Everyone goes quiet" [29]) punctuate the chapter, acting as a commentary on the characters' exchanges and the gaps and silences they leave.

Swift is also adept at constructing his dialogue so as to create the impression of intimacy as well as routine and habit. Lenny is repeatedly described as a "stirrer" (7, 21), while Vic is cast in the role of "referee" (31), reinforcing the idea that in their relations with one another these men have fallen into a familiar pattern—a pattern that is consolidated by their verbal interactions. This is observable particularly at the level of turn taking, where it appears that the rights and roles of the participants have been preordained. Although Vince might appear to have some degree of control over the other men as the driver of the car, Lenny is the dominant figure in the group exchanges. From the outset, Lenny seems intent on controlling the conversation. When Vince tries to address Vic's question about the purpose of their journey, Lenny self-selects,[1] responding to Vince's statement as though it has the illocutionary force of an accusation ("Think I don't remember?"), when Vince's words were not obviously directed at Lenny at all. As Goodwin and Goodwin (1982) have claimed, this sort of move demonstrates that hearers may transform prior utterances for their own purposes, actively reworking their meaning rather than passively decoding them.

Elsewhere, Lenny relies on more overt means of control; for example, he threatens Vince's positive face wants by belittling him with name-calling ("Big Boy") and bald assertions of his superior knowledge: "I know that, don't I" (29). He also uses sarcasm ("Raysy here's a mine of information"), flouting Grice's ([1963] 1975, 45) maxim of quality ("Be truthful") to convey to the others his suspicion that Ray is withholding information from them. Lenny's utterances in this chapter are characterized by a high incidence of questions, used primarily it seems to tease and probe his companions, and showing no respect for their sensitivities. In fact, in the course of this short scene Lenny commits several face-threatening acts,[2] such as directly challenging Vince's memories of his parents and their relationship ("You were there, were you, Big Boy?") and openly contradicting Vince ("this aint a Sunday outing"). He also attempts to control the conversational floor by seizing on Ray's reference to his closeness to Amy to return to the controversial subject raised in earlier chapters of "why she aint come along an' all?" What we seem to have here, then, is a clear example of Fogel's (1985) notion of the "coercion to speak," discussed previously (especially in chapters 2 and 6), with Lenny refusing to back off and almost relishing his ability to make his companions squirm and feel uncomfortable. For Vince in particular, some of the exchanges with Lenny seem excruciating, as Lenny issues a series of what discourse analysts call "challenging moves" (see chapter 1), combining these with insinuations about Jack and about Vince's relationship with him to open up some painful memories and unresolved tensions, later leading to a fistfight between the two men.

Lenny's stirring and Vic's attempts at appeasement often lead to clashes, where instead of adjacency pairs and recipient design,[3] which conversation analysts see as crucial to the efficient management of talk, we find self-selection and the men's contributions running in parallel with one another, as in the following sequence:

> Vic says, "You shouldn't judge."
> Lenny says, "Ashes is ashes."
> Vic says, "And best to do things prompt."
> Lenny says, "And wishes is wishes."

Despite the layout of this exchange, conveying the impression of the utterances as consecutive turns at talk, the conjunctions suggest almost a single continuous utterance rather than links across different utterances, and the reporting clauses only seem to exaggerate the men's childish competitiveness to finish what it is they each want to say. Moreover, Lenny's repeated use of tautologies flouts Grice's ([1963] 1975, 45) maxim of Quantity ("Make your contribution as informative as is required for the purposes of the talk at hand") and suggests that for him, maintaining control over the conversation is of the utmost importance.

Elsewhere, too, we see that the trajectory of the conversation is not unidirectional, with the characters taking the conversation back to recurring topics ("She's seeing June" from Raysy, or "Why Margate?" from Vic), as though each is caught up in his own world and is not listening to or attending to what the others are saying. As has already been suggested, frequently the impoliteness and lack of regard for one another is more overt, as when Lenny seems to completely ignore Vince's question concerning Jack ("How do we know he'd be none the wiser?"), continuing as though uninterrupted with his own train of thought ("Not that I'm saying . . . "). This kind of inattention is not confined to Lenny, however, as Raysy also disrupts the flow by taking the conversation back to an earlier topic ("It wasn't specific"), leading Lenny to demand what conversational analysts (Sacks, Schegloff, and Jefferson 1978) call a repair ("What weren't specific?"). Here Swift seems to present us with a conversation that is not textbook in any sense, where each of the characters except for Vic seems to use the exchanges to taunt and hurt one another, and where the management of the

talk seems to be more about disruption and thwarting progress than about coopera-
tion in the Gricean (1975) sense.

Throughout the chapter we see a curious interplay between the characters' references to their shared knowledge (as in Lenny's "I know that, don't I") and the fact that
in the organization of the talk in particular, familiar tensions seem to resurface. Vince
contributes least in terms of conversational turns, but his silent observation of the
others and his abrupt interjections "How do we know he'd be none the wiser?" convey
his simmering resentment regarding their ownership of memories about Jack as well
as his desperate and rather poignant determination to keep believing that somehow
Jack remains among them: "So you think he does know? You think he can see us?"

The ending to the chapter is highly effective, requiring some realignment of our
previous attempts at contextual framing (Emmott 1997, discussed in chapter 5). Lenny's apparent tormenting of Vince emerges in a slightly different light as Lenny reacts
to the younger man's desperate attempt to cling to the belief that Jack "does know"
and "can see us." Once again, Swift relies on paralinguistic information to convey the
impression that Lenny is caught off guard (i.e., he "blinks and pauses a moment") as he
looks to Ray for support and to Vic "as if he needs some of that refereeing." Although
Lenny resorts to his tactic of repeating himself ("Manner of speaking, Vincey, manner
of speaking") to buy himself some conversational time, and he returns to what appears
to be provocation, calling Vince "Big Boy" once again and accusing him once more
of showing off ("why'd you go and borrow a Merc?"), here Lenny's behavior seems
defensive and even protective of Vince, in contrast to earlier in the scene, where it
appeared as nothing more than mindless cruelty.

In "Blackheath" Ray's narrative framing is barely noticeable, apart from the occasional witticism ("Blackheath isn't black and it isn't a heath"). However, at the end of
the chapter he indulges in an unexpectedly rich description ("The sun's sparkling on
the grass") that seems to offer the possibility of a more positive conclusion, even if it
is immediately countered by a negative ("Jack can't see it"). Similarly, Vic's "slow and
gentle" attempt to present Vince's actions in a positive light ("It's a fine gesture. It's a
beautiful car") seems to offer the possibility of the scene closing on a more harmonious note. However, Swift chooses to end the scene with Vince rejecting this "gesture," highlighting his semi-detached position in relation to the rest of the group,
as he responds with a negative ("It aint a meat van") which simultaneously acts as
a rebuff to Lenny's insults and Vic's refereeing while also suggesting that his resentment toward Jack remains.

As was said earlier, many of the tensions hinted at in the chapter are returned to
later in the novel, as we find out more about the nature of Jack's daughter June's problems, the reasons why Vince feels resentment, and the nature of Ray's relationship
with Amy. Although Ray's contributions are few, his quiet assertiveness ("It wasn't
specific"; "Amy showed me") suggests that despite the protestations of the others, he

is the character who is closest to understanding the motives for Jack's actions as well as the secrets and sadnesses that continue to haunt Jack's family.

Swift's chapter, exposing as it does the conflicts and tensions underlying the surface talk of this group of men, does so not with any dramatic departure from convention or any overt stylistic experimentation, but through a finely tuned understanding of how minute modulations within the management of talk can produce conversations that set one's teeth on edge in terms of their sharpness, cruelty, and pain. This is not something that is confined exclusively to this chapter, and many of its effects rely on the reader's ability to react to the subtly shifting contextual frames of the narrative as we not only relate what the characters say to what we already know but also reframe what we have heard and seen as the subsequent chapters unfold. Swift presents us with a version of talk that in many respects challenges the prevailing idea of dialogue discussed earlier. Here, the exchanges between the men not only disrupt notions of parity and harmony but also resist closure and resolution, requiring the reader to revisit and reinterpret rather than assume that the words represented on the page offer us some kind of transparent window into the men's minds or their mutual relations. Furthermore, the chapter offers us a view of the men's talk not as a working through of problems or a therapeutic exercise but as an ongoing struggle for power, control, and a sense of self-worth.

Notes

3. Speech, Character, and Intention

1. "If a writer of prose knows enough about what he is writing about he may omit things that he knows and the reader, if the writer is writing truly enough, will have a feeling of those things as strongly as though the writer had stated them. The dignity of movement of an iceberg is due to only one eighth of it being above water."

4. Dialogue in Action

1. For a fuller analysis of this scene from *Black Mischief* see Thomas (2002).
2. Most notorious was E. M. Forster's expression of impatience that "Yes—oh dear yes—the novel tells a story . . . and I wish that it was not so" ([1927] 1963, 34).
3. Brown and Levinson (1978, 66) define "face" as "the public self image that every member wants to claim for himself." They subdivide this further into positive and negative face wants. "Positive face wants" refer to the desire to be appreciated and approved of by others. "Negative face wants" refer to the desire to be unimpeded by others.

5. Framing

1. George Vallins (1960, 91) uses the metaphor of the stage, claiming that the narrator must know when to step aside, "realising that his interference would only distract the reader, much as an actor's over-attention to stage 'business' is apt to distract the attention of the audience." Meanwhile, Frederick Stopp (1958) refers to the narrator in the novels of Evelyn Waugh as a kind of compère.

6. Dialogue and Genre

1. This was also, of course, a major theme of Francis Ford Coppola's film *The Conversation* (1974).
2. The film version of *The Friends of Eddie Coyle* appeared in 1973, and the film version of *Get Shorty* appeared in 1995.
3. Victor Yngve (1970) coined the term "back-channel communication" to refer to an indication, either verbal or nonverbal, that the listener is paying attention.
4. This technique is later taken up by Quentin Tarantino in the famous scene from

Pulp Fiction (1994) where Jules and Vincent, gangsters played by John Travolta and Samuel L. Jackson, discuss cultural variations on well-known fast-food burgers.

7. The Alibi of Interaction

1. There is, of course, a long tradition of responding to (and anticipating) new technologies in science fiction. For example, Ray Bradbury's *Fahrenheit 451* (1953) depicts a society in which television provides a literal "fourth wall" for its viewers and where television appears to directly engage with viewers, for whom it substitutes for real-life social networks.

2. This response was not always a positive one. Writing of the emergence of the "talkies," Waugh claimed that they would "set back by twenty years the one vital art of the century" ([1929] 1946, 13).

3. The term "a babel of voices" was introduced in previous chapters in relation to a technique devised by the novelist Ronald Firbank. The technique is reminiscent of film's treatment of background dialogue and the "polylogue," where, as Kozloff (2000, 72) puts it, "the individual lines are less important than the group flavor."

4. Waugh makes this claim in the preface to *Vile Bodies*. The telephone had featured in earlier novels, e.g., Michael Arlen's *The Green Hat* (1924), P. G. Wodehouse's *Summer Lightning* ([1929] 1988), and Joyce's *Ulysses* ([1922] 1985). Despite Danius's (2002) claim that the telephone conversation is fully naturalized in Joyce's novel, when Bloom telephones the newspaper office only one side of the call is reported and it appears in a section called "A Distant Voice" (137). Moreover, as Brooks (1977) points out, Joyce anthropomorphizes the telephone in much the same way that DeLillo was later to do with television: the phone rings out "rudely" in Miss Dunne's (229) office. The telephone was also commonly used as a plot device on the stage and screen, but Waugh's claim that he was the first to give the device "a large part" seems justified.

5. Waugh shows how the telephone can facilitate deception in *A Handful of Dust*, in particular in the scene where Brenda Last talks to her husband while fending off her lover. Telephone conversations between the characters are also important indicators of the state of their relationships in this novel.

6. For a more exhaustive analysis of this scene, see Thomas (1997).

7. For example, Nick Hornby uses telephone conversations in both *High Fidelity* (1995) and *How to Be Good* (2001). In the former, the narrator engages in a series of excruciatingly awkward conversations with his mother, his ex-girlfriend's mother, and his ex-girlfriend. Telephone conversations also feature extensively in Douglas Coupland's *All Families Are Psychotic* (2001) and are crucial to conveying the emotional distance between the various members of the family in question. Bringing the technology up to date, Bret Easton Ellis's

Lunar Park (2005) has a chapter titled "The Phone Call" in which the narrator, "Bret," receives a menacing anonymous call on his cell phone.

8. See, e.g., Pool (1977).

9. "Para-social interaction" or "intimacy at a distance" refers to the various ways in which broadcast media create the illusion of a face-to-face relationship for their audiences.

10. Susan Blackmore (2000, 211) claims that "the telegraph and telephone, radio and television, are all steps towards spreading memes more effectively."

11. Debates about the potentially empowering nature of TV talk largely center on the talk show (Shattuc 1997), which licenses frank and full discussions of taboo subjects but is accused by some of being exploitative (Dovey 2000).

12. In Irvine Welsh's *Trainspotting* ([1993] (1996), Mark Renton's withdrawal symptoms are exacerbated as he is made to sit through hours of televisual "light entertainment" in his parents' home. More recently, British novelists have begun experimenting with incorporating TV shows into their fictions. Andrew O'Hagan's *Personality* (2003), a novel about a child star, features fictionalized interviews from the Johnny Carson and Terry Wogan shows, among others. *Dead Famous* (2001) by Ben Elton features a murder on the set of a reality TV show and intersperses a narrative of the investigation with excerpts from the show.

13. Tichi (1989) has argued that television is often associated with nostalgia for childhood in contemporary fiction.

14. The spelling of the TV show's name, *Catweazel*, is changed here to convey how the characters would pronounce the name of the character.

15. Other examples of novels featuring computer-mediated communication are Jeanette Winterson's *The Powerbook* (2000), Helen Fielding's *Bridget Jones's Diary* (1996), and Russell Hoban's *Angelica's Grotto* (1999), as well as Matt Beaumont's *e* (2000), a novel composed entirely of e-mails.

16. ELIZA was a computer program developed in 1966 by Joseph Weizenbaum to mimic naturally occurring conversation. Many see it as the prototype for the "chatterbot."

8. Stuck in a Loop?

1. As the technology becomes more sophisticated, it will be interesting to see how far writers exploit the potential to use sounds and visuals in representing the speech of their characters—e.g., so that readers can hear how a line is spoken or see the gestures and facial expressions that accompany what is said.

2. Angle brackets replace quotation marks. Square brackets denote lexias, i.e., textual units within the hypertext.

3. This section of *afternoon, a story* is also where we have the most overt (and joyous) intertextual references to James Joyce, blending dialogue with interior monologue and providing both wordplay and orthographic variation.

4. Yellowlees Douglas may be alluding here to an idiomatic expression in American English, "That's all she wrote," meaning "That's all there is" or "That's the end of it."

Appendix

1. According to conversation analysts (e.g., Sacks, Schegloff, and Jefferson 1978), the management of talk relies on participants negotiating the floor and sharing turns at talk. When one participant self-selects repeatedly, this may be therefore be interpreted as competitive or selfish.

2. A face-threatening act (Brown and Levinson 1978) may be committed verbally or nonverbally, "off record" or "on record."

3. Adjacency pairs are utterances that are closely linked together, such that where the first pair part occurs there is a strong expectation of the second—for example, an answer to a question or an acceptance of an offer. Recipient design refers to the fact that "talk by a party in a conversation is constructed or designed in ways which display an orientation and sensitivity to the particular other(s) who are the co-participants" (Sacks, Schegloff, and Jefferson 1978, 43).

Bibliography

Fiction

Arlen, Michael. 1924. *The Green Hat*. London: Collins.

Baker, Nicholson. (1992) 1994. *Vox*. London: Granta.

———. 2004. *Checkpoint*. London: Chatto & Windus.

Beaumont, Matt. 2000. *e*. London: Harper Collins.

Bradbury, Ray. 1953. *Fahrenheit 451*. New York: Ballantine Books.

Byatt, A. S. 1990. *Possession*. London: Chatto & Windus.

Compton-Burnett, Ivy. (1929) 1984. *Brothers and Sisters*. London: Allison & Busby.

Coupland, Douglas. (1995) 1996. *Microserfs*. London: Flamingo.

———. 2001. *All Families Are Psychotic*. London: Flamingo.

DeLillo, Don. (1984) 1986. *White Noise*. London: Picador.

———. 2004. *Cosmopolis*. London: Picador.

Douglas, Jane Yellowlees. 1994. *I Have Said Nothing*. Watertown MA: Eastgate.

Doyle, Roddy. (1996) 1998. *The Woman Who Walked into Doors*. London: Vintage.

———. (2006) 2007. *Paula Spencer*. London: Vintage.

Ellis, Bret Easton. 2005. *Lunar Park*. New York: Random House.

Elton, Ben. 2001. *Dead Famous*. London: Bantam Press.

Fielding, Helen. 1996. *Bridget Jones's Diary*. London: Picador.

Firbank, Ronald. (1915) 1988. *Vainglory*. In *The Complete Firbank*. London: Picador.

———. (1919) 1988. *Valmouth*. In *The Complete Firbank*. London: Picador.

Forster, E. M. (1910) 1986. *Howards End*. Harmondsworth: Penguin Classics.

Gaddis, William. (1975) 2003. *JR*. London: Atlantic Books.

———. (1985) 2003. *Carpenter's Gothic*. London: Atlantic Books.

Green, Henry. (1939) 1978. *Party Going*. London: Picador.

———. (1950) 1979b. *Nothing*. London: Picador.

———. (1952) 1979a. *Doting*. London: Picador.

Hardy, Thomas. (1886) 2007. *The Mayor of Casterbridge*. London: Penguin Popular Classics.

Hemingway, Ernest. (1925) 1987. "Cat in the Rain." In *The Complete Short Stories of Ernest Hemingway*, 129–31. New York: Scribner.

———. (1927) 1987. "Hills Like White Elephants." In *The Complete Short Stories of Ernest Hemingway*, 211–14. New York: Scribner.

Higgins, George V. (1970) 2001. *The Friends of Eddie Coyle*. London: Robinson.

Hoban, Russell. 1999. *Angelica's Grotto*. London: Bloomsbury.

Hornby, Nick. 1995. *High Fidelity*. London: Gollancz.

———. 2001. *How to Be Good*. London: Viking.

Jackson, Shelley. 1995. *Patchwork Girl*. Watertown MA: Eastgate.

Joyce, James. (1916) 1966. *A Portrait of the Artist as a Young Man*. Harmondsworth: Penguin.

———. (1922) 1985. *Ulysses*. Harmondsworth: Penguin.

Joyce, Michael. 1987. *afternoon, a story*. Watertown MA: Eastgate.

Kesey, Ken. 1962. *One Flew Over the Cuckoo's Nest*. London: Methuen.

Kosinsky, Jerzy. (1970) 1997. *Being There*. London: Black Swan.

Leonard, Elmore. (1990) 1991. *Get Shorty*. London: Penguin.

Lodge, David. (1984) 1985. *Small World*. London: Penguin.

———. (1988) 1989. *Nice Work*. London: Penguin.

O'Hagan, Andrew. 2003. *Personality*. London: Faber and Faber.

Orwell, George. 1949. *Nineteen Eighty-Four*. London: Secker & Warburg.

Puig, Manuel. (1976) 1991. *Kiss of the Spider Woman*. Trans. Thomas Colchie. London: Vintage.

Pynchon, Thomas. 1990. *Vineland*. London: Secker & Warburg.

Roth, Philip. (1990) 1992. *Deception*. London: Vintage.

Saramago, José. 1997. *Blindness*. Trans. Giovanni Pontiero. London: Harvill Press.

Swift, Graham. 1996. *Last Orders*. London: Picador.

Walker, Alice. 1983. *The Color Purple*. London: The Women's Press.

Waugh, Evelyn. (1928) 1983. *Decline and Fall*. Harmondsworth: Penguin.

———. (1930) 1987. *Vile Bodies*. Harmondsworth: Penguin.

———. (1932) 1986. *Black Mischief*. Harmondsworth: Penguin.

———. (1934) 1987. *A Handful of Dust*. Harmondsworth: Penguin.

———. (1942) 1982. *Put Out More Flags*. Harmondsworth: Penguin.

———. (1957) 1988. *The Ordeal of Gilbert Pinfold*. Harmondsworth: Penguin.

Welsh, Irvine. (1993) 1996. *Trainspotting*. London: Minerva.

Winterson, Jeanette. 2000. *The Powerbook*. London: Jonathan Cape.

Wodehouse, P. G. (1929) 1988. *Summer Lightning*. In *Life at Blandings*. London: Penguin.

———. (1933) 1988. *Heavy Weather*. In *Life at Blandings*. London: Penguin.

———. (1952) 1957. *Pigs Have Wings*. Harmondsworth: Penguin.

Nonfiction

Abercrombie, David. 1966. *Studies in Phonetics and Linguistics*. Oxford: Oxford University Press.

Antaki, Charles, and Susan Widdicombe. 1998. *Identities in Talk*. London: Sage.

Atkinson, Maxwell J., and John Heritage. 1984. *Structures of Social Action: Studies in Conversational Analysis*. Cambridge: Cambridge University Press.

Austin, John Langshaw. 1962. *How to Do Things with Words*. Oxford: Oxford University Press.

Bakhtin, Mikhail. 1968. *Rabelais and His World*. Trans. Hélène Iswolsky. Cambridge: MIT Press.

——. 1981. *The Dialogic Imagination*. Ed. Michael Holquist. Trans. Caryl Emerson and Michael Holquist. Austin: University of Texas Press.

——. 1984. *Problems of Dostoevsky's Poetics*. Ed. Caryl Emerson. Trans. Caryl Emerson. Manchester: Manchester University Press.

——. 1986. *Speech Genres and Other Late Essays*. Ed. Caryl Emerson and Michael Holquist. Trans. Vern W. McGee. Austin: University of Texas Press.

Barnett, Louise K. 1993. *Authority and Speech: Language, Society, and Self in the American Novel*. Athens: University of Georgia Press.

Baron, Naomi. 2000. *Alphabet to Email*. London: Routledge.

Barthes, Roland. 1977. "Introduction to the Structural Analysis of Narratives." In *Image-Music-Text*, trans. Stephen Heath, 20–30. London: Fontana.

Bell, Alice. 2010. *The Possible Worlds of Hypertext Fiction*. Basingstoke: Palgrave Macmillan.

Bernard, Catherine. 1997. "An Interview with Graham Swift." *Contemporary Literature* 38 (2): 217–31.

Bishop, Ryan. 1991. "There's Nothing Natural about Natural Conversation: A Look at Dialogue in Fiction and Drama." *Oral Tradition* 6 (1): 58–78.

Blackmore, Susan. 2000. *The Meme Machine*. Oxford: Oxford University Press.

Blake, Norman F. 1981. *The Use of Non-Standard Language in English Literature*. London: Andre Deutsch.

Bolter, Jay David. 2001. *Writing Space: The Computer, Hypertext, and the History of Writing*. 2nd ed. Hillside NJ: Lawrence Erlbaum.

Bolter, Jay David, and Richard Grusin. 2000. *Remediation*. Cambridge: MIT Press.

Bourdieu, Pierre. 1986. "The Forms of Capital." In *Handbook of Theory and Research for the Sociology of Education*, ed. John G. Richardson, 241–58. New York: Greenwood Press.

Bradbury, Malcolm. 1992. "Writing Fiction in the '90s." In *Neo-Realism in Contemporary American Fiction*, ed. Kristiaan Versluys, 13–25. Amsterdam: Rodopi.

Brantlinger, Patrick. 1983. *Bread and Circuses: Theories of Mass Culture as Social Decay*. Ithaca: Cornell University Press.

Brooke-Rose, Christine. 1978. "Transgressions: An Essay-Say on the Novel Novel Novel." *Contemporary Literature* 19 (3): 378–407.

Brooks, John. 1977. "The First and Only Century of Telephone Literature." In *The Social Impact of the Telephone*, ed. Ithiel deSola Pool, 208–24. Cambridge: MIT Press.

Brown, Penelope, and Stephen Levinson. 1978. "Universals in Language Use: Politeness Phenomena." In *Questions and Politeness: Strategies in Social Interaction*, ed. Esther N. Goody, 56–311. Cambridge: Cambridge University Press.

Bruck, Jan. 1982. "From Aristotelean Mimesis to 'Bourgeois' Realism." *Poetics* 11 (3): 189–202.

Burke, Peter. 1993. *The Art of Conversation*. London: Polity.

Burton, Deirdre. 1980. *Dialogue and Discourse*. London: Routledge & Kegan Paul.

Cameron, Deborah. 2000. *Good to Talk? Living and Working in a Communication Culture*. London: Sage.

Carens, James. 1966. *The Satiric Art of Evelyn Waugh*. Seattle: University of Washington Press.

Carpenter, H. 1990. *The Brideshead Generation*. Boston: Houghton, Mifflin.

Chafe, Wallace. 1982. "Integration and Involvement in Speaking, Writing, and Oral Literature." In *Spoken and Written Language: Exploring Orality and Literacy*, ed. Deborah Tannen, 35–53. Norwood NJ: Ablex.

Chapman, Raymond. 1984. *The Treatment of Sounds in Language and Literature*. Oxford: Blackwell.

———. 1989. "The Reader as Listener: Dialect and Relationships in *The Mayor of Casterbridge*." In *The Pragmatics of Style*, ed. Leo Hickey, 159–78. London: Routledge.

———. 1994. *Forms of Speech in Victorian Fiction*. Harlow: Longman.

Collins, Randall. 1988. "Theoretical Continuities in Goffman's Work." In *Erving Goffman: Exploring the Interaction Order*, ed. Paul Drew and Anthony Wootton, 41–63. Cambridge: Polity.

Coste, Didier. 1989. *Narrative as Communication*. Minneapolis: University of Minnesota Press.

Coulmas, Florian, ed. 1981. *Conversational Routine: Explorations in Standardized Communication Situations and Prepatterned Speech*. The Hague: Mouton.

Coupe, Stuart, and Julie Ogden, eds. 1992. *Hardboiled*. London: Allen & Unwin.

Crystal, David. 2001. *Language and the Internet*. Cambridge: Cambridge University Press.

Cuddy-Keane, Melba. 1996. "The Rhetoric of Feminist Conversation: Virginia Woolf and the Trope of the Twist." In *Ambiguous Discourse: Feminist Narratology and British Women Writers*, ed. Kathy Mezei, 137–61. Chapel Hill: University of North Carolina Press.

Culpeper, Jonathan. 2002. "A Cognitive Stylistic Approach to Characterisation." In *Cognitive Stylistics: Language and Cognition in Text Analysis*, ed. Elena Semino and Jonathan Culpeper, 251–77. Amsterdam: John Benjamins Publishing Company.

Danius, Sara. 2002. *The Senses of Modernism: Technology, Perception, and Aesthetics*. Ithaca: Cornell University Press.

Davis, Lennard J. 1987. *Resisting Novels: Ideology and Fiction*. London: Methuen.

Dawson, Jeffrey. 1995. *Quentin Tarantino: The Cinema of Cool*. New York: Applause Books.

Dennett, Daniel. 1996. *Elbow Room: Varieties of Free Will Worth Wanting.* Cambridge: MIT Press.

Dentith, Simon. 1995. *Bakhtinian Thought.* London: Routledge.

de Zengotita, Thomas. 2005. *Mediated: How the Media Shapes Your World and the Way You Live in It.* London: Bloomsbury.

Douglas, Susan J. 1999. *Listening In: Radio and the American Imagination.* New York: Times Books, Random House.

Dovey, Jon. 2000. *Freakshow: First Person Media and Factual Television.* London: Pluto Press.

Eco, Umberto. 1984. Postscript to *The Name of the Rose.* New York: Harcourt Brace Jovanovich.

Edelsky, Carole. (1981) 1993. "Who's Got the Floor?" In *Gender and Conversational Interaction,* ed. Deborah Tannen, 189–227. Oxford: Oxford University Press.

Edwards, Derek. 1997. *Discourse and Cognition.* London: Sage.

Edwards, Derek, and Jonathan Potter. 1992. *Discursive Psychology.* London: Sage.

Emmott, Catherine. 1997. *Narrative Comprehension: A Discourse Perspective.* Oxford: Clarendon Press.

Ensslin, Astrid. 2007. *Canonizing Hypertext: Explorations and Constructions.* London: Continuum.

Ermida, Isabel. 2006. "Linguistic Mechanisms of Power in *Nineteen Eighty-Four*: Applying Politeness Theory to Orwell's World." *Journal of Pragmatics* 38 (6): 842–62.

Fiske, John. 1987. *Television Culture.* London: Routledge.

Fitzpatrick, Kathleen. 2006. *The Anxiety of Obsolescence: The American Novel in the Age of Television.* Nashville: Vanderbilt University Press.

Fludernik, Monika. 1993. *The Fictions of Language and the Languages of Fiction.* London: Routledge.

———. 1996. *Towards a "Natural" Narratology.* London: Routledge.

Fogel, Aaron. 1985. *Coercion to Speak: Conrad's Poetics of Dialogue.* Cambridge: Harvard University Press.

Forster, Edward Morgan. (1927) 1963. *Aspects of the Novel.* Harmondsworth: Penguin.

Foucault, Michel. 1978. *The History of Sexuality.* Vol. 1. Trans. R. Hurley. London: Allen Lane.

Fowler, Roger. 1989. "Polyphony in *Hard Times.*" In *Language, Discourse, and Literature,* ed. Ron Carter and Paul Simpson, 75–92. London: Unwin Hyman.

Frank, Arthur W. 1995. *The Wounded Storyteller.* Chicago: University of Chicago Press.

French, Marilyn. 1978. "The Voices of Sirens in Joyce's *Ulysses.*" *Journal of Narrative Technique* 8 (1): 1–10.

Frow, John. 2002. "The Literary Frame." In *Narrative Dynamics: Essays on Time, Plot, Closure, and Frames,* ed. Brian Richardson, 333–38. Columbus: Ohio State University Press.

Frye, Northrop. 1957. *The Anatomy of Criticism.* Princeton: Princeton University Press.

Furedi, Frank. 2004. *Therapy Culture.* London: Routledge.

Gadamer, Hans-Georg. (1975) 2004. *Truth and Method.* London: Continuum.

Genette, Gérard. 1980. *Narrative Discourse: An Essay on Method.* Trans. Jane E. Lewin. Ithaca: Cornell University Press.

Geraghty, Christine. 1991. *Women and Soap Opera.* London: Polity.

Geyh, Paula, ed. 1997. *Postmodern American Fiction: A Norton Anthology.* London: Norton.

Giddens, Anthony. 1992. *The Transformation of Intimacy.* Cambridge: Polity Press.

Goffman, Erving. 1959. *The Presentation of Self in Everyday Life.* New York: Doubleday.

———. 1967. *Interaction Ritual: Essays in Face-to-Face Behavior.* Chicago: Aldine.

———. 1974. *Frame Analysis.* New York: Harper Colophon.

———. 1981. *Forms of Talk.* Blackwell. London.

Goodwin, Charles, and Marjorie Harness Goodwin. 1982. "Concurrent Operations on Talk: Notes on the Interactive Organization of Assessments." Paper presented at the Seventy-Seventh Annual Meeting of the American Sociological Association, San Francisco, September 9.

Green, Henry. 1992. "A Novelist to His Readers: 1." In *Surviving: The Uncollected Writings of Henry Green,* ed. Matthew Yorke. London: Chatto & Windus.

Grice, Paul. (1963) 1975. "Logic and Conversation." In *Syntax and Semantics: Speech Acts,* ed. Peter Cole and Jerry L. Morgan, 41–45. New York: Academic Press.

Grishakova, Marina. 2009. "Beyond the Frame: Cognitive Science, Common Sense, and Fiction." *Narrative* 17 (2): 188–99.

Grosjean, Michèle. 2004. "From Multi-Participant Talk to Genuine Polylogue: Shift-Change Briefing Sessions at the Hospital." *Journal of Pragmatics* 36 (1): 25–52.

Gumperz, John J. 1982. *Discourse Strategies.* Cambridge: Cambridge University Press.

Hall, Stuart. 1980. "Encoding/Decoding." In *Culture, Media, Language,* ed. Stuart Hall, Dorothy Hobson, Alan Lowe, and Paul Willis, 128–39. London: Hutchinson.

Haraway, Donna. 1991. *Simians, Cyborgs, and Women: The Reinvention of Nature.* London: Free Association Books.

Hartley, Lucy. 2000. "Conflict Not Conversation: The Defeat of Dialogue in Bakhtin and DeMan." *New Formations* 41: 71–82.

Heath, Jeffrey M. 1982. *The Picturesque Prison: Evelyn Waugh and His Writing.* London: Weidenfeld and Nicolson.

Hemingway, Ernest. 1932. *Death in the Afternoon.* New York: Scribner.

Heritage, John, and Rod Watson. 1979. "Formulations as Conversational Objects." In *Everyday Language,* ed. George Psathas, 123–62. New York: Irvington Press.

Herman, David. 1994. "The Mutt and Jute Dialogue in Joyce's *Finnegans Wake*: Some Gricean Perspectives." *Style* 28 (2): 219–41.

———. 2003. *Narrative Theory and the Cognitive Sciences*. Stanford: CSLI Publications.

———. 2006. "Dialogue in a Discourse Context: Scenes of Talk in Fictional Narrative." *Narrative Inquiry* 16 (1): 79–88.

Higgins, George V. 1991. *On Writing*. London: Bloomsbury.

Hirschkop, Ken. 1992. "Is Dialogism for Real?" *Social Text* 30: 102–13.

Hobson, Dorothy. 1980. "Housewives and the Mass Media." In *Culture, Media, Language*, ed. Stuart Hall, Dorothy Hobson, Alan Lowe, and Paul Willis, 105–14. London: Hutchinson.

Holmesland, Oddvar. 1986. *A Critical Introduction to Henry Green's Novels*. London: Macmillan.

Horton, Donald, and Richard Wohl. 1957. "Mass Communication and Para-Social Interaction: Observations on Intimacy at a Distance." *Psychiatry* 19: 215–29.

Hudson, Richard A. 1980. *Sociolinguistics*. Cambridge: Cambridge University Press.

Hummel, Volker. n.d. "Television and Literature: David Foster Wallace's Concept of Image-Fiction, Don deLillo's *White Noise* and Thomas Pynchon's *Vineland*." http://home.foni.net/~vhummel/Image-Fiction/TOC.html.

Iser, Wolfgang. 1974. *The Implied Reader*. Baltimore: Johns Hopkins University Press.

———. 1978. *The Act of Reading*. Baltimore: Johns Hopkins University Press.

Ives, Sumner. 1971. "A Theory of Literary Dialect." In *A Various Language: Perspectives on American Dialects*, ed. Juanita Williamson and Virginia M. Burke, 145–77. New York: Holt, Rinehart, and Winston.

Jahn, Manfred. 2005a. "Cognitive Narratology." In *Routledge Encyclopedia of Narrative Theory*, ed. David Herman, Manfred Jahn, and Marie-Laure Ryan, 67–71. London: Routledge.

———. 2005b. "Quotation Theory." In *Routledge Encyclopedia of Narrative Theory*, ed. David Herman, Manfred Jahn, and Marie-Laure Ryan, 479–80. London: Routledge.

Jefferson, Gail. 1973. "A Case of Precision Timing in Ordinary Conversation." *Semiotica* 9 (1): 47–96.

Johnston, John. 1998. *Information Multiplicity: American Fiction in the Age of Media Saturation*. Baltimore: Johns Hopkins University Press.

Joyce, Michael. 1995. "Nonce Upon Some Times: Rereading Hypertext Fiction." *Modern Fiction Studies* 43 (3): 579–97.

Kacandes, Irene. 2001. *Talk Fiction: Literature and the Talk Explosion*. Lincoln: University of Nebraska Press.

Kennedy, Andrew. 1983. *Dramatic Dialogue: The Duologue of Personal Encounter*. Cambridge: Cambridge University Press.

Kermode, Frank. 1976. *The Genesis of Secrecy*. Cambridge: Harvard University Press.

Kozloff, Sarah. 2000. *Overhearing Film Dialogue*. Berkeley: University of California Press.

Kress, G. 2003. *Literacy in the New Media Age*. London: Routledge.

Lacey, Nick. 2000. *Narrative and Genre*. Basingstoke: Macmillan.

Lambert, Mark. 1981. *Dickens and the Suspended Quotation*. New Haven: Yale University Press.

Laver, John. 1975. "Communicative Functions of Phatic Communion." In *Organization of Behavior in Face-to-Face Interaction*, ed. Adam Kendon and Richard M. Harris, 215–38. The Hague: Mouton.

———. 1981. "Linguistic Routines and Politeness in Greeting and Parting." In *Conversational Routine*, ed. Florian Coulmas, 289–304. The Hague: Mouton.

Lea, Daniel. 2005. *Graham Swift*. Manchester: Manchester University Press.

Leavis, Q. D. (1932) 1965. *Fiction and the Reading Public*. London: Chatto & Windus.

Leech, Geoffrey, and Mick Short. 1981. *Style in Fiction*. Harlow: Longman.

Leonard, Elmore. 2000. "Introduction to *The Friends of Eddie Coyle*," by George V. Higgins, v–vii. Owl Books. New York: Henry Holt.

Levinson, Stephen. 1983. *Pragmatics*. Cambridge: Cambridge University Press.

Lodge, David. 1990. *After Bakhtin: Essays on Fiction and Criticism*. London: Routledge.

———. 1992. *The Art of Fiction*. Harmondsworth: Penguin.

MacCabe, Colin. 1974. "Realism and the Cinema: Notes on Some Brechtian Theses." *Screen* 15 (2): 7–27.

Magnusson, Lynne. 1999. *Shakespeare and Social Dialogue: Dramatic Language and Elizabethan Letters*. Cambridge: Cambridge University Press.

Marcus, Steven. 1965. *Dickens from Pickwick to Dombey*. New York: Basic Books.

Mazzon, Gabriella. 2009. *Interactive Dialogue Sequences in Middle English Drama*. Philadelphia: John Benjamins.

McDowell, John Holmes. 1985. "Verbal Dueling." In *Handbook of Discourse Analysis*. Vol. 3, *Dialogue and Discourse*, ed. Teun vanDijk, 203–11. London: Academic Press.

McHale, Brian. 1978. "Free Indirect Discourse: A Survey of Recent Accounts." PTL: *Journal For Descriptive Poetics and the Theory of Literature* 3: 249–87.

———. 1992. *Constructing Postmodernism*. London: Routledge.

McIntyre, Dan. 2010. "Dialogue and Characterisation in Quentin Tarantino *Reservoir Dogs*: A Corpus Stylistic Analysis." In *Language and Style*, ed. Dan McIntyre and Beatrix Busse, 162–82. Basingstoke: Palgrave.

McLuhan, Marshall. 1964. *Understanding Media: The Extensions of Man*. New York: McGraw-Hill.

Mepham, John. 1997. "Novelistic Dialogue: Some Recent Developments." In *New Developments in English and American Studies*, ed. Zygmunt Mazur and Teresa Bela, 411–31. Krakow: Proceedings of the Seventh International Conference of English and American Literature.

———. 1998. "Psychoanalysis, Modernism, and the Defamiliarisation of Talk." *Hungarian Journal of English and American Studies* 4 (1–2): 105–19.

Miall, David S. 1999. "Trivializing or Liberating? The Limitations of Hypertext Theorizing." *Mosaic* 32 (3): 157–72.

Middleton, Peter. 2000. "The Burden of Intersubjectivity: Dialogue as Communicative Ideal in Postmodern Fiction and Theory." *New Formations* 41: 31–56.

Miller, Vincent. 2008. "New Media, Networking, and Phatic Culture." *Convergence* 14 (4): 387–400.

Mills, Sara. 2004. "Class, Gender, and Politeness." *Multilingua* 23: 171–90.

Modleski, Tania. 1983. "The Rhythms of Reception: Daytime Television and Women's Work." In *Regarding Television*, ed. E. Ann Kaplan, 67–75. Los Angeles: American Film Institute/University Publications of America.

Mohammed, Patricia, ed. 2002. *Gendered Realities: Essays in Caribbean Feminist Thought*. Kingston: University of West Indies Press.

Moore, Stephen. 1989. *William Gaddis*. Boston: Twayne.

Moran, Charles, and Gail E. Hawisher. 1998. "The Rhetorics and Languages of Electronic Mail." In *Page to Screen: Taking Literacy into the Electronic Era*, ed. Ilana Snyder, 80–101. London: Routledge.

Morley, David. 1986. *Family Television*. London: Comedia.

Morson, Gary, and Caryl Emerson, eds. 1989. Introduction. *Rethinking Bakhtin*, 1–60. Evanston IL: Northwestern University Press.

Moulthrop, Stuart. 1995. "Traveling in the Breakdown Lane: A Principle of Resistance for Hypertext." *Mosaic* 28 (4): 57–77.

Mullan, John. 2003. "Talking Sense." *The Guardian*. April 5. www.guardian.co.uk/books/2003/apr/05/grahamswift/print.

Nash, Walter. 1985. *The Language of Humour*. London: Longman.

Noah, Timothy. 2004. "Assassination Porn." *Slate Magazine*. www.slate.com/id/2104805.

Ochs, Elinor. 1979. "Transcription as Theory." In *Developmental Pragmatics*, ed. Elinor Ochs and Bambi Schieffelin, 43–72. New York: Academic Press.

Ong, Walter.1982. *Orality and Literacy*. London: Methuen.

Osteen, Mark. 2000. *American Magic and Dread: Don DeLillo's Dialogue with Culture*. Philadelphia: University of Pennsylvania Press.

Page, Norman. 1988. *Speech in the English Novel*. 2nd ed. London: Macmillan.

Palmer, Alan. 2004. *Fictional Minds*. Lincoln: University of Nebraska Press.

———. 2005. "Philosophical Novel." In *Routledge Encyclopedia of Narrative Theory*, ed. David Herman, Manfred Jahn, and Marie-Laure Ryan, 426–27. London: Routledge.

———. 2007. "Attribution Theory: Action in Charles Dickens' *Little Dorrit* and Emotions in Thomas Pynchon's *The Crying of Lot 49*." In *Contemporary Stylistics*, ed. Peter Stockwell and Marina Lambrou, 81–92. London: Continuum.

Parker, Emma. 2003. "No Man's Land: Masculinity and Englishness in Graham Swift's *Last Orders*." In *Posting the Male: Masculinities in Post-War and Contemporary British Literature*, ed. Daniel Lea and Berthold Schoene-Harwood, 89–104. Amsterdam: Rodopi.

Pool, Ithiel desola, ed. 1977. *The Social Impact of the Telephone*. Cambridge: MIT Press.

Preston, Dennis R. 1982. "'Ritin' Fowklower Daun 'Rong: Folklorists' Failures in Phonology." *Journal of American Folklore* 95: 304–26.

Pritchett, Victor Sawdon. 1980. *The Tale Bearers*. London: Chatto & Windus.

Pugh, Sheenagh. 2005. *The Democratic Genre: Fanfiction in a Literary Context*. Bridgend: Seren Books.

Rée, Jonathan. 1990. "Funny Voices: Stories, Punctuation and Personal Identity." *New Literary History* 21 (4): 1039–58.

Richardson, Brian, ed. 2002. *Narrative Dynamics: Essays on Time, Plot, Closure, and Frames*. Columbus: Ohio State University Press.

Richardson, Kay. 2010. *Television Dramatic Dialogue*. Oxford: Oxford University Press.

Ronen, Ruth. 1995. "Philosophical Realism and Postmodern Anti-Realism." *Style*. http://findarticles.com/p/articles/mi_m2342/is_n2_v29/ai_17842019/.

Rossen-Knill, Deborah. 1999. "Creating and Manipulating Fictional Worlds: A Taxonomy of Dialogue in Fiction." *Journal of Literary Semantics* 28 (1): 20–45.

Ryan, Marie-Laure. 2002a. "Beyond Myth and Metaphor: Narrative in Digital Media." *Poetics Today* 23 (4): 581–609.

———. 2002b. "Stacks, Frames, and Boundaries." In *Narrative Dynamics: Essays on Time, Plot, Closure, and Frames*, ed. Brian Richardson, 366–85. Columbus: Ohio State University Press.

Sacks, Harvey, Emmanuel Schegloff, and Gail Jefferson. 1978. "A Simplest Systematics for the Organization of Turn-Taking for Conversation." In *Studies in the Organization of Conversational Interaction*, ed. Jim Schenkein, 7–55. New York: Academic Press.

Sarraute, Nathalie. 1963. *Tropisms and the Age of Suspicion*. Trans. Maria Jolas. London: John Calder.

Scannell, Paddy. 1996. *Radio, Television and Modern Life*. Oxford: Blackwell.

Schank, Roger C., and Robert P. Abelson. 1977. *Scripts, Plans, Goals and Understanding: An Enquiry into Human Knowledge Structures*. Hillsdale NJ: Lawrence Erlbaum.

Schechner, M. 2003. *Up Society's Ass, Copper*. Madison: University of Wisconsin Press.

Schegloff, Emmanuel. 1967. "The First Five Seconds: The Order of Conversational Opening." PhD diss., University of California, Berkeley.

———. 1992. "Repair after Next Turn: The Last Structurally Provided Defense of

Intersubjectivity in Conversation." *American Journal of Sociology* 97 (5): 1295–1345.

Schiffrin, Deborah. 1990. "The Principle of Intersubjectivity in Communication and Conversation." *Semiotica* 80 (1–2): 121–51.

Scollon, Ron. 1981. "The Rhythmic Integration of Ordinary Talk." In *Analyzing Discourse: Text and Talk*, ed. Deborah Tannen, 335–49. Washington DC: Georgetown University Press.

Shattuc, Jane. 1997. *The Talking Cure: Television Talk Shows and Women*. London: Routledge.

Simmons, Philip E. 1997. *Deep Surfaces: Mass Culture and History in Postmodern American Fiction*. Athens: University of Georgia Press.

Sinclair, John McH., and Malcolm Coulthard. 1977. *An Introduction to Discourse Analysis*. Harlow: Longman.

Spitulnik, Debra. 1997. "The Social Circulation of Media Discourse and the Mediation of Communities." *Journal of Linguistic Anthropology* 6 (2): 161–87.

Stanzel, Franz Karl. 1984. *A Theory of Narrative*. Trans. Charlotte Goedsche. Cambridge: Cambridge University Press.

Steiner, George. 1975. *After Babel: Aspects of Language and Translation*. Oxford: Oxford University Press.

Sternberg, Meir. 1981. "Polylingualism as Reality and Translation as Mimesis." *Poetics Today* 2 (4): 221–39.

———. 1982a. "Point of View and the Indirections of Direct Speech." *Language and Style* 15 (2): 67–117.

———. 1982b. "Proteus in Quotation Land: Mimesis and the Forms of Represented Discourse." *Poetics Today* 3 (2): 107–56.

———. 1986. "The World from the Addressee's Viewpoint: Reception as Representation, Dialogue as Monologue." *Style* 20 (3): 295–318.

Stopp, Frederick J. 1958. *Evelyn Waugh: Portrait of an Artist*. London: Chapman & Hall.

Stuart-Smith, Jane, and Claire Timmins. 2004. *Investigating the Role of Television as a Factor in Language Change*. Fachbereich Literatur- und Sprachwissenschaften. Universität Hannover. http://strath.academia.edu/CTimmins/Papers/246243/Analysing_the_Language_of_Television_The_Case_of_Media_Cockney.

Tannen, Deborah. 1989. *Talking Voices: Repetition, Dialogue and Imagery in Conversational Discourse*. Cambridge: Cambridge University Press.

———. 1993. *Framing in Discourse*. Oxford: Oxford University Press.

———. 1994. *Gender and Discourse*. Oxford: Oxford University Press.

———. 1998. *The Argument Culture*. London: Virago.

———. 1999. "New York Jewish Conversational Style." In *The Discourse Reader*, ed. Adam Jaworski and Nikolas Coupland, 459–73. London: Routledge.

———. 2004. "Talking the Dog: Framing Pets as Interactional Resources in Family Discourse." *Research on Language and Social Interaction* 37 (4): 399–420.

———. 2005. *Conversational Style*. New edition. Oxford: Oxford University Press.

———. 2006. "Intertextuality in Interaction: Reframing Family Arguments in Public and Private." *Text and Talk* 26 (4–5): 597–617.

Thomas, Bronwen. 1995. "The Use of Dialogue in the Comic Novels of Ronald Firbank, P. G. Wodehouse, Evelyn Waugh, and Henry Green." PhD diss., Manchester University.

———. 1997. "It's Good to Talk? An Analysis of a Telephone Conversation from Evelyn Waugh's *Vile Bodies*." *Language and Literature* 6 (2): 105–19.

———. 2002. "Multiparty Talk in the Novel: The Distribution of Tea and Talk in a Scene from Evelyn Waugh's *Black Mischief*." *Poetics Today* 23 (14): 657–84.

———. 2007. "Dialogue." In *The Cambridge Companion to Narrative*, ed. David Herman, 80–93. Cambridge: Cambridge University Press.

Tichi, Cecelia. 1989. "Television and Recent American Fiction." *American Literary History* 1 (1): 110–30.

Tolson, Andrew. 1991. "Televised Chat and the Synthetic Personality." In *Broadcast Talk*, ed. Paddy Scannell, 178–200. London: Sage.

Toolan, Michael. 1985. "Analyzing Fictional Dialogue." *Language and Communication* 5: 193–206.

———. 1987. "Analyzing Conversation in Fiction." *Poetics Today* 8 (2): 393–416.

———. 1988. *Narrative: A Critical Linguistic Introduction*. London: Routledge.

Tovares, Alla V. 2006. "Public Medium, Private Talk: Gossip about a TV Show as 'Quotidian Hermeneutics.'" *Text and Talk* 26 (4–5): 463–91.

Turkle, Sherry. 1995. *Life on the Screen: Identity in the Age of the Internet*. New York: Simon and Schuster.

Vallins, George H. 1960. *The Best English*. London: André Deutsch.

Voloshinov, Valentin. (1930) 1973. *Marxism and the Philosophy of Language*. Trans. Ladislav Matejka and Irwin Titunik. New York: Seminar Press.

Wallace, David Foster. 1993. "E Unibus Pluram: Television and U.S. Fiction." *Review of Contemporary Fiction* 13 (2): 151–94.

Wardaugh, Ronald. 1985. *How Conversation Works*. Oxford: Blackwell.

Watson, Colin. 1971. *Snobbery with Violence: English Crime Stories and Their Audience*. London: Eyre Methuen.

Waugh, Evelyn. (1929) 1990. Letter to Henry (Yorke) Green. Quoted in Humphrey Carpenter, *The Brideshead Generation*, 183. Boston: Houghton Mifflin.

———. (1929) 1946. "A Pleasure Cruise in 1929." *When the Going Was Good*. London: Reprint Society.

———. (1929) 1983. "Ronald Firbank." In *The Essays, Articles, and Reviews of Evelyn Waugh*, ed. Donat Gallagher, 57–58. London: Methuen.

———. 1930. *Labels*. London: Duckworth.

Weinstein, Arnold L. 1993. *Nobody's Home: Speech, Self, and Place in American Fiction from Hawthorne to DeLillo*. New York: Oxford University Press.

Weldon, Fay. 1990. "Talk before Sex and Talk after Sex." *New York Times*, March 11.

Wieseltier, Leon. 2004. "The Extremities of Nicholson Baker." *New York Times*, Books, August 8.

Wilde, Alan. 1980. "Surfacings: Reflections on the Epistemology of Late Modernism." *boundary 2*, 209–27. Durham NC: Duke University Press.

Williams, Raymond. (1974) 1990. *Television*. 2nd ed. London: Routledge.

Worpole, Ken. 1983. *Dockers and Detectives: Popular Reading, Popular Writing*. London: Verso.

Yellowlees Douglas, Jane. 1992. "What Hypertext Can Do That Print Narratives Cannot." *The Reader* 42: 1–23.

———. 1994. "'How Do I Stop This Thing?' Closure and Indeterminacy in Interactive Narratives." In *Hyper/Text/Theory*, ed. George Landow, 159–88. Baltimore: Johns Hopkins University Press.

———. 1998. "Will the Most Reflexive Relativist Please Stand Up: Hypertext, Argument, and Relativism." In *Page to Screen: Taking Literacy into the Electronic Era*, ed. Ilana Snyder, 144–62. London: Routledge.

Yngve, Victor H. 1970. "On Getting a Word in Edgewise." *Papers for the Sixth Regional Meeting of the Chicago Linguistic Society*, 567–77.

Young, Kay. 2001. *Ordinary Pleasures: Couples, Conversation, and Comedy*. Columbus: Ohio State University Press.

Zeldin, Theodore. 1998. *Conversation*. London: Harvill Press.

Zunshine, Lisa. 2003. "Theory of Mind and Experimental Representations of Fictional Consciousness." *Narrative* 11 (3): 270–91.

Index

Abercrombie, David, 23
action: and "booby traps," 89–90; in
  Checkpoint, 90–93; and coercion to
  speak, 84; and contextualization of
  speech, 78–81, 84–86, 89–90, 91–92;
  conversational interaction as, 75–76,
  77, 78, 80–85, 90–93; in crime fiction, 115; juxtaposition of, with
  speech, 89; in Modernist novels, 74;
  and multi-party talk, 85, 88; oral
  accounts of, 82–83; and pacing, 76,
  77, 87–88, 90–91; and plot, 74–75, 88;
  in Postmodernist novels, 74, 75; priority of speech over, 77–78, 93; and
  "scene" organization, 76, 77, 83–89,
  90–91, 93; and speech act theory, 78
addressee, role of the, 46–47, 62, 64, 71;
  and superaddressee, 148–49
afternoon, a story (Joyce), 152, 185n3;
  and anxiety about speaking, 162,
  163–64; and coercion to speak, 163;
  and contextualization of speech,
  158–60; conversational interaction
  in, 157–59, 162, 163–67; narration of,
  155, 158, 162; plot line of, 154–55, 159–
  60; representation of speech in, 155–
  57, 158; and sequencing of dialogue,
  159–60, 164–67; speech tags in, 158;
  and the "talking cure," 162, 163. *See
  also* hypertext fiction
"alibi of interaction," 11, 130, 137–38. *See
  also* technology

attribution theory, 67, 71, 83

"babel of voices" technique, 65, 107–8,
  132, 184n3. *See also* multi-party talk
Baker, Nicholson, vii, 10, 75; *Checkpoint*,
  19, 90–93, 102; and script form, 19,
  90, 102; *Vox*, 58, 135
Bakhtin, Mikhail, 4–5, 40, 42, 170, 175;
  and addressivity, 148–49, 160; and the
  carnivalesque nature of dialogue, 120;
  critiques of, 5, 40–41; and dialogical
  principle, 36; and dialogism, 57–58,
  79, 99, 106, 177; and heteroglossia, 4,
  39, 99, 156, 170, 175; idealism of, 40;
  and polyphony, 99, 170; and skaz, 175;
  and superaddressee, 148–49
Barnett, Louise, 34
Beckett, Samuel, 153
Being There (Kosinsky), 57, 133, 139, 141
Bishop, Ryan, 1–2, 17
Black Mischief (Waugh), 85–86
Blake, N. F., 31
Blindness (Saramago), 25
Bolter, Jay, 169
"booby traps," 89–90, 113–14. *See also*
  devices
Brantlinger, Patrick, 129
broadcast media. *See* radio; television
Brothers and Sisters (Compton-Bur-
  nett), 68–69; family interactions in,
  70–72, 172; self-discovery in, 72–73;
  vocalization of secrets in, 69–71, 81

norms, 26. *See also* conversational interaction; discourse analysis

cooperative principle, 3, 26, 27, 43; maxims of the, 122, 135, 146, 178, 179. *See also* politeness principle

Cosmopolis (DeLillo), 81, 89

Coste, Didier, 62, 68–69

Coupland, Douglas: *Microserfs*, 133, 149–50, 151

crime fiction, 10, 83; and coercion to speak, 117–19; euphemism and vagueness in, 121–22; experimentation with dialogue in, 116–17; and humor, 117, 119, 127; and idiom, 114, 116; obscenities in, 115–16; power relations in, 118–19, 122–23, 126–27; and reader as outsider, 120–21, 122; and realism in dialogue, 114–15, 124; scene construction in, 124–26; speech tags in, 120; storytelling in, 120, 123–24, 127–28. *See also* genre

Cuddy-Keane, Melba, 32, 167

dashes, 19–20, 30, 103–4, 105, 106, 155–56. *See also* punctuation

Davis, Lennard J., 33, 77, 88; and the idea of dialogue, 38–39, 40, 41

Deception (Roth), 38, 47, 81, 171, 176; characterization in, 67–68; and coercion to speak, 52; as compared to *Last Orders*, 176; composition of, as duologue, 68; critical reception of, 49–50, 53; and cultural differences in conversation, 44, 52; experimentation with dialogue in, 49–53; game-playing in, 50–51; and gender differences in conversation, 44, 52; power relations in, 51–52; and the "talking cure," 51, 52–53

Decline and Fall (Waugh), 83

defamiliarization, 104; and script form,

101, 105; of technologies, 131, 138, 148. *See also* devices

DeLillo, Don, 75; *Cosmopolis*, 81, 89; *White Noise*, 133, 136–37, 138, 139, 141

devices: "booby traps," 89–90, 113–14; and characterization, 59, 68; defamiliarization, 101, 104, 105, 131, 138, 148; footnotes, 105; "free run" dialogue, 100–102; and the integrity of speech, 38; juxtaposition of conversation and action, 89; merging voices, 101; phonetic transcription, 22–24; punctuation, 19–20, 29–30, 103–4, 105, 106, 155–56; script form, 19, 90, 101, 102, 105, 125–26; speech tags, 20–22, 29, 49, 65, 79–80, 104; suspended quotation, 21–22, 79–80, 102; technological, 133, 134, 135, 184n4. *See also* typography

de Zengotita, Thomas, 140

dialect, 22, 24–25, 33, 113; and framing of dialogue, 103, 106; phonetic transcription of, 22–23; and social class, 2, 23, 31–32, 59. *See also* speech

dialogical principle, 36. *See also* dialogism

dialogism, 57–58, 79, 177; critique of, 41; and the dialogical principle, 36; framing of dialogue, 99, 106. *See also* Bakhtin, Mikhail

dialogue: boundaries of, 1–2, 20, 32, 36, 49, 57, 79, 86–87, 125, 138, 147; as compared to naturally occurring speech, 15, 17, 18, 22–23, 39; in crime fiction, 114–15, 116–20; and dialogism, 41, 57–58, 79, 99, 106, 177; and the direct discourse fallacy, 5, 16–17; etymology of the term, 36, 41; experimentation with, 1, 8–9, 25, 31–33, 34, 49–50, 53, 75, 101–2, 113, 153, 169; "free run," 100–102; as inherent-

dialogue (*cont.*)

ly good, 5, 8, 39, 40–41, 44–46, 61; juxtaposition of, with incongruous action, 89; layout of, 20, 24, 38, 48, 102, 156; and mimesis, 15–16, 18, 22–23; and pacing, 16, 24, 76, 77, 87–88, 90–91, 177; and phonetic transcription, 22–24; and plot, 74, 75, 76–77, 81–86, 89–94; political connotations of, 40–42; and punctuation, 19–20, 29–30, 103–4, 105, 106, 155–56; and routine talk, 8, 27–28, 124; and "scene" concept, 16, 76, 77, 83–89, 90–91, 93, 101–2, 108, 124–26, 177; unmediated, vii, 4–5. *See also* conversational interaction; devices; framing; idea of dialogue; speech

dialogue novel: and "booby traps," 89–90; characterization in the, 67–73; and comic writing, 10, 87, 89, 113–14; and context, 76, 84, 88, 89–90, 91; cult following of the, vii; and dialogue as action, 74, 75–76, 81, 83–84, 87–88, 90, 93, 94; duologues in the, 50, 68; and framing, 104; intentionality in the, 65, 66, 69; pacing in the, 87–88; and resolution of issues, 93; set-piece scenes in, 83–84, 93; valuation of, by academic critics, vii, 11; and verbal interplay, 31–32, 75. See also *Brothers and Sisters* (Compton-Burnett); *Checkpoint* (Baker); *Deception* (Roth); dialogue

Dickens, Charles, 20, 22, 24, 31, 102, 103

direct discourse fallacy, 5, 16–17

direct speech, 29. *See also* speech

discourse analysis, 18–19, 26, 27, 43, 86–87. *See also* conversation analysis

discursive psychology, 79

Doting (Green), 88–89

Douglas, Susan J., 138, 149

Doyle, Roddy: *Paula Spencer*, 106; *The Woman Who Walked into Doors*, 106, 142–46, 147

dramatic script. *See* script form

duologue, 36, 50, 68. *See also* dialogue; dialogue novel

Edelsky, Carole, 43, 172

e-mail exchanges, 131, 149–51. *See also* computer-mediated communication

Emmott, Catherine, 98–99, 109, 159

Ermida, Isabel, 84

ethnography, 3, 98, 139–40, 147

fictional minds, 1, 6–7, 30–31, 66–67, 69. *See also* characters, fictional

film, 7, 132, 133, 138; dialogue in, 60, 76–77, 132, 133; genres, 113, 115–16

Firbank, Ronald, 10, 89, 130; and the "babel of voices" technique, 65, 107, 184n3; and the sequencing of utterances, 65, 88, 107; *Vainglory*, 65, 107–8; *Valmouth*, 80

Fitzpatrick, Kathleen, 151

Fludernik, Monika, 3, 17, 21, 30; direct discourse fallacy critique of, 5, 16

Fogel, Aaron: on coercion to speak, 39–40, 41, 52, 64, 84, 118, 179; and conversational idealism, 32, 39–40

Forster, E. M., 183n2 (chap. 4); *Howards End*, 28–29, 106

Foucault, Michel, 118, 150–51, 170

Fowler, Roger, 25

framing, 10, 95–96; in cognitive psychology, 95; and dialogism, 99; within frames, 106–8; and "free run" dialogue, 100–102; and humor, 103; as "interference," 100, 103–4; metaphors of, 96–97, 99, 183n1 (chap. 5); and narration, 10, 86, 95, 98, 101, 102, 103–7, 108–9, 127; in Postmodernist fiction, 104–5; and power relations, 99–100; and reader response, 109, 110; and realism, 20–22; in sociolinguistics, 97–98; and suspended quotation device, 102; theories of, 97–99; and typographical devices, 95; varieties of, 100–110. *See also* dialogue

free direct speech, 29–30. *See also* speech

The Friends of Eddie Coyle (Higgins), 116–17; and coercion to speak, 118, 119; euphemism and vagueness in, 121–22; film version of, 183n2 (chap. 6); power relations in, 122–23; scene construction in, 124–25; and solidarity through talk, 123, 127; and storytelling, 120, 123–24, 127. *See also* crime fiction

Frow, John, 99, 105

Frye, Northrop, 75

Gadamer, Hans-Georg, 46

Gaddis, William, vii, 5, 108; *Carpenter's Gothic*, 25, 61–62, 63, 81; *JR*, 101–2

gear shifting, viii, 67; and framing, 95, 97, 105–6

Genette, Gérard, 1, 16, 76, 77, 90–91, 177

genre, 10, 113, 114–16, 127–28, 173; romantic comedy, 37, 173; and technology, 184n1. *See also* crime fiction

Get Shorty (Leonard), 116–17, 124; euphemism in, 121; film version of, 183n2 (chap. 6); humor in, 117, 119, 127; scene construction in, 125–26; and script form, 125–26; and solidarity through talk, 123, 127; and storytelling, 120, 127–28; verbal play in, 119, 126–27. *See also* crime fiction

Giddens, Anthony, 130

Goffman, Erving, 62, 66, 171; and boundaries of conversation, 86, 175; frame theory of, 97

Green, Henry, vii, viii, 10, 88, 171; and "booby traps" device, 89; *Doting*, 88–89; experimentation of, with dialogue, 31–32, 132; and framing, 104; *Nothing*, 74, 83, 89; *Party Going*, 88, 104

Greene, Graham, 103

Grice, Paul, 38; and the cooperative principle, 3, 26, 27, 43, 122, 135, 146, 178, 179

group talk. *See* multi-party talk

Gumperz, John J., 97–98

A Handful of Dust (Waugh), 81–82, 89, 109, 184n5

Haraway, Donna, 149

hard-boiled crime fiction. *See* crime fiction

Hardy, Thomas: *The Mayor of Casterbridge*, 59

Hartley, Lucy, 40, 42

Heath, Jeffrey, 82

Heavy Weather (Wodehouse), 103

Hemingway, Ernest, viii, 66, 117, 132, 183n1 (chap. 3)

Heritage, John, 46

Herman, David, 38, 147; holistic approach of, to narrative, 6, 78, 87

heteroglossia, 4, 39, 99, 170; in hypertext fiction, 156; in *Last Orders*, 175. *See also* Bakhtin, Mikhail

Higgins, George V.: *The Friends of Eddie Coyle*, 116–17, 118, 119–20, 121–25, 127; influence of, on Elmore Leonard, 124

"Hills Like White Elephants" (Hemingway), viii

Hirschkop, Ken, 5, 40–41

Howards End (Forster), 28–29, 106

Hummel, Volker, 138

humor, 22, 49, 80, 89; and "booby traps," 89, 113–14; in crime fiction,

humor (*cont.*)
117, 119, 127; in dialogue novels, 10,
113–14; in routine talk, 27–28; and
tempo of comic dialogue, 24, 173;
and verbal indiscretions, 103; in
Waugh, 31, 133; in Wodehouse, 22,
27–28, 31, 103. *See also* satire
Huxley, Aldous, 38, 75
hypertext fiction, 11, 173; anxiety about
speaking in, 162–64; common plot
lines in, 154–55; and contextualization of speech, 158–61, 168–69; conversational scripts in, 157; criticisms
of, 153; and framing, 98–99; heteroglossia in, 156; interactivity of, 152–
53, 154, 169; narrator's role in, 155,
157–58, 162–63, 164, 168; representation of speech in, 155–57, 168–69,
185n2; and sequentiality of dialogue,
153–54, 164–67; and the "talking
cure," 161–62

"iceberg" theory, 66, 183n1 (chap. 3)
idea of dialogue: and coercion to speak,
39–40, 49, 52; critiques of the, 38–39,
40–43, 52–53; in *Deception*, 49–53;
ethico-political baggage of the, 5,
6, 40–42; history of the, 9, 36–38,
42, 53; as inherently good, 6, 39,
40–42, 45–46, 93; and intersubjectivity, 36, 41–42, 43; and linguistics,
43–44; and power relations, 39–40,
51–52; and relational scripts, 42–43;
and the role of the addressee, 46–47;
and speech as equal to moral virtue,
37–38, 45; and the "talking cure," 8,
44–46, 51. *See also* dialogue
I Have Said Nothing (Yellowlees Douglas), 152, 167; anxiety about speaking
in, 162, 163, 164; and contextualization of speech, 160–61; narration in,

155, 161, 163; plot line of, 154–55; representation of speech in, 156, 157–58.
See also hypertext fiction
intentionality, 46, 62, 65–66, 69, 96, 119;
in *Checkpoint*, 90, 93; and conversation analysis, 87; and intersubjectivity, 63, 64; multi-layered nature of, 47
interactional sociolinguistics, 98. *See
also* sociolinguistics
interiority, 32; and technology, 138, 151
intersubjectivity, 43, 62–63, 177; and
coercion to speak, 64; and cognitive theory, 36, 41, 43; within families, 63–64; and linguistic theories,
43; understanding of, from novels,
41–42. *See also* idea of dialogue
Iser, Wolfgang, 71, 76
Ives, Sumner, 23

James, Henry, 17
Joyce, James, 17, 32–33, 75, 153, 185n3;
and dash use, 19–20, 30, 103–4, 105,
155–56; and flow between scenes,
101–2, 108; *A Portrait of the Artist as
a Young Man*, 27; and speech tags,
21; *Ulysses*, 19, 21, 30, 101, 184n4
Joyce, Michael, 153; *afternoon, a story*,
152, 154–60, 162–67, 185n3
JR (Gaddis), 101–2

Kacandes, Irene, 8
Kesey, Ken: *One Flew Over the Cuckoo's Nest*, 27
Kiss of the Spider Woman (Puig), 58,
82, 105, 107; composition of, as duologue, 68, 92; punctuation use in,
80–81
Kosinsky, Jerzy: *Being There*, 57, 133,
139, 141
Kozloff, Sarah, 60, 76–77, 82, 132; on
genre, 113, 115, 120

narrator, 19–20, 48; commentary of the, 27, 28, 29, 65, 95, 106; and framing, 10, 86, 95, 98, 101, 102, 103–7, 108–9, 127; in hypertext fiction, 155, 157–58, 162–63, 164, 168; and interference, 103–4; relationship of, with reader, 19, 81, 98, 104, 109, 155, 157; role of the, 4–5, 6–7, 16, 69, 89, 101, 108, 158, 162; similarity of, to characters, 105–6; and storytelling, 82–83; and the suspended quotation, 21–22, 80, 102

Nash, Walter, 24

naturally occurring speech, 15, 17, 18, 22–23, 29, 95. *See also* realism; speech

Nice Work (Lodge), 134–35

Nineteen Eighty-Four (Orwell), 84

non-ratified participants, 62, 85

Nothing (Green), 74, 83, 89

Ochs, Elinor, 23–24

One Flew Over the Cuckoo's Nest (Kesey), 27

online interaction. *See* computer-mediated communication

orality, 129–30, 133

The Ordeal of Gilbert Pinfold (Waugh), 136

Orwell, George: *Nineteen Eighty-Four*, 84

overlapping speech, 25, 44, 172. *See also* speech

pacing, 77, 87–88, 177; and equivalence of story time to discourse time, 16, 76, 90–91. *See also* action

Page, Norman, 116, 136, 149; and comic writing, 113–14; on speech varieties, 2, 19–20, 23, 24–25, 31, 59; and theater's influence on novels, 19, 79–80

Palmer, Alan, 75, 79, 172–73; and fictional minds, 1, 6–7, 30–31, 67, 83

Party Going (Green), 88, 104

Paula Spencer (Doyle), 106

phatic communion, 28–29, 130

Pigs Have Wings (Wodehouse), 103

plot. *See* action

politeness principle, 44, 84, 91, 183n3 (chap. 4). *See also* cooperative principle

polyphony, 99, 170, 175

A Portrait of the Artist as a Young Man (Joyce), 27

Possession (Byatt), 25

postcolonial novels, 33–34

Postmodernist fiction, 20, 57, 65–66, 69; experimentation with dialogue in, 9, 34, 75; and framing, 95, 104–5; and genre, 117, 128; plot in, 74, 75; and realism, 19, 34; and the talking cure, 45; and technology, 130, 131, 138, 141. *See also* hypertext fiction; Modernist fiction

power relations, 26, 43, 61–62, 63, 72, 91–92, 170; and coercion to speak, 39–40, 49, 51–52, 64, 84, 117–18, 144, 163, 179; and collaborative storytelling, 123–24; in crime fiction, 118–19, 122–23, 126–27; and framing, 99–100; and hyptertext fiction, 169; and speech and action, 78; and technology, 135–36. *See also* conversational interaction

pragmatics, 3, 26, 77–78

Pritchett, V. S., 88

Puig, Manuel, 75; *Kiss of the Spider Woman*, 58, 68, 80–81, 82, 92, 105, 107

punctuation, 25; dashes, 19–20, 30, 103–4, 105, 106, 155–56; quotation marks, 19–20, 29–30, 103–4. *See also* typography

Put Out More Flags (Waugh), 133, 136

Pynchon, Thomas: *Vineland*, 139, 141

social class, 29, 44, 136, 141–42; and coercion to speak, 40; and crime fiction, 115; and dialect, 2, 23, 31, 32, 59–60; and framing, 106; and speech varieties, 2, 25, 29, 31

sociolinguistics, 97–98, 141

Socratic dialogue, 37, 75

speech: and action, 77–78, 79, 93; categorization of, 29–31, 32–34, 58–59; and characterization, 57–60, 68, 73; concealing nature of, 57, 68; connection of, to moral virtue, 37–38, 45; and context, 78–81, 84–85, 89–90, 97–98, 128, 171; and dialect, 2, 22–23, 24–25, 31–32, 33, 59, 103, 106, 113; direct, 29; and framing, 10, 95; free direct, 29–30; overlapping, 25, 44, 172; phonetic transcription of, 22–24; and previous literary representations, 24–25; replication of, in prose, 2–3, 8, 9, 22–23, 34, 114; and social class, 2, 23, 25, 29, 31, 32, 59–60; and technology, 133; and television, 141; and thought, 1, 6, 7, 20, 30, 32–33, 47, 49, 57, 62, 65–66, 67, 138; varieties of, 2–3, 19–20, 23, 24–25, 29, 31, 59. See also conversational interaction; dialogue; speech tags

speech act theory, 3, 10, 27, 29, 78, 165, 170; and realism, 18; and the role of the addressee, 46. See also pragmatics

Speech in the English Novel (Page), 2

speech tags, 20–22, 29, 30; in *afternoon, a story*, 158; in *Brothers and Sisters*, 70; and contextualization, 79–80, 104; in *Deception*, 49; in *The Friends of Eddie Coyle*, 120; in hypertext fiction, 158; and intentionality, 65; and realism, 20–21. See also devices; speech

spontaneous speech. See naturally occurring speech

Stanzel, Franz Karl, 24

Stein, Gertrude, 153

Sternberg, Meir, 30, 78; direct discourse fallacy critique of, 5, 16; and mimesis in dialogue, 15–16, 22; and quotation theory, 16, 100; and role of the addressee, 47, 62; and translation issues, 22

storytelling, 82–83; in crime fiction, 120, 123–24, 127–28

Style in Fiction (Leech and Short), 3

stylistics, 3, 19, 26. See also linguistics

Summer Lightning (Wodehouse), 21–22, 27–28, 184n4

superaddressee, 148–49. See also addressee, role of the

suspended quotation, 21–22, 79–80, 102. See also devices

Swift, Graham: *Last Orders*, 172, 175–81

table talk, 38, 44. See also multi-party talk

Talk Fiction (Kacandes), 8

"talking cure," 8, 44–46, 51, 72, 140, 161–62, 185n11

Tannen, Deborah, 97–98, 108; and family interactions, 63; and intertextuality, 87; and power relations, 92; and turn-taking, 44

Tarantino, Quentin, 115–16, 183n4 (chap. 6)

technology: and an "alibi of interaction," 11, 130, 137–38; and cognitive science, 138; computer-mediated communication, 129–30, 131, 147–51; and the cyborg concept, 149; defamiliarization of, 131, 138, 148; development of, 130–31; and disembodied voices, 154; and experimentation with representing, 131–33, 171; and interiority, 138, 151; and memes, 185n10; mobile communications, 134–35; and Modernism, 130, 131; and orality, 129–30; and Postmodernism, 130, 131; and radio, 130, 131, 132, 136–37, 138; remediation of, in fiction, 9, 11, 129, 131, 132, 151; in science fiction, 184n1; and the "talk explosion," 131–32; telegraph, 130–32, 138; telephone, 27, 58, 130–32, 133–36, 138, 157, 161; television, 63–64, 130, 131, 132, 133, 136–37, 138–42, 143–47

telegraph, 130–32, 138

telephone, 130–32, 138, 184n5, 184n7; in *afternoon, a story,* 157; in *I Have Said Nothing,* 157, 161; in *Nice Work,* 134–35; and power relations, 135–36; and stylistic (verbal) play, 134; in *Summer Lightning,* 27; in *Vile Bodies,* 58, 133–34, 184n4; in *Vox,* 58, 135. *See also* technology

television, 130, 131, 132, 133, 137, 185n9, 185n12; defamiliarization of, 138; and ethnography, 139–40, 147; and family relationships, 142–46; and linguistics, 140; and nostalgia, 185n13; and Postmodernist fiction, 138, 141; and rituals of viewing, 142, 143–44; and social class, 141–42; and sociolinguistics, 141; talk around the, 63–64, 140–41, 146–47; and the talking cure, 140, 185n11; in *White Noise,* 136–37, 139, 141; in *The Woman Who Walked into Doors,* 142–46. *See also* technology

theater, 19, 20–21, 59, 76, 79–80

Tolson, Andrew, 140

Toolan, Michael, 3, 19, 46, 66, 78; and conversational management, 26–27, 43, 85; and non-routine talk, 27, 88

Tovares, Alla, 63–64, 140–41

Trainspotting (Welsh), 59, 106, 172, 185n12; and script form, 19, 101

Turkle, Sherry, 149

turn-taking, 24, 26, 38, 43, 44, 60, 98, 172, 178. *See also* conversational interaction

typography, 22–24, 80–81, 95; and layout, 20, 24, 38, 48, 102, 156; and punctuation, 19–20, 25, 30, 80–81, 103–4, 105, 106, 155–56. *See also* devices

Ulysses (Joyce), 19, 21, 30, 101, 184n4

universality, 43–44

utterances, 60, 68, 71, 170, 186n3; addressivity of, 160; and analysis of dialogue, 3–4, 30, 53, 79, 85; and context, 4–5, 6, 73, 81, 122, 158, 159, 163, 167, 168, 171; in *Deception,* 51, 52; and dialogic theory, 57–58, 99; in Firbank's novels, 65, 88, 107–8; and framing, 101, 104, 107–8, 110; in hypertext fiction, 153, 156, 158–59, 160, 163, 167, 168; in *Last Orders,* 176–77, 178, 179; and layout, 24, 179; and realism, 18, 21, 38, 124; relevance of, 88; sequentiality of, 26, 28, 46–47, 65, 86–87; and taboo subjects, 103; and television, 147; and vagueness, 122. *See also* dialogue; speech

Vainglory (Firbank), 65, 107–8

Valmouth (Firbank), 80

verbal dueling, 75, 144, 157

Vile Bodies (Waugh), 58, 67, 101, 133–34, 184n4

Vineland (Pynchon), 139, 141

virtual interactions. *See* computer-mediated communication

Voloshinov, Valentin, 5, 79

IN THE FRONTIERS OF NARRATIVE SERIES:

To order or obtain more information
on these or other University
of Nebraska Press titles, visit
www.nebraskapress.unl.edu.